"I am delighted to see Vern Poyt
edge of the Scriptures and the in
responsibly is unsurpassed. He p.........
clearly and simply so that laypeople and scholars alike will benefit. This is a
book that you will not want to miss."

   Richard L. Pratt Jr., President, Third Millennium Ministries

"As readers learn how the New Testament relates to the Old, they will encounter the subject and language of typology. I'm grateful for Vern Poythress
providing this accessible resource so that interpreters can think about how
the patterns and shadows of the Old Testament point to Christ, the church,
and the new creation. The divine author of Holy Scripture is summing up all
things in his Son. Let Poythress help you identify key symbols and types along
the storyline of redemption."

   Mitchell L. Chase, Associate Professor of Biblical Studies, The
   Southern Baptist Theological Seminary; author, *Short of Glory:
   A Biblical and Theological Exploration of the Fall*

Crossway Books by Vern S. Poythress

Biblical Typology

Chance and the Sovereignty of God

In the Beginning Was the Word

Inerrancy and the Gospels

Inerrancy and Worldview

Interpreting Eden

Logic

The Lordship of Christ

The Miracles of Jesus

Reading the Word of God in the Presence of God

Redeeming Mathematics

Redeeming Our Thinking about History

Redeeming Philosophy

Redeeming Reason

Redeeming Science

Redeeming Sociology

Theophany

Truth, Theology, and Perspective

Biblical Typology

Biblical Typology

How the Old Testament Points to Christ,
His Church, and the Consummation

Vern S. Poythress

WHEATON, ILLINOIS

Library of Congress Cataloging-in-Publication Data
Names: Poythress, Vern S., author.
Title: Biblical typology : how the Old Testament points to Christ, his church, and the consummation / Vern S. Poythress.
Description: Wheaton, Illinois : Crossway, 2024. | Includes bibliographical references and index.
Identifiers: LCCN 2023020517 (print) | LCCN 2023020518 (ebook) | ISBN 9781433592423 (trade paperback) | ISBN 9781433592430 (pdf) | ISBN 9781433592447 (epub)
Subjects: LCSH: Typology (Theology) | Theophanies. | Bible. Old Testament—Criticism, interpretation, etc.
Classification: LCC BT225 .P69 2024 (print) | LCC BT225 (ebook) | DDC 220.6/4—dc23/eng/20231120
LC record available at https://lccn.loc.gov/2023020517
LC ebook record available at https://lccn.loc.gov/2023020518

To my wife, Diane

Contents

APPENDICES

Tables and Illustrations

Tables

Illustrations

Introduction: What Is Typology?

WHAT IS *TYPOLOGY*? Typology is the study of *types*. This study belongs to the larger subject of principles for interpreting the Bible. And what is a type? Roughly speaking, a *type* is a symbol specially designed by God to point forward to a fulfillment.[1] The word *type* is used here as a technical term. It is not to be confused with the more common meaning of the English word *type*, such as when we say, "A nail is one *type* of fastener," that is, one *kind* of fastener, one *category* of fastener.

Priests as Types

What is one example of a type? The priests in the Old Testament are *types* pointing forward to Christ. God specially appointed Aaron, the brother of Moses, and Aaron's sons, as priests (Num. 8–9). The priests

---

1 There is more than one way of defining the technical word *type*. And there are disputes about whether it should encompass a wider or narrower group of events and institutions and personages, together with the texts that discuss them. The simple description that we have just provided can suffice for a starting point. It has an affinity to Patrick Fairbairn's description, which singles out two elements: resemblance and divine design. Under the aspect of design he says, "[Types] were designed by Him to foreshadow and prepare for the better things of the Gospel" (Fairbairn, *The Typology of Scripture: Viewed in Connection with the Whole Series of . . . The Divine Dispensations* [New York and London: Funk & Wagnalls, 1911], vol. 1, book 1, ch. 2, p. 46 [1.1.2.46]; we will include volume, book, and chapter numbers to help readers who may have a different edition). Fairbairn includes in his picture the idea of temporal unfolding in the history of redemption. He also affirms that types are "symbols" (1.1.2.52).

Complexities will be considered later. For more on the underlying Greek words, see our appendix B. For the relationship with analogy, see chapters 15, 25, and 29, and appendix C.

were symbolic personages. They symbolized the need that people have for a mediator to represent them and reconcile them to God through the forgiveness of their sins. Christ is the final great priest, who actually accomplished forgiveness and reconciliation by his own death and resurrection (Heb. 4:14–10:39). Before Christ came, God appointed priests to symbolize what Christ would do. That is the basic idea: a type symbolizes something beforehand. It *prefigures* or foreshadows something else still to come.

The Larger Picture

In this book we explore how to find types in the Bible and how to interpret them. Our exploration is for practical purposes. We want to understand the Old Testament more deeply and to profit spiritually from it. We want to be able to show others how to grow in understanding it. This book is for ordinary readers of the Bible and for pastors and teachers who guide others in understanding the Bible. It builds on a long and helpful history of interpretation of biblical types. That history must be left to other books.[2] Readers who want to know how this book differs from past studies of types are referred to appendix C.

2   Fairbairn, *Typology of Scripture*, 1.1.1.1–41; Richard M. Davidson, *Typology in Scripture: A Study of Hermeneutical Τύπος Structures* (Berrien Springs, MI: Andrews University Press, 1981), 17–93; K. J. Woollcombe, "The Biblical Origins and Patristic Development of Typology," in G. W. H. Lampe and K. J. Woollcombe, *Essays on Typology*, Studies in Biblical Theology 22 (Naperville, IL: Alec R. Allenson, 1957), 39–75; Jean Danielou, *From Shadows to Reality: Studies in the Biblical Typology of the Fathers* (London: Burns & Oates, 1960); Leonhard Goppelt, *Typos: The Typological Interpretation of the Old Testament in the New*, trans. Donald H. Madvig (Grand Rapids, MI: Eerdmans, 1982), 23–58. For an analysis of the recent state of discussion, see G. K. Beale, *Handbook on the New Testament Use of the Old Testament* (Grand Rapids, MI: Baker, 2012), 13–27.

PART I

INTRODUCING THE CHALLENGE OF THE OLD TESTAMENT

It is a major challenge to see the relevance of the Old Testament to our lives in Christ. Types are one important way in which we may read the Old Testament as a testimony to Christ, not merely as historical records or instances of moral examples.

1

Understanding the Old Testament

BEFORE WE FOCUS MORE DIRECTLY ON TYPES, let us consider briefly a larger question: Why is it important to understand the Old Testament?

The Challenge of Jesus's Understanding of the Old Testament

On two separate occasions, recorded in Luke 24, Jesus indicates that the Old Testament is about him. The first of these occurred as he encountered two disciples on the road to Emmaus:

> And he said to them, "O foolish ones, and slow of heart to believe all that the prophets have spoken! Was it not necessary that the Christ should suffer these things and enter into his glory?" And *beginning with Moses and all the Prophets*, he interpreted to them in all the Scriptures the things *concerning himself*. (Luke 24:25–27)

Later, he spoke in similar terms to a larger group of disciples:

> Then he said to them, "These are my words that I spoke to you while I was still with you, that everything *written about me* in the Law of Moses and the Prophets and the Psalms must be fulfilled." Then he opened their minds to understand *the Scriptures*, and said to them, "*Thus it is written*, that *the Christ* should suffer and on the third day

rise from the dead, and that repentance for the forgiveness of sins should be proclaimed in his name to all nations, beginning from Jerusalem." (Luke 24:44–47)

It is worth looking at these two passages more carefully, especially the second one. "The Scriptures" here are the Old Testament. The Jews of Jesus's time recognized three major divisions in the Old Testament. The "Law of Moses" contains the first five books, Genesis through Deuteronomy. "The Prophets" includes both what the Jews call the "Former Prophets," namely the historical books Joshua, Judges, 1–2 Samuel, and 1–2 Kings; and the "Latter Prophets," the prophetical books Isaiah, Jeremiah, Ezekiel, and Hosea through Malachi. The third division in the Jewish reckoning is "the Writings," which is more miscellaneous and includes all the other books of the Jewish canon (Ruth, 1–2 Chronicles, Ezra, Nehemiah, Esther, Job, Psalms, Proverbs, Ecclesiastes, Song of Solomon, Lamentations, and Daniel). The Psalms is the most prominent in this third group, "the Writings." According to Jesus, all three groups testify to his suffering and his resurrection. In Luke 24:44–47, the phrase "Thus it is written" introduces a summary of the thrust of the whole Old Testament, that is, "the Scriptures" that existed at the time when Jesus spoke, the time before the composition of any New Testament books.[1]

We may believe that what Jesus said is true, but still not see *how* it is true. How can it be that "the Scriptures" as a whole are about his suffering and his resurrection?

After Jesus spoke with the disciples on the road to Emmaus, they said to each other, "Did not our hearts burn within us while he talked to us on the road, while he opened to us the Scriptures?" (v. 32). They saw the true meaning of the Old Testament, and they were transformed. But we were not there with them to hear what Jesus said.

Jesus, however, taught not only these two disciples, but, as we have seen, a larger group, during the time between his resurrection and his ascension (Luke 24:44–51; see also Acts 1:3). Among these people

---

1   Iain M. Duguid, *Is Jesus in the Old Testament?* (Phillipsburg, NJ: P&R, 2013), 9.

were some of the human authors of New Testament books. The New Testament was written by people inspired by the Holy Spirit. Jesus sent the Spirit to continue his teaching, and this includes teaching them the meaning of the Old Testament:

> "I [Jesus] still have many things to say to you, but you cannot bear them now. When the Spirit of truth comes, he will *guide you into all the truth*, for he will not speak on his own authority, but whatever he hears he will speak, and he will declare to you the things that are to come. He will glorify me, for he will take what is mine and declare it to you. All that the Father has is mine; therefore I said that he will take what is mine and declare it to you." (John 16:12–15)

So through the New Testament we have instruction that enables us rightly to appreciate the Old Testament. And that appreciation means understanding how the Old Testament points to Christ.

The Old Testament Designed for Us

We should understand that God gave us the whole Bible for our instruction, not only the New Testament. Romans 15:4 says,

> For whatever was written in former days was written *for our instruction*, that through endurance and through the encouragement of the Scriptures we might have hope.

Likewise 1 Corinthians 10 indicates the value of the record of Israel in the wilderness:

> Now these things [written in the books of Moses] took place as examples *for us*, that we might not desire evil as they did. (v. 6)

> Now these things happened to them as an example, but they were written down *for our instruction*, on whom the end of the ages has come. (v. 11)

Other Approaches to the Old Testament

God designed the Old Testament Scriptures for us. But *how* are we supposed to profit from them?

Luke 24 indicates that their meaning is found in their pointing forward to Christ. But in the church through the centuries, this meaning has not always been fully understood. We may consider various alternative paths that Christians have followed.

1. Use Just the New Testament

One path is to use just the New Testament. Quite a few pastors give sermons and teaching almost exclusively from the New Testament. Likewise, ordinary Bible readers may ignore the Old Testament and read only from the New.

The New Testament is indeed the word of God. But it makes up less than a third of the whole. This strategy of ignoring the Old Testament is not compatible with what God himself says in Romans 15:4 and elsewhere about the continuing value of the Old Testament.

2. Use the Old Testament for Moral Examples, Good and Bad

A second path is to use the Old Testament as a series of moral examples. This approach is called "exemplary preaching." How should we evaluate it? Indeed, there are good and bad moral examples in the Old Testament. And there are quite a few mixed examples as well. There are people like Abraham and David who are examples of faith but who had serious moral failures at some time in their life. There are people like Ahab who were wicked, but who humbled themselves (1 Kings 21:27–29). The mixed examples are in fact quite confusing if what we want are clear, black-and-white moral examples.

But the main trouble is deeper. Such use of the Bible runs a serious danger of seeming to have a message that says we are supposed to save ourselves by our own strength in moral striving. "Be good like these good examples." It ends up being moralism, with the message, "Save yourself," not the good news of what God has done in Christ. Man, not

God, ends up being at the center of the picture. The Bible does contain moral examples, but the point in recording them is never *merely* to be an example. There is instruction about God and his ways, ways that come to a climax in the work of Christ. Christ is the Savior. He, not our own moral striving, rescues us from sin and death.

3. Use the Old Testament Simply as a Historical Record

A third path is to use the Old Testament simply as a historical record. The Old Testament records what people said and did long ago. If we choose to, we can read it merely for information. Some people enjoy reading history. There is nothing wrong in studying the Bible for its historical information. But if that is *all* we do, we are treating the Bible as no different from any other record of the past. So this path of study is not adequate.

4. Use the Old Testament for What It Teaches Us about God's Nature

A fourth path is to use the Old Testament to teach us about God. The Old Testament does teach us about God. And God is the same throughout all time. So the Old Testament teaching about God is relevant to us now. Still, this approach does not yet do justice to what Jesus indicates in Luke 24—that the Old Testament is not just about God in general, but more specifically about Jesus's suffering and glory. It points forward to the redemption that he accomplished in history, once and for all.

5. Be Clever: Find Strange Secrets

A fifth path is to find special secrets in the Old Testament. Some people study the Old Testament to find secrets. They find things there that few other people have found. Their interpretations are clever and colorful, but strange. The trouble here is the obvious one: Are the "secrets" that they claim to find, secrets from the mouth of God, or are they secrets invented by the cleverness and overactive imagination of the person who is searching for them?

The Accessibility of the Bible

How do we evaluate the idea of secret messages? We might consider again the key passages in the New Testament about the value of the Old Testament: not only Luke 24, Romans 15:4, 1 Corinthians 10:1–11, but also Matthew 5:17–20, 19:3–9, 2 Timothy 3:15–17, and others. Such passages confirm that God caused the Bible to be written for everyone, not just for a special spiritual elite who allegedly would have secret access to secret truths. The New Testament writers were specially inspired by the Holy Spirit. But when they appeal to a passage from the Old Testament, the atmosphere is one in which they expect their audience to see the truth on the basis of what the Old Testament passage actually says. For example, the Bereans in Acts 17 are commended for "examining the Scriptures daily to see if these things were so" (v. 11). And as a consequence, "Many of them therefore believed, with not a few Greek women of high standing as well as men" (v. 12). The Old Testament passages they examined had meanings open to examination, not secret meanings that had no connection with what an ordinary person could see.

We must also pay attention to a complementary truth. The work of the Holy Spirit is essential in bringing to life people who are spiritually dead (Eph. 2:1). Concerning Lydia, the seller of purple goods, the Bible says, "The Lord opened her heart to pay attention to what was said by Paul" (Acts 16:14). The Holy Spirit has to work. His work is essential if people are going to be saved by placing their trust in Christ. But the hearts and minds of the hearers are also active. Lydia paid attention.

A similar principle holds for us as modern readers. We are supposed to ask God to help us and to send his Holy Spirit to open our hearts. We are not going to understand as we should unless the Holy Spirit gives us understanding:

> [Paul prays] that the God of our Lord Jesus Christ, the Father of glory, may give you the *Spirit* of wisdom and of revelation in the *knowledge* of him, having the eyes of your hearts *enlightened*, that you may *know* . . . (Eph. 1:17–18)

In addition, as the Holy Spirit works in us, we are supposed to "pay attention." Lydia paid attention to what Paul said, words inspired by the Spirit. We are supposed to pay attention to everything the Bible says. The problem is not that the message of the Bible is inaccessible, but that our hearts can be hardened by sin.

How to Use the Old Testament Wisely

In sum, the alternative paths do not really do justice to the role that God intended the Old Testament to have. We need to grow in our ability to understand the meaning of the Old Testament in relation to its fulfillment in Christ. One of the principal paths for this purpose is typology, the study of *types* (in the special sense of the word). The main purpose of this book is to develop skill in the study of types.

2

Interpreting Noah's Flood

BEFORE TURNING TO THE BROADER PRINCIPLES for the study of types, we may briefly consider two examples of passages that point forward to Christ. The first passage is Genesis 6:9–22, which leads up to Noah's flood. What do we do with a passage like this one?

> These are the generations of Noah. Noah was a righteous man, blameless in his generation. Noah walked with God. And Noah had three sons, Shem, Ham, and Japheth.
>
> Now the earth was corrupt in God's sight, and the earth was filled with violence. And God saw the earth, and behold, it was corrupt, for all flesh had corrupted their way on the earth. And God said to Noah, "I have determined to make an end of all flesh, for the earth is filled with violence through them. Behold, I will destroy them with the earth. Make yourself an ark of gopher wood. Make rooms in the ark, and cover it inside and out with pitch. . . . For behold, I will bring a flood of waters upon the earth to destroy all flesh in which is the breath of life under heaven. Everything that is on the earth shall die. But I will establish my covenant with you, and you shall come into the ark, you, your sons, your wife, and your sons' wives with you. And of every living thing of all flesh, you shall bring two of every sort into the ark to keep them alive with you. They shall be male and female. . . . (Gen. 6:9–14, 17–19)

This passage may serve as an illustration of the alternative paths that we laid out in the previous chapter.

Path 1: Ignore the Old Testament

The first path is simply to ignore the Old Testament. We would then ignore this passage, as well as every other part of the Old Testament. We regard it simply as past and gone and irrelevant. But that is not right. We have seen that God has a design for us to learn from it.

Path 2: Look for a Moral Example

Can we find a moral example in the passage? We find a morally good example in Noah. And we find a morally bad example in the people around him:

> And God saw the earth, and behold, it was corrupt, for all flesh had corrupted their way on the earth. (Gen. 6:12)

The morally bad people experience a suitably bad end:

> And God said to Noah, "I have determined to make an end of all flesh, for the earth is filled with violence through them. Behold, I will destroy them with the earth." (v. 13)

The moral lesson is obvious: do not be morally corrupt, or you will be destroyed by God; be righteous like Noah, and you will be saved from destruction.

The general moral principle is valid. God rewards righteousness and punishes wickedness. We may not always see just rewards in the short run, but we will see them at the time of final judgment (Rev. 20:11–15). But this truth is insufficient. Each of us comes into the world already corrupted by sin (Ps. 51:5; Rom. 3:10–11). We need to know how we can be saved from the sin in which we are already immersed. We cannot save ourselves. Noah is a worthy example. But his example cannot save us. And even Noah would not survive a minute inspection according to the perfect holiness of God (Ex. 33:20).

Well, then, shall we use Noah not as an example of righteousness, but as an example of faith? Hebrews 11:7 uses Noah in this way:

> By *faith* Noah, being warned by God concerning events as yet unseen, in reverent fear constructed an ark for the saving of his household. By this he condemned the world and became an heir of the righteousness that comes by *faith*.

This appeal to Noah is a valid use of the passage in Genesis. But it does not show us how the passage is fulfilled in Christ, in the way that Luke 24:44–49 indicates.

Path 3: Find Historical Information

A third path is to use the Bible for its historical information. There was a flood. Noah and his family survived, but the rest did not. That will be interesting to historians, and also indirectly for people who are looking for historical remains from the flood. But is that all?

Path 4: Find Teaching about God

A fourth path is to ask what the passage teaches us about God. The passage illustrates that God is righteous. He will not always put up with human sin, especially as it multiplies. God pays attention to righteous people like Noah. He is a God who can and does save people from calamity.

All these principles are true, but they do not yet tell us how this passage points forward to Christ.

Path 5: Find a Clever, Strange Meaning

As an example of strange interpretation, we may consider an interpretation of Philo of Alexandria (first century AD). Philo is commenting on Genesis 6:9, "These are the generations of Noah. Noah was a righteous man, blameless in his generation." Philo explains the passage this way:

The offspring [generations] indeed of creatures compounded of soul and body, must also themselves be compound; horses necessarily beget horses, lions beget lions, bulls beget bulls, and so too with men. Not such are the offspring proper to a good mind; but they are the virtues mentioned in the text, the fact that he was just, that he was perfect, that he was well pleasing to God.[1]

Philo interprets the word "generations" (offspring) as referring to a kind of spiritual offspring produced by "a good mind." The "offspring" consists in the virtues of being just and perfect. In this interpretation, Philo ignores the fact that Genesis 6:9 is the opening of an entire section of Genesis, and as such is parallel to 5:1 and 10:1, etc. He also ignores the fact that the next verse, verse 10, supplies the names of the actual sons of Noah: Shem, Ham, and Japheth.

Philo's interpretation seems really strange until we set it in the context of what Philo is doing in his whole treatise, "The Unchangeableness of God," and his treatises on other sections of Genesis. He consistently finds in the text in Genesis a second level of meaning, a meaning having to do with the purification of the mind by seeking God and by proper contemplation. The good mind and its virtues are regularly contrasted with base passions. In dealing with text after text, Philo sees in the text the schema of virtue and vice, and an emphasis on mental purification. The message that Philo supplies veers toward moralism.

Philo does affirm the centrality of God. God supplies us moral instruction. Everything has its source in God. God is good to those who seek him. But it is easy to read Philo and to think that it is up to us to save ourselves from sin and corruption by mental purification and seeking virtue. This is not the true message of salvation. Philo's message aptly illustrates how arbitrary meanings can be imported into the Bible if we already have a schema that endorses such a mode of interpretation.

---

1 Philo of Alexandria, "The Unchangeableness of God," 25:118, in *Philo*, vol. 3, Loeb Library (London: William Heinemann; Cambridge, MA: Harvard University Press, 1968), 69.

Typology

In sum, there are mistaken ways of dealing with this text. There are also ways that use the text only in one narrow aspect of its total value. Is there a better and more robust way?

In an approach that is sensitive to typology, we consider whether texts like Genesis 6:9–22 have a symbolic dimension in their literary and historical context. Is there anything here more than a bare account of events?

One of the more obvious aspects in Genesis 6 is the theme of God's judgment. God evaluates the wickedness: "The LORD saw that the wickedness of man was great in the earth, and that every intention of the thoughts of his heart was only evil continually" (v. 5). Then he brings judgment: "Behold, I will destroy them with the earth" (v. 13). He saves Noah (v. 18). Both the judgment and the salvation have a symbolic depth. The judgment is not the final judgment. But it symbolizes and makes known the nature of God as Judge. In this way, it anticipates the final judgment:

> . . . that the heavens existed long ago, and the earth was formed out of water and through water by the word of God, and that by means of these the world that then existed was deluged with water and perished. But by the same word the heavens and earth that now exist are stored up for fire, being kept until the day of judgment and destruction of the ungodly. (2 Pet. 3:5–7)

Likewise, the salvation of Noah and his family is not a salvation that gives them eternal life. But it symbolizes the power of God to give eternal life (see Gen. 3:22).

Because of this symbolic dimension, the story contains a typological aspect. It points forward to salvation and the judgment that take place in Christ. And indeed, this is how the New Testament treats the flood of Noah in more than one place:

> For as were the days of Noah, so will be the coming of the Son of Man. (Matt. 24:37)

. . . if he did not spare the ancient world, but preserved Noah, a herald of righteousness, with seven others, when he brought a flood upon the world of the ungodly; . . . (2 Pet. 2:5)

. . . when God's patience waited in the days of Noah, while the ark was being prepared, in which a few, that is, eight persons, were brought safely through the water. Baptism, which corresponds to this, now saves you, . . . (1 Pet. 3:20–21)

All of the above New Testament passages indicate that there is a correspondence between Noah's flood and later judgment. But none of them explains completely just how the personages and events of Noah's flood correspond to later judgment. We can see some further correspondences. Noah, the righteous man, saves not only himself but also his family. Christ, the final, perfect righteous man, saves his spiritual family, namely all the saints who belong to him.

But we may also note elements of difference between the two events. Noah's salvation is temporary. On the other side of the flood, we still see signs that human nature as a whole remains sinful: "The intention of man's heart is evil from his youth" (Gen. 8:21). Noah's family has been saved from a watery death. But they will still have to face a future in which their bodies will eventually die, and they will have to face God's eternal judgment. The underlying difficulty of sin has not been overcome. Christ's salvation is superior because it deals with the root, not just the fruit, of sin. He has conquered death forever (Rom. 6:5–11; Heb. 2:14–15; Rev. 1:18).

Noah, then, is a type of Christ. And the flood is a type of judgment. Both Noah and the flood are forward-pointing symbols. This aspect of meaning enables us to see how the story of Noah anticipates and foreshadows the work of Christ. In this way, a typological analysis can go beyond the unsatisfying alternatives in how we treat the Old Testament.

It is appropriate, then, that we take time to consider principles for interpreting typological meanings in the Old Testament.

3

The Bronze Serpent (Numbers 21:4–9)

LET US CONSIDER ANOTHER EXAMPLE of an Old Testament passage that points forward to redemption in Christ. Our passage is Numbers 21:4–9:

> From Mount Hor they [the people of Israel] set out by the way to the Red Sea, to go around the land of Edom. And the people became impatient on the way. And the people spoke against God and against Moses, "Why have you brought us up out of Egypt to die in the wilderness? For there is no food and no water, and we loathe this worthless food." Then the LORD sent fiery serpents among the people, and they bit the people, so that many people of Israel died. And the people came to Moses and said, "We have sinned, for we have spoken against the LORD and against you. Pray to the LORD, that he take away the serpents from us." So Moses prayed for the people. And the LORD said to Moses, "Make a fiery serpent and set it on a pole, and everyone who is bitten, when he sees it, shall live." So Moses made a bronze serpent and set it on a pole. And if a serpent bit anyone, he would look at the bronze serpent and live.

Context

This passage is part of the book of Numbers. The book as a whole recounts various episodes that happen and arrangements that are made while the people of Israel are in the wilderness, on their way from Egypt to the land of Canaan. They have been delivered from slavery in Egypt (Exodus). They are destined to go to the land of Canaan, which God had promised to the descendants of Abraham. They are thus in a situation where they have already experienced a fundamental deliverance. But they have not yet arrived at a situation of complete fulfillment.

The book as a whole is a nonfiction prose Hebrew narrative. So the passage records actual events that happened to the people. It is one of a number of passages that illustrate a repeated problem of grumbling and faithlessness on the part of the people. God has appointed Moses to lead the people, under God's direction. But the people repeatedly complain about both Moses and God.

A Major Theme: Sin and Deliverance

The context of the wilderness and the theme of complaining are both important. God is caring for his people in the wilderness, a region that presents the people with difficulties. The people repeatedly fail to trust God and obey him. Sin is there, in all its ugliness. The events are actual, unrepeatable events in history and also illustrations of the broader principles of sin and redemption. God's relation to Israel illustrates principles for God's relation to his people all the way through history, from the initial entrance of sin in Adam to the final triumph over sin in the new heaven and the new earth.

The events in the wilderness have symbolic depth. On the surface, the issues are issues of physical survival. To put it simply, the people need continued life. And for this purpose, they need food, water, health, protection from sickness and plague, protection from people groups who may oppose or attack them, and guidance to find a way to the land of Canaan.

The physical supplies come in the context of communion with God. It is not merely a matter of surviving physically in an inhospitable territory. It is a matter of surviving as a sinful people who have a holy God in their midst (Ex. 25:8–9). Israel is not just any people, but the special people of God (19:5–6). Israel is God's "firstborn son," as God instructs Moses to say to Pharaoh (4:22). God provides the physical provisions for Israel as one aspect and one expression of personal communion between himself and his people. There is a deep personal and spiritual dimension to the relation. So the issue in the wilderness is never merely a matter of continued physical life. Physical life symbolizes the deeper theme of true life in the presence of God.

This symbolic dimension to physical life comes to the surface already in Genesis 2–3, in what is said about the tree of life and the tree of the knowledge of good and evil. Eating from the second of the two results in death (2:17; 3:19). Eating from the first means life, as the name of the tree indicates. But what kind of life? When the tree of life is first mentioned, in 2:9, one might guess that only physical life is in view. After all, the other trees with their fruits are intended in an obvious way to nourish physical life. But when one arrives at 3:22, one finds that the endpoint is eternal life: "Now, lest he reach out his hand and take also of the tree of life and eat, and *live forever* . . ." Likewise, the death that comes from eating from the tree of the knowledge of good and evil encompasses both physical death and spiritual death. Physical death comes eventually, as 3:19 indicates. But spiritual death has come already, as the alienation of Adam and Eve from God signifies (3:8). The symbolic depth attached to the theme of life means that life in communion with God is signified by life in its physical dimension.

Likewise, when we come to the experience of Israel in the wilderness, the issue for Israel is *both* physical life and spiritual life. Except for Joshua and Caleb, the whole generation that came out of Egypt is condemned to die in the wilderness, in the sense of physical death. And why do they experience physical death? Because they have not trusted in God (Num. 14:5–12). Their physical death symbolizes the appropriate penalty of spiritual death, for people who rebel against God.

That is why the New Testament indicates that the events in the wilderness in some ways express principles concerning the people of God throughout the ages:

Now these things [events in the wilderness] took place as examples for us, that we might not desire evil as they did. (1 Cor. 10:6)

Now these things happened to them as an example, but they were written down for our instruction, on whom the end of the ages has come. (1 Cor. 10:11)

For good news came to us just as to them [in the wilderness], but the message they heard did not benefit them, because they were not united by faith with those who listened. (Heb. 4:2; see 3:1–4:11)

The Need in Numbers 21:4–9

With this larger picture in view, we can consider the particular episode narrated in Numbers 21:4–9. In this incident, the people of Israel are faithless to God and show that they despise his care. In his holiness he sends them punishment in the form of "fiery serpents" (venomous serpents). The serpents are fitting vehicles for the punishment. The record from the past goes back to the original serpent in the garden of Eden, the serpent who tempted Eve. And behind this physical serpent stood Satan himself, who used the serpent as his mouthpiece. If the people of Israel want to follow evil, they get a fit punishment in the form of an animal who is a symbol of evil. And the animal brings death to them, death that is the punishment specified by God for violating his command in Genesis 2:17.

So the conflict in Numbers 21 has resonances with the initial conflict between mankind and the serpent, which took place in Genesis 3. The conflict continues, according to the promise in Genesis 3:15, as a conflict between the offspring of the woman and the offspring of the serpent. The offspring of the woman will triumph over Satan. This triumph takes place in Christ. He is the offspring of the woman and the chief offspring of Abraham (Gal. 3:16). But there are preliminary stages of the conflict in the time of Abel, and the time of Noah, and the time of Abraham. So likewise, the conflict continues in the time of Israel's trek in the wilderness. Israel is supposed to be God's special son. But Israel is continually slipping back into rebellion. Their hearts are not inclined to God.

The symbolic depth in Numbers 21:4–9 involves the issue of life with God, or death as the punishment for rebellion against God. So the physical death from the bites of the serpents symbolizes the ultimate penalty of spiritual death in alienation from God, who is the true source of life.

The people deserve to die. But they admit their sin. They call out to Moses to intercede. Of course, Moses himself is not sinlessly perfect. Nonetheless, he is a symbol of the final intercession of Christ (Heb. 7:25).

The Lord instructs Moses to "make a fiery serpent" (Num. 21:8). The bronze serpent is a symbolical representation of the serpents that bit the people. The remedy for sin comes in the form of a symbol of sin and death. This bronze serpent is put on a pole so that everyone can see it. "And if a serpent bit anyone, he would look at the bronze serpent and live" (v. 9).

The bronze serpent is a temporary remedy for a physical affliction of death. But the story of redemption, and the promise of the offspring of the woman (Gen. 3:15), implies that there will be a final remedy, supplied by God. This final remedy will itself achieve redemption through a cursed object that people can view spiritually. The use of a cursed object on a pole anticipates the role of Christ, who undertakes to bear the curse of sin and death on our behalf:

> Christ redeemed us from the curse of the law by becoming a curse for us—for it is written, "Cursed is everyone who is hanged on a tree"— so that in Christ Jesus the blessing of Abraham might come to the Gentiles, so that we might receive the promised Spirit through faith. (Gal. 3:13–14)

Jesus explains the function of the curse beforehand to Nicodemus:

> And as Moses lifted up the serpent in the wilderness, so must the Son of Man be lifted up, that whoever believes in him may have eternal life. (John 3:14–15)

The Son of Man, Jesus himself, is "lifted up" on the cross, which in the Roman Empire was an instrument for crucifying notorious criminals. On the cross, Jesus is actually forsaken by God because he bears the curse for us (Matt. 27:46; 1 Pet. 2:24). By looking to Jesus in faith, believing that he can give us life through his death, we are healed spiritually (Gal. 3:2–3, 9). So we may conclude that the bronze serpent in Numbers 21:8–9 is a symbol pointing to Christ. God designed it beforehand, and gave the instructions to Moses, in order that the people of Israel at that time and forever after might have a picture not only of a remedy for a snake bite, but also of the deeper remedy—the final remedy for sin, found only in Christ. Praise the Lord!

PART II

—————

A FRAMEWORK
FOR TYPOLOGICAL
INTERPRETATION

*We survey some of the main biblical doctrines that offer a framework
for interpreting types.*

4

Basic Theology for Typology

IN PREPARATION FOR VENTURING into the details of types and the details of biblical passages, we should survey the larger framework for biblical interpretation. We must refer people to other books for a more thorough discussion of the larger issues of interpretation.[1] But we may mention some particular principles that have an important influence as we come to study typology.

God as Ruler

Since typology studies connections between earlier and later events in history, we have to understand something about the nature of history. So the first principle of importance is that God rules history. He rules it from the very beginning and forever into the future:

> Lord, you have been our dwelling place
> in all generations.
> Before the mountains were brought forth,
> or ever you had formed the earth and the world,
> from *everlasting to everlasting* you are God. (Ps. 90:1–2)

---

1 Vern S. Poythress, *God-Centered Biblical Interpretation* (Phillipsburg, NJ: P&R, 1999); Vern S. Poythress, *Reading the Word of God in the Presence of God: A Handbook for Biblical Interpretation* (Wheaton, IL: Crossway, 2016). On types in the Pentateuch, see Vern S. Poythress, *The Shadow of Christ in the Law of Moses* (repr., Phillipsburg, NJ: P&R, 1995). For a short introduction, see Iain Duguid, *Is Christ in the Old Testament?* (Phillipsburg, NJ: P&R, 2013).

Remember this and stand firm,
    recall it to mind, you transgressors,
    remember the former things of old;
for I am God, and there is no other;
    I am God, and there is none like me,
declaring *the end from the beginning*
    and from ancient times things not yet done,
saying, "My counsel shall stand,
    and I will accomplish all my purpose." (Isa. 46:8–10)

God works out both the great sweep of historical development and every minuscule event within it:

Who has spoken and it came to pass,
    unless the Lord has commanded it?
Is it not from the mouth of the Most High
    that good and bad come? (Lam. 3:37–38)

In him we have obtained an inheritance, having been predestined according to the purpose of him who works *all things* according to the counsel of his will, . . . (Eph. 1:11)

Are not two sparrows sold for a penny? And not one of them will fall to the ground apart from your Father. But even the hairs of your head are all numbered. Fear not, therefore; you are of more value than many sparrows. (Matt. 10:29–31)

God has a plan encompassing all of history:

"*My counsel* shall stand,
    and I will accomplish *all my purpose*, . . ." (Isa. 46:10)

. . . the *purpose* of him who works all things according to *the counsel of his will*. (Eph. 1:11)

His plan is to sum up all things in Christ:

> . . . as a plan for the fullness of time, to *unite all things in him* [Christ],
> things in heaven and things on earth. (Eph. 1:10)

So there is a unity to God's plan. Earlier and later events are connected, even across vast stretches of time, because God is orchestrating all events for his own glory (Eph. 1:6, 12) and for the blessing of his people (Eph. 1:22–23; Rom. 8:28).

The Outline of History: Creation, Fall, Redemption, and Consummation

Every particular event in history has meaning given by God in his plan. Every event is related to every other event within a vast panorama. God alone knows his plan comprehensively. But he reveals key aspects of his plan to us, through what he says in the Bible.

We can therefore obtain from the Bible a basic outline of history. History consists in creation, fall, redemption, and consummation.

God has a plan, before history ever begins.

As the first step in executing his plan, there is creation. God creates the world (Gen. 1). As a climactic act of creation, he creates mankind in Adam (vv. 26–27).

Second, there is the fall. Adam and Eve fall into sin after being tempted by the serpent (Gen. 3).

Third, God works redemption. Beginning with the promise of redemption in Genesis 3:15, God speaks and acts over a long period of time to begin to work out his plan for redeeming human beings from their sin, guilt, and alienation from him. God's works of redemption, together with his words explaining his works, extend from Genesis through the whole history of the Old Testament. All of this history is leading up to Christ. Christ comes into the world in his incarnation. He takes on our human nature. But, unlike us, he is perfectly obedient and without sin. His righteousness substitutes for our unrighteousness. As the bearer of our sins, he suffers and is put to death on the cross.

He rises on the third day for our justification (Rom. 4:25). He ascends to heaven and rules from there (Eph. 1:20–22).

All of this is the grand story of redemption. The process extends from the fall onward, but it comes to its definitive climax in the work of Christ on earth. He has defeated death and sin and the devil once and for all. We now await his return.

Fourth, there is the consummation, still to come.[2] The consummation, the new heaven and the new earth (Rev. 21:1), represents the final stage of history. Sin and death are completely eliminated in the new world. The saints enjoy the presence of God forever (Rev. 22:1–5). The consummation can be treated as the final stage of redemption. But it goes on forever, after redemption is completed. So it is aptly considered to be a fourth stage, in addition to creation, fall, and redemption.

Old Testament and New Testament

Within this grand outline, we can make a further distinction between the Old Testament period of redemption (from the fall onward) and the New Testament period (beginning with the announcement of the kingdom of God by John the Baptist). The major division is found in the coming of Christ. Everything before his coming is leading up to his coming. Everything after his first coming is built on what he achieved in that first coming. It is also looking forward to his second coming.

Already and Not Yet

It has become customary to speak of "already" and "not yet." Already Christ has come. Already he has defeated death in his resurrection. Already he has poured out the Holy Spirit and commissioned his disciples to spread the gospel to all nations. Already, in union with Christ, we have eternal life (John 6:35, 40, 47–51; 11:25–26). But all of this has not yet been wrapped up, as it will be in the consummation. What remains is called "not yet," or (more positively) "yet to come."

2   Premillennialists teach about a distinct epoch, which they associate with the "millennium," in between the second coming of Christ and the creation of the new heaven and the new earth.

Accordingly, there are several aspects of the application of redemption that are spoken of both as already here and as still to come. For example, we are already adopted as sons (Rom. 8:15–17; Gal. 4:5–7), but the fullness of adoption is yet to come (Rom. 8:23). We have eternal life now (John 6:47), but the resurrection of the body remains future (vv. 39–40).

Movements within the Old Testament

We may also observe major movements in the history of redemption that take place within the Old Testament period. Noah's flood marks a watershed. So does the call of Abraham, the exodus under Moses, the establishment of the monarchy with David (after Saul's failure), the exile, and the restoration from exile (Ezra). All of these stages take place according to God's plan. Each of them has a distinctive flavor. But God's unified plan for salvation remains the same. Through the whole Old Testament, generation after generation of people find salvation by believing in God's promise of a Savior who will accomplish climactic salvation. All the stages are moving forward toward this climax.

Meaning within History

Each event in history, such as the preservation of Noah in the flood, and the lifting up of the bronze serpent in Numbers 21, has meaning in the mind of God. Each event fits into his overall plan. Each event takes place within the context of creation, which has preceded it. Each event is part of a sequence leading to the consummation, which sums up the meaning of it all in Christ (Eph. 1:10).

Each event in the middle period, the period of redemption, has a role in the working of God's purposes of redemption. The Bible records both events of deliverance and salvation and events of judgment and destruction. Events of salvation look forward to climactic salvation in Christ. Instances of judgment look forward to the last judgment (Rev. 20:11–15). Also, Christ in his death bore judgment on behalf of sinners. Each event is related to the work of Christ, who is the center. We may not be able to discern this meaning. The meaning is ultimately God's meaning, not ours. And God is infinite. But by instructing us about his plan in the Bible, God does show us aspects of his purposes.

The Role of the Bible

What part does the Bible play in God's plan for history? God acts in history. God also speaks in history. He spoke to Adam and Eve (Gen. 3). He spoke to Noah (6:13–21). He spoke to Abraham (12:1–3). He spoke to Moses (Ex. 3). These words were passed on to their descendants. In addition, God caused his words to be written down, as we see with the Ten Commandments and Moses's writings (Deut. 31:9, 24–26). Over time, God caused more books to be added. The result is now the completed canon of Scripture. The Bible is the very word of God (2 Tim. 3:16; 2 Pet. 1:21). God designed it to have a central role in guiding our lives (Ps. 119:105; Matt. 4:4).

As a result, it is to the Bible that we turn in order to understand the meaning of the Old Testament. The general principle is that Scripture interprets Scripture. What is said in one place in the Bible helps us to understand better what is said in other places. The Bible is in one way a single book, because it has a single divine author, namely God, who wrote it over a period of centuries to be a permanent guide for us. It is also many books, written by a number of distinct human authors. God raised up each distinctive human author with his own distinctive personality and his own distinctive gifts. So we should pay attention to each human author in his distinctiveness. But we pay primary attention to God, who guided each human author: "For no prophecy was ever produced by the will of man, but men spoke from God as they were carried along by the Holy Spirit" (2 Pet. 1:21). It is appropriate, therefore, for us to use the whole Bible when we are trying to appreciate more deeply the implications of any one passage from any one book of the Bible.

Progressive Revelation

The Bible and the history of redemption go together, according to the unified plan of God. God's work of redemption in history, and God's *words* in history, go together in harmony. As one aspect of this joint work, God spread out his words over time. He did not reveal the whole Bible for all time suddenly to Adam and Eve. He did reveal some aspects of the promise of redemption in Genesis 3:15, but more revelation was to follow. We must respect this progressive character of the working of redemption, and with it respect the progressive character of God's speech. He shows more and more, over time, as he speaks through the centuries, through different human authors and prophets.

What is added in later parts of the Old Testament, and then what is added in the New Testament, is not merely more bits of information. Certainly there *is* more information. But later words often spiral back around the themes of earlier words. They enrich the understanding of themes already mentioned, rather than merely adding some new theme with no relation to what came earlier. This enrichment is more challenging than if God had just added new bits, unrelated to the old. But it is in accord with the unity of his plan. God in fact is surveying his *whole* plan, rather than just small bits, when he gives the promise in Genesis 3:15. Later revelation does not change the whole plan, but it does enrich our understanding of it. The enrichment is often holistic, not merely adding an isolated new bit.

In the time of the Old Testament, God is already at work to save a people for his own possession (Gen. 4:26; 5:22–24; 6:9; 12:1–3; Ex. 19:5–6). He shows them enough about himself and his ways so that they can trust him and be saved. So it is natural that his communication to them would be holistic. After all, his saving relation to them is holistic. He promises Abraham and his offspring that he will "be God to you" (Gen. 17:7).

God establishes a multifaceted, rich personal relation with his people. It has many implications. The implications *in detail* are only gradually revealed, over time. This gradual work is called *progressive revelation*. God himself designed revelation to have this progressive character. Therefore, the earlier revelations do not have any faults in them, contrary to what some people have alleged. The earlier revelations are exactly what God wants, each one appropriate to its particular time in the history of redemption. But each one is *incomplete* in comparison with the history as a whole. And the people at the earlier times would have intuitively sensed that it was incomplete. For them much was still mysterious, and the promises of God are magnificent in their scope.

A Summary by G. K. Beale

G. K. Beale aptly summarizes this whole theological framework in a few sentences, as follows:

> . . . there is one grand assumption of all: Jesus and the apostles believed that the OT Scriptures were "sacred" and were the Word of God. Therefore all authoritative theological discussion had to be based on and proceed from this sacred body of literature. . . .

1. There is the apparent assumption of *corporate solidarity* or *representation*.
2. In the light of corporate solidarity or representation, Christ as the Messiah is viewed as representing the *true Israel* of the OT *and* the true Israel—the church—in the NT.
3. *History is unified* by a wise and sovereign plan so that the earlier parts are designed to correspond and point to the later parts (cf., e.g., Matt. 5:17; 11:13; 13:16–17).
4. The age of *eschatological fulfillment* has come in Christ.
5. As a consequence of the preceding presupposition, it follows that the later parts of biblical history function as the broader context for interpreting earlier parts because they all have the same, ultimate divine author who inspires the various human authors. One deduction from this premise is that Christ is the goal toward which the OT pointed and is the end-time center of redemptive history, which is the *key to interpreting the earlier portions of the OT and its promises.*[3]

---

3 G. K. Beale, *Handbook on the New Testament Use of the Old Testament* (Grand Rapids, MI: Baker, 2012), 95–97, emphasis original.

5

The Shape of Our Response to the Bible

OUR INTERPRETATIONS OF TYPOLOGY should fit into a broader context of how we respond to God and to his word. We will briefly consider our response using three perspectives on ethics: the normative perspective, the situational perspective, and the existential perspective.

The Three Perspectives on Ethics

As developed by John Frame, the three perspectives on ethics each look at the whole field of ethics, but in three distinct ways.[1] The normative perspective focuses on *norms*. These are found in the contents of Scripture. (Conscience is a kind of subordinate norm, but due to the corruption of sin, it is no longer fully reliable.) The situational perspective focuses on *the situation*. It asks concerning the situation, "What will promote the glory of God within the situation?" The existential perspective, also called the personal perspective, focuses on the *persons* and their attitudes and motives. So each individual asks, "What are my motives, and what should they be, in guiding my thoughts and actions?" According to this third view, the primary motive should be love.

---

1 John M. Frame, "A Primer on Perspectivalism (Revised 2008)," §7, www.frame-poythress.org; John M. Frame, *Perspectives on the Word of God: An Introduction to Christian Ethics* (repr., Eugene, OR: Wipf & Stock, 1999); John M. Frame, *The Doctrine of the Christian Life* (Phillipsburg, NJ: P&R, 2008).

These three perspectives imply one another; in a sense, they include each other. For example, if we pay careful attention to the moral standards in the Bible, which are in focus in the normative perspective, we find that these standards tell us to have the motive of love, which is in focus in the existential perspective. The standards also tell us that we should pay attention to the situation in order better to understand our neighbor's needs and to love him effectively. So if we diligently follow the normative perspective, we will find within that perspective that it tells us to begin using the situational and existential perspectives.

Or suppose that we start with the existential perspective. We should have the motive of love. And if we do, and we love God, we will pay attention to what he says. So we will develop the normative perspective. If we love our neighbor, it leads us to pay attention to his situation in order to help. So we will develop the situational perspective.

Thus the three perspectives are perspectives on the whole challenge of how to think and act in the presence of God, who governs all three perspectives.

The Normative Perspective for Bible Study

We may now apply all three of these perspectives to see their implications for the study of typology. Actually, the three perspectives have something to say about how we interpret the Bible in general, not just about how we interpret passages that may include types.

First, in the normative perspective, we focus on God and his norms, which are in the Bible. In a typical study of the Bible, we have before us one main passage, such as the passage in Genesis 6:9–22 leading to Noah's flood. We have to pay attention to the passage. We are supposed to submit to what it says, as a norm. We take care not merely to avoid injecting our own ideas, but to listen to what God says. So we will not do as Philo did, by importing his own ideas about spiritual generation of virtues.

The Situational Perspective for Bible Study

The situational perspective focuses on the situation. This includes the historical and cultural environment to which our passage belongs.

The surrounding culture and its history is not itself a norm that we are supposed to conform to. Any culture and any extended historical sequence of events is going to include both good and bad, often in complex mixtures. But a Bible passage that God gives us originally addresses people within a cultural context. For the events in Genesis 6, the nearby context is the increasing wickedness of the people of the time of Noah. But the *words* of Genesis 6 come from a somewhat later time, when the book of Genesis was originally written. The book of Genesis is addressed to the people of Israel. (And, as we have observed, it was written by God "for our instruction," Rom. 15:4.) The Bible comments in various ways on the context of Noah's time and the context of the people of Israel as a nation. The Bible may ask the people to change in some way in relation to their context. If we fail to pay attention to the context, it is easy to inject our own modern meanings and our own modern context as a substitute. And then we will not get typology right—in fact, we will not get right the interpretation of any passage in the Bible.

The Existential Perspective for Bible Study

The existential perspective for Bible study tells us to pay attention to the motives of the people about whom the passages speak. But, more important, it tells us to pay attention to our own motives. It is very easy to find ourselves trying to make the Bible say what we want it to say rather than what it does say.

The study of types is a particularly challenging area because people can easily go in one of two extreme directions. In one direction, they become so timid that they cannot see typological meaning at all. They do not see anything beyond the obvious surface. In the other direction, people can develop overheated imaginations. They find all kinds of meanings that are not really there. We saw an instance of excessive imagination in Philo of Alexandria's interpretation of Genesis 6:9 (see chapter 2).

So what do we do? We must ask God for wisdom. Proverbs repeatedly stresses the value of wisdom and exhorts us to seek it:

My son, if you receive my words
and treasure up my commandments with you,
making your ear attentive to wisdom
    and inclining your heart to understanding;
yes, if you call out for insight
    and raise your voice for understanding,
if you seek it like silver
    and search for it as for hidden treasures,
then you will understand the fear of the LORD
    and find the knowledge of God.
For the LORD gives wisdom;
    from his mouth come knowledge and understanding;
he stores up sound wisdom for the upright;
    he is a shield to those who walk in integrity,
guarding the paths of justice
    and watching over the way of his saints.
Then you will understand righteousness and justice
    and equity, every good path;
for wisdom will come into your heart,
    and knowledge will be pleasant to your soul;
discretion will watch over you,
    understanding will guard you,
delivering you from the way of evil,
    from men of perverted speech,
who forsake the paths of uprightness
    to walk in the ways of darkness,
who rejoice in doing evil
    and delight in the perverseness of evil,
men whose paths are crooked,
    and who are devious in their ways. (Prov. 2:1–15)

Wisdom, which comes from the Lord, guides us not only in just dealings with other people but also in having discretion in how we interpret the Bible.

We could add also the need for patience, for humility, and in general for the fruits of the Spirit (Gal. 5:22–23). We need patience, because a deep and sound understanding of the Bible does not come in a single moment. We are committing ourselves to a lifetime of study. This patience is needed in typology. Not all typological meanings are obvious. We have to grow in understanding the Bible as a whole.

We also need humility. We need to recognize that we are limited, especially as we face the majesty of God in reading the Bible. Not every thought that comes into our minds is directly an indication of what God actually means.

PART III

INTRODUCING THE PRACTICE OF TYPOLOGICAL INTERPRETATION

We introduce Edmund Clowney's triangle and illustrate how to use it with various passages that involve types.

6

Introducing Clowney's Triangle

IT IS NOW TIME to see how to interpret types in practice. Later, we will add a few more principles that will help us to refine typological interpretation. But at this point we want to concentrate on the most basic principles for types, plus examples that illustrate how the principles work. The general pattern for interpreting types is called "Clowney's triangle."

Clowney's Triangle

"Clowney's triangle" is the usual label for a triangle diagram first introduced by Edmund P. Clowney in order to illustrate how to interpret types.[1] (See fig. 6.1.)

We will first illustrate the use of the triangle with a particular example, and then consider its general principles.

Clowney's Triangle Illustrated with the Passover Lamb

As our example, let us consider the Passover lamb, described in Exodus 12:1–13. The purpose for the lamb is especially in focus in the key verses, 11–13:

> . . . It is the LORD's Passover. [12] For I will pass through the land of Egypt that night, and I will strike all the firstborn in the land of Egypt, both

---

1 Edmund P. Clowney, *Preaching and Biblical Theology* (Grand Rapids, MI: Eerdmans, 1961), 110 (explained on 98–112).

man and beast; and on all the gods of Egypt I will execute judgments: I am the LORD. [13] The blood shall be a sign for you, on the houses where you are. And when I see the blood, I will pass over you, and no plague will befall you to destroy you, when I strike the land of Egypt.

The Passover lamb is an instance of a type. It is a symbol of divine truth, and it points forward to the climactic manifestation of truth in Christ, at the climax of history: "For Christ, our Passover lamb, has been sacrificed" (1 Cor. 5:7).

Figure 6.1: Clowney's Triangle (Altered)[2]

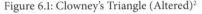
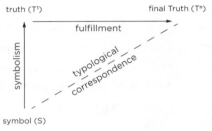

Clowney's Triangle, First Step

The first step in interpreting a type is to ask what the type symbolizes. Every type is a symbol. So for something to be a type, it must symbolize something. Verse 13 indicates that the blood of the lamb has a symbolic meaning: "when I see the blood, I will pass over you." What does it mean that God "will pass over you"? The land of Egypt experiences a plague, namely the death of the firstborn. Israel experiences no plague. God passes over them. Why?

Leviticus 17:11 and Deuteronomy 12:23 indicate that blood symbolizes life. The Passover lamb dies, and the blood is a symbol of its life. Its death functions to deliver the people of Israel from death. So a symbolic meaning attaches not only to the blood of the lamb but also to the lamb itself. The lamb is a substitute for the firstborn. Its

---

2   We have slightly relabeled the pieces for the sake of clarity. See appendix D.

death substitutes for the death of the firstborn among the Israelites. The truth symbolized is that by a substitute death the people can be delivered from death.

This first step in interpretation is represented by the vertical leg, the vertical side, of Clowney's triangle. The symbol (S) is the lamb with its blood. The truth symbolized (T[1]) is that God spares his people Israel on account of the death of a substitute.

We may thus begin to fill out the contents of Clowney's triangle in the vertical leg or vertical side, as indicated in fig. 6.2.

Figure 6.2: The Symbolic Meaning of the Passover (Step 1)

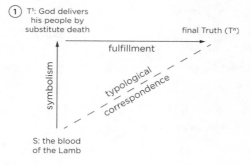

It is important to focus on the meaning of the symbol at the time and within the text in which it is originally given.[3] We are asking what the blood of the lamb means in the light of Exodus 12:1–13 and the surrounding portions of Exodus. We are not yet asking what it means in the light of progressive revelation leading to Christ and the New Testament.

Clowney's Triangle, Second Step

Our second step is to move forward in time. In the light of progressive revelation, we ask how the truth that has been manifested in Exodus (T[1]) is fulfilled in a later climactic manifestation (T[n]). Especially we are interested in fulfillment in Christ.

---

3 Patrick Fairbairn, *The Typology of Scripture: Viewed in Connection with the Whole Series of . . . The Divine Dispensations* (New York and London: Funk & Wagnalls, 1911), 1.1.2.53.

In the case of the Passover lamb, the central fulfillment is found in Christ. God delivered his people from death in Old Testament times. But the supreme deliverance comes with Jesus Christ. As 1 Corinthians 5:7 indicates, "For Christ, our Passover lamb, has been sacrificed." This connection between Christ and the Passover lamb is confirmed by the announcement of John the Baptist: "Behold, the Lamb of God, who takes away the sin of the world!" (John 1:29, referring to Jesus). Moreover, the Last Supper is a Passover meal (Luke 22:8, 15). Jesus reinterprets its significance in terms of his death: "This cup that is poured out for you is the new covenant in *my blood*" (v. 20).

We can therefore fill out the next portion of the triangle, the horizontal leg or horizontal side, as indicated in fig. 6.3.

The Significance of Two Steps

We use two steps for an obvious reason. There are two aspects to a type. A type is (1) a symbol and is (2) forward-pointing. Step 1 asks for the meaning of the symbol. Step 2 asks how the meaning points forward, and what it points forward to. Together, the two steps lead to determining the relation of the type (S) to its fulfillment (T^n). The Passover lamb points forward to God delivering his people through the death of Christ.

Special Terms

The third side of Clowney's triangle is the diagonal side, or hypotenuse. It is labeled "typological correspondence." The typological correspondence is the correspondence between the blood of the lamb (S), which is the "type," and its fulfillment (T^n), which is found in God delivering his people by the blood of Christ. The fulfillment (T^n) is called the *antitype*. The label *antitype* can be confusing to some people, because the English prefix *anti-* frequently has the sense of "being opposed to" or "in conflict with." But that is not the sense here. In Greek, *anti-* can mean "in place of." The *antitype* is the thing that arises later and replaces the type—it is the thing to which the type points forward.

The relation between the type and the antitype is traditionally called a "typical relation." "Typical" is the adjective form derived from "type."

But the more common meaning of "typical" is "combining or exhibiting the essential characteristics of a group [for example] *typical* suburban houses."[4] To avoid evoking this other meaning, we use the expression "typological correspondence" or "typological relation." *Typology* is the study of types and the related topics, such as antitypes and typological relations.

Figure 6.3: The Fulfillment of the Passover Lamb (Step 2)

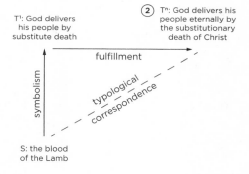

The Importance of Two Steps

It is important to have two steps, because together they guide the proper interpretation of types. Interpreters may be tempted to run directly from the concrete symbol (S) to its fulfillment (T^n), that is, to use the diagonal side of the triangle right away. But if they do, they may miss the actual meaning. They need step 1 so as not to leap to some meaning that comes into their mind that is not the actual meaning intended by God when he provided the symbol. (For the function of two steps in Patrick Fairbairn's approach to typology, see appendix A.)

A Third Step: Application

Clowney's triangle in its original form was a triangle with three sides. But at some point someone added a fourth, vertical line, in order to

4   *Merriam-Webster Dictionary*, online, https://www.merriam-webster.com/dictionary, accessed February 7, 2023.

represent application. Application assesses how typological meaning applies to individual believers and to the church as the corporate body of believers. We may denote the application by *A*. The reasoning from fulfillment to application takes the form of a vertical arrow, running from fulfillment (T^n) to application (A). (See fig. 6.4.)

Figure 6.4: Adding Application (Step 3)

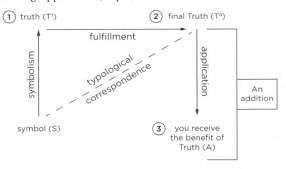

It would be appropriate to have the arrow for application run from the truth (T^n) out of the page, pointing to the reader. But one cannot achieve this effect with a two-dimensional diagram.

Application for the Passover Lamb

What is the application for the Passover lamb? We ask, "How does the fulfillment in Christ's blood apply to us?" It does apply. When we are united to Christ, we receive cleansing and deliverance from eternal death. The New Testament speaks of this reality as cleansing by the blood of Christ (Heb. 9:12–14).

On this basis we can fill out the text (3) to which the downward vertical arrow in the diagram points, the arrow representing application. (See fig. 6.5.) It is important to delay the third step (*application*) until after the completion of the first two steps (*symbolic meaning* and *fulfillment*). The first two steps serve as guides that help us to make applications that actually derive from the meaning of the type in the Bible. They are not simply invented by an overactive imagination.

Figure 6.5: Application for the Passover Lamb

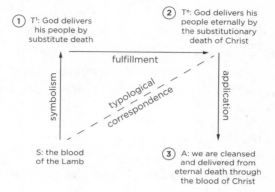

The General Principles for Clowney's Triangle

We may now generalize on the basis of the example of the Passover lamb that we have just worked through. The analysis of a type consists of three distinct steps.

Step 1: The meaning of a symbol. In step 1, we ask what is the divine truth symbolized in a type (because a type is also a symbol). We are seeking the meaning of the symbol at the time when God first gave it in the text that we are studying. (See fig. 6.6.)

Figure 6.6: Step 1: The Meaning of a Symbol

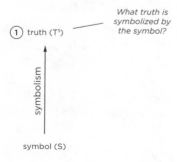

Step 1 is based on the fact that what God says and does has a meaning at the time when he first speaks and acts within the history of redemption.

What he says, he says to the people that he initially addresses. It makes sense at the time. Further revelation may throw further light on its meaning. But further revelation never dispenses with or overthrows the meaning initially given. Everything that God says and does is in harmony with who he always is. God speaks earlier to the people in the original situation. With the same words, he *also* speaks to us, according to Romans 15:4.

Step 2: From truth to fulfillment. In step 2, we ask how the truth finds fulfillment. To what does it point forward? We are seeking to follow the line of progressive revelation and the progressive work of God in the history of redemption. (See fig. 6.7.)

Figure 6.7: Step 2: From Truth to Fulfillment

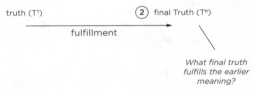

Step 2 is based on the reality of progressive revelation and the progressive working out of the plan of God in history. The earlier revelation looks forward to greater revelation to come. Step 2 tells us to pay attention to the growth of revelation and its climax in Christ. The same or similar symbols may reoccur throughout the Bible, and later occurrences may enrich the meaning that we associate with the symbol. In accord with the emphasis in Luke 24:44–49 on fulfillment in Christ, we ask especially how the symbol points forward to Christ and finds fulfillment in him.

Step 3: From fulfillment to application. In step 3, we ask how the truth that we have discovered applies to us, both individually and corporately (as the church). (See fig. 6.8.)

Step 3 is based on God's purpose for the Bible—that it will nourish us. Romans 15:4 says, "For whatever was written *in former days* was written *for our instruction*, that through endurance and through the encouragement of the Scriptures we may have hope." The Bible also teaches that we who

INTRODUCING CLOWNEY'S TRIANGLE 51

are believers are united through the Spirit with Jesus Christ (Rom. 8:9–11). We participate in the benefits of his work. "[Y]ou have been filled in him [Christ]" (Col. 2:10). So what is fulfilled in Christ has relevance for us.

Figure 6.8: Step 3: From Fulfillment to Application

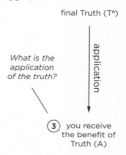

Harmony in the Three Steps

The three steps are in harmony with the principles that we already discussed (chapter 4) in sketching the larger theological framework for typological interpretation. Step 1 is based on the conviction that God spoke to people at earlier times, and spoke in terms that they could understand (when illumined by the Holy Spirit). Step 2 is based on the principle of progressive revelation, the principle of the unity of God's plan, and the principle that it is in Christ and his work that salvation is definitively accomplished. Step 3 is based on the principle that God already had us in mind when he wrote the Old Testament (Rom. 15:4).

7

The Tabernacle and Its
Furniture (Exodus 25)

WE MAY NOW ILLUSTRATE the function of Clowney's triangle by applying it to the tabernacle and some of its furniture.[1] We first consider the tabernacle as a whole (Ex. 25–40). Then we consider the ark (Ex. 25:10–22), the table for bread (vv. 23–30), and the lampstand (vv. 31–40).

The Tabernacle as a Whole: Step 1

Is the tabernacle a type? And if it is, what is its typological meaning? The key introductory explanation for the tabernacle is found in Exodus 25:8–9:

> [8] And let them [the people of Israel] make me a sanctuary, that I may dwell in their midst. [9] Exactly as I show you concerning the pattern of the tabernacle, and of all its furniture, so you shall make it.

The first step in interpreting a type is to ask what the type symbolizes. Verse 8 indicates that the tabernacle has a symbolic meaning, namely, "that I may dwell in their midst." The tabernacle is a tent structure. The tent symbolizes that God dwells in the midst of the people of Israel.

---

1 Vern S. Poythress, *The Shadow of Christ in the Law of Moses* (repr., Phillipsburg, NJ: P&R, 1995); see also appendix D.

So, for the tabernacle, the symbol (S) is the tent. The truth symbolized (T^1) is that God dwells in the midst of his people Israel.

We may thus begin to fill out the contents of Clowney's triangle in the vertical leg or vertical side, as indicated in fig. 7.1.

Figure 7.1: The Symbolic Meaning of the Tabernacle (Step 1)

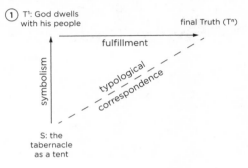

As in the case of the Passover lamb, it is important to focus on the meaning of the symbol at the time and in the text in which it is originally given. We are asking what the tabernacle means in the light of Exodus 25:8–9 and the surrounding portions of Exodus. We are not yet asking what it means in the light of progressive revelation leading to Christ and the New Testament.

The Tabernacle as a Whole: Step 2

Our second step is to move forward in time. In the light of progressive revelation, we ask how the truth that has been manifested in Exodus (T^1) is fulfilled in a later climactic manifestation (T^n).

In the case of the tabernacle, the central fulfillment is in Christ. God was dwelling with his people in Old Testament times. But the supreme dwelling of God with man is announced in the name Immanuel given to Jesus:

All this [concerning Jesus's conception] took place to fulfill what the Lord had spoken by the prophet [Isa. 7:14]:

> "Behold, the virgin shall conceive and bear a son,
>> and they shall call his name Immanuel"

(which means, *God with us*). (Matt. 1:22–23)

We find a similar idea in the Gospel of John:

> And the Word became flesh and *dwelt* among us, and we have seen
> his glory, glory as of the only Son from the Father, full of grace and
> truth. (John 1:14)

The mention of glory includes an allusion to the glory of the Lord that filled the tabernacle once it was completed (Ex. 40:35). John 2:21 indicates that the true temple is Jesus's body.

We can therefore fill out the next portion of the triangle, the horizontal leg or horizontal side, as indicated in fig. 7.2.

Figure 7.2: The Fulfillment of the Tabernacle (Step 2)

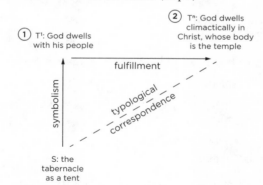

The Tabernacle as a Whole: Step 3

As our third step, we ask, "What is the application for the tabernacle?" We ask how the fulfillment in Christ, as the final temple, applies to us. It does apply. When we are united to Christ, we receive the gift of the Holy Spirit. The Spirit dwells in us and makes us a temple.

God makes the church a temple (1 Cor. 3:16), and the body of the individual Christian is a temple as well (6:19). There is both a corporate application to the church, and an individual application to each believer. Both are temples through the indwelling of the Holy Spirit, who is the Spirit of Christ. On this basis, we can fill out the downward vertical arrow on the righthand side of the diagram, the arrow representing application. (See fig. 7.3.)

Figure 7.3: Application for the Tabernacle (Step 3)

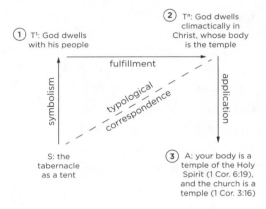

As in the case of the Passover lamb, it is important to delay the third step until after the completion of the first two steps. The first two steps serve as guides that help us to make applications that actually derive from the meaning of a type. They are not simply invented by an overactive imagination.

The Ark of the Covenant

Next, we consider some of the furniture in the tabernacle, as described in Exodus 25:10–40. The pieces of furniture for the tabernacle fit into the picture provided by the tabernacle as a whole. As we have seen, the meaning of the tabernacle as a whole is to show God dwelling with his people. So we expect that the items of furniture will show one or more aspects of the meaning of God's communion with his people.

The first item of furniture to consider is the ark of the covenant. It is described in Exodus 25:10–22. In some ways there are challenges about its meaning. Why is it shaped like a box? Why does it have the dimensions of 2½ cubits by 1½ cubits by 1½ cubits (v. 10)?

The most informative verses about the ark come later. It is a depository for "the testimony": "And you shall put into the ark the testimony that I shall give you" (v. 16). The "testimony" is the Ten Commandments (31:18; 32:15). Moses broke the original copy of the Ten Commandments (32:19). So the Lord commissioned a second copy (34:29). It consisted of two tablets that were later deposited in the ark (40:20). The Lord provides further information about its function:

> There I will meet with you, and from above the mercy seat, from between the two cherubim that are on the ark of the testimony, I will speak with you about all that I will give you in commandment for the people of Israel. (25:22)

The testimony itself consists in the Ten Commandments; it is what God says. It is both law and a covenant between God and the people. The further interaction described in 25:22 is therefore an extension of this core communication.

With this much information, we have enough to begin to see the symbolic meaning of the ark. At the very least, it symbolizes that God speaks to his people as one aspect of dwelling with them. So we may complete step 1 by indicating the meaning of the symbol. (See fig. 7.4.)

Figure 7.4: The Ark, Step 1 (Symbolic Meaning)

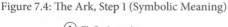

① T¹: God speaks
to his people

symbolism

S: the ark

In step 2, we ask how the truth comes to fulfillment. The climactic speaking of God is in Christ, as indicated in Hebrews 1:1–2:

> Long ago, at many times and in many ways, God spoke to our fathers by the prophets, but in these last days he has spoken to us by his Son, . . .

So we can add step 2, as indicated in fig. 7.5.

Figure 7.5: The Ark, Step 2 (Fulfillment)

What is the application to us? God speaks to *us* in Christ. And as we have the word written on our hearts, we may begin to speak it to others as well (Col. 3:16; Heb. 8:10–11). (See fig. 7.6.)

Figure 7.6: The Ark, Step 3 (Application)

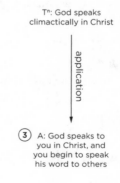

We may summarize the analysis in all three steps with a single complete diagram (fig. 7.7).

More Meaning in the Ark

If we look at the full passage in Exodus 25:10–22, further meanings are discernible. The ark is plated all over with gold (v. 11). To an Israelite, this would signify expense and beauty. It is a testimony to the greatness of God as King.

Figure 7.7: The Ark, All Three Steps

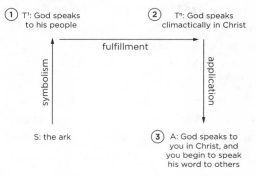

The theme of God's kingship also leads to a further explanation of the shape of the ark. The ark has to be a box in order to provide a depository for the testimony, the Ten Commandments. But within the environment of the ancient Near East, its shape is reminiscent of the footstool of a king. Indeed, Psalm 132:7–8 indicates a close relationship between the ark and the idea of a footstool:

> Let us go to his dwelling place;
>> let us worship at his *footstool*!
> Arise, O Lord, and go to your resting place,
>> you and the *ark* of your might.

The ark is the lower point of God's throne. And so it reinforces the point of the testimony. God is *ruling* over his people through his speech and his commandments.

Consider a second feature. There are two statues of cherubim attached to the "mercy seat," the cover of the ark (Ex. 25:18–21). These are images of the real cherubim, who are heavenly creatures who serve God in his presence in heaven. They are a reminder that the earthly tabernacle is a representation or image of God's dwelling in heaven. God is exalted in his holiness. The people of Israel have to be holy, as the law indicates (19:5–6, 10, 22, etc.; Lev. 19:2). God's holiness means that sinners need atonement. The term in Hebrew for mercy seat is related to atonement (so also in the Septuagint, the ancient Greek translation). Leviticus 16 specifies that on the Day of Atonement (and only on that special day) the blood of a bull and of a goat are to be taken into the Most Holy Place and sprinkled in front of the mercy seat, to "make atonement" (vv. 6, 10, 11, 16, 17, 18).

The symbolism says that the people need atonement. They need atonement in particular for their violations of the commandments that God has given in the Ten Commandments and in the other Mosaic instructions added to them. The fellowship between God and Israel includes both speech and provision for cleansing for their violations of God's holiness.

We may therefore add to our analysis information concerning atonement. (See fig. 7.8.)

Figure 7.8: The Ark, All Three Steps with Atonement

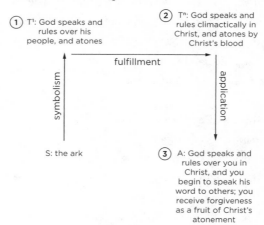

The Table for Bread

Next let us consider the table for bread, as described in Exodus 25:23–30. The provisions for placing bread on the table are discussed in Leviticus 24:5–9. Once again we need to move through the three steps in succession.

The first step is to consider the symbolic meaning of this table. The table is a piece of furniture within the tabernacle as a whole, which is the tent that symbolizes God dwelling with his people. The people themselves are living in tents. Their lives are supposed to reflect their communion with God. The table provides food, week by week. To the Israelites as a whole, God provides food in the form of manna from heaven (Ex. 16). The point of the table within the tabernacle is similar to the meaning of the manna. The meaning is that God provides food for his people. The bread that was put on the table consisted of twelve loaves (Lev. 24:5–6), corresponding to the twelve tribes of Israel. This number reinforced the point that God was providing for his people, who comprised twelve tribes.

At the end of each week, the priests removed the bread and ate it: "And it shall be for Aaron and his sons, and they shall eat it in a holy place, since it is for him a most holy portion out of the LORD's food offerings, a perpetual due" (Lev. 24:9). In the ancient Near East, eating a meal together was a sign of personal fellowship. God expressed his fellowship and friendship with the people of Israel. A more intensive case of a meal with God occurred in Exodus 24:11: "And he did not lay his hand on the chief men of the people of Israel; they beheld God, and ate and drank." The threat of people dying as a result of beholding God is there in the background. They could die because they were not qualified to stand before the holiness of God. But in the case in Exodus 24:11, they did not die. God established a relation of blessing with his people Israel, and the tabernacle was a permanent symbol of it.

So the table signifies both that God provides food for his people and that he provides fellowship, overcoming the barrier of sin.

We can now move to the second step. We ask, "How does this truth about God come to fulfillment?" It comes to fulfillment in Christ, who says, "I am the bread of life" (John 6:35). Christ himself is the bread that does not merely sustain physical life for a day but provides eternal life (vv. 50–51). Christ is also the one who brings atonement for sin and in this way establishes peaceful fellowship between God and his people.

The third step is application. The application is that we eat the bread of life, which is Christ. We feed on Christ by exercising faith in Christ: "Truly, truly, I say to you, whoever believes has eternal life" (John 6:47).

We may summarize the results of these three steps in a single diagram (fig. 7.9).

Figure 7.9: The Table, All Three Steps

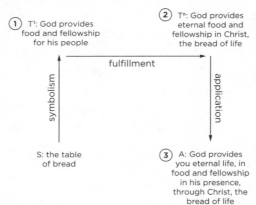

The Lampstand and Its Lights

Next we come to a third piece of furniture, the lampstand, described in Exodus 25:31–40. It is easy to see what its main function is: "And the lamps shall be set up so as to give light on the space in front of it" (v. 37). The lampstand was in the Holy Place. The Holy Place had no window. There were walls of boards on two of the sides; there was the main curtain or "veil" on the west side (26:31–33), separating the Holy Place from the Most Holy Place; there was another curtain or "screen," which served as the entrance to the Holy Place from the courtyard. Only a bit of daylight would have filtered in through cracks.

What is the symbolic meaning? The Israelites in their tents had lamps. God is signifying that he provides light for his people. The meaning is more evident when we remember that the tabernacle as a whole is an earthly representation of God's dwelling in heaven. The courtroom of God's presence in heaven is filled with the light of his presence. But there are also lights in the visible heavens—the sun and the moon and the stars. These lights are there by the provision of God in creation (Gen. 1:14–19).

In the wilderness, God provided light at night in the pillar of fire. The pillars of cloud and fire led the way through the wilderness, providing the light of guidance:

And the LORD went before them by day in a pillar of cloud to *lead them* along the way, and by night in a pillar of fire to give them light, that they might travel by day and by night. The pillar of cloud by day and the pillar of fire by night did not depart from before the people. (Ex. 13:21–22)

As a second step, we ask how the theme of God providing light is fulfilled later in history. The answer is that Christ is the light of the world (John 8:12; 9:5).

As a third step, we ask how this truth applies to believers. The answer is that we receive light from Christ. In union with Christ, we also become lights ourselves:

You are the light of the world. (Matt. 5:14)

. . . for at one time you were darkness, but now you are light in the Lord. Walk as children of light. (Eph. 5:8)

. . . the seven lampstands are the seven churches. (Rev. 1:20)

We may summarize the results in a single diagram (fig. 7.10).

Figure 7.10: The Lampstand, All Three Steps

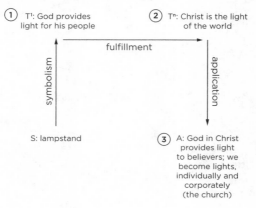

The Tree of Life

The description of the lampstand in Exodus 25:31–40 contains some additional features. The lampstand is like a tree. It has branches and almond blossoms. Why the blossoms? The text specifies carefully that the blossoms have both calyxes and flowers. There is attention to detail.

We may recall that the tabernacle as a whole is the dwelling place of God. Genesis 3 indicates that Adam and Eve originally dwelt in the presence of God. But their sin led to their being cast out of his presence. The tabernacle instructions come with this original fellowship with God in the background. The tabernacle promises a renewal of fellowship—though the continued presence of sin in the people makes the situation more complicated and subject to danger. The lampstand as a tree is placed within the sphere of the more intense presence of God in the Holy Place. It stands, then, as a reminder of the original garden of Eden and its trees. The close association between light and life in the Old Testament suggests that the lampstand symbolizes the tree of life (Job 33:30; Ps. 56:13; compare 27:1; 36:9).

Note that this meaning association with the tree of life would have been available to the Israelites at the time. The tree of life is mentioned in Genesis 2:9, 3:22, and 3:24. The people need both light and food in order to live.

The theme of the tree of life can therefore be added to the information that we have already accumulated. In the fulfillment, Christ is "the life" (John 14:6) and he freely offers eternal life to his people. (See fig. 7.11.)

Figure 7.11: The Tree of Life, All Three Steps

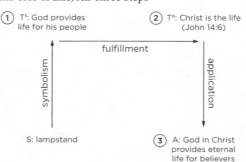

8

Clowney's Triangle for
Episodes in Genesis

WE NOW ILLUSTRATE the use of Clowney's triangle in analyzing some of the narrative portions in Genesis.

Noah's Flood (Gen. 6:9–22)

First, consider the narrative introducing Noah's flood in Genesis 6:9–22. Noah is declared to be a righteous man, whom God chooses to be the means for saving his family.

In our earlier discussion of Noah's flood (chapter 2), we saw that it had symbolic dimensions. Noah's flood is a symbol of God's righteous judgment. Noah as a righteous man is a symbol of the final deliverer, promised in Genesis 3:15. This symbolism already gives us step 1 in the steps delineated in Clowney's triangle.

Step 2 involves asking about fulfillment. The fulfillment comes in two stages. At his first coming, Christ as the righteous man delivers his spiritual family, the church, from the wrath of God. At the second coming there is a final judgment. Those who have trusted in Christ are again delivered. The deliverance at Christ's first coming is a deliverance in which Christ himself first bears the wrath of God. Then there is application (step 3) to the people of God.

We may summarize the entire picture using the points in Clowney's triangle (fig. 8.1).

Figure 8.1: Noah's Flood, Three Steps

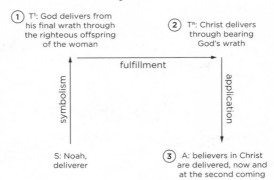

Melchizedek

As a second example, consider Melchizedek. Melchizedek appears in Genesis 14:17–20, Psalm 110:4, and Hebrews 5–7. Genesis 14:18 indicates that "he was priest of God Most High." As we saw in the introduction to this book, the Old Testament priests are types. So we can use Clowney's triangle on the passage in Genesis 14:17–20.

Step 1 asks, what is the significance of Melchizedek within his own time frame? He is a somewhat mysterious figure, appearing suddenly after Abram's military victory, and then disappearing. He is a priest. That means he symbolizes mediation between God and man. He is not the final, sufficient mediator, but he foreshadows this mediation.

We may note that even if Hebrews did not directly teach about Melchizedek in Hebrews 5–7, we could work out the basic meaning of Melchizedek in the context of Genesis 14. Genesis 14:18 indicates that he is both priest and king. This exalted combination contrasts with the separation of the offices of priest and king established in Leviticus and Deuteronomy. Psalm 110:4 adds to the picture by mentioning Melchizedek at a point in time long after both Melchizedek himself and the establishment of the Aaronic priesthood. Melchizedek contrasts with the Aaronic priests in that he receives his priesthood on his own, rather than as a result of a succession of generations. In this respect, he more directly anticipates the final priesthood described in Psalm 110:4.

Step 2 considers how Melchizedek foreshadows and anticipates a later fulfillment. This step is pretty straightforward, because the New Testament clearly teaches in Hebrews 5–7 that Melchizedek foreshadows the final priesthood of Christ.

Step 3 asks about application. The application to us is that Christ through his priesthood gives us free access to God (Heb. 10:19–25). The results from all three steps can be summarized using Clowney's triangle (fig. 8.2).

Figure 8.2: Clowney's Triangle for Melchizedek

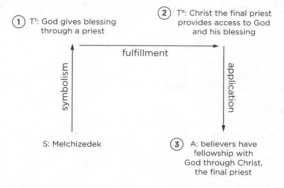

Sarah and Hagar

Let us now consider the narrative of Sarah and Hagar in Genesis 16. It is of some significance, because the apostle Paul comments on it in Galatians 4:21–31, drawing attention to its relation to Isaiah 54:1.

The use of Clowney's triangle means that first, in step 1, we consider Genesis 16 within its own historical and literary environment. We bring in Isaiah 54:1 and Galatians 4:21–31 only at later stages (steps 2 and 3). What is the significance of this episode? Does it have any symbolic overtones?

It does have symbolic overtones, because a contrast runs through Genesis between what springs from Adam by merely natural powers, and what springs up by the supernatural activity of God. God is working in history to bring small instances of supernatural deliverance, in anticipation of his climactic deliverance through the offspring of the woman (Gen. 3:15).

The issue of barrenness comes up with Sarah, Rebekah, and Rachel. The deliverer who is the offspring of the woman will come through the offspring of Abraham. But he must come as if by life from the dead. God repeatedly overcomes barrenness within the line of promise. Barren wombs are associated symbolically with death: "Sheol [the realm of the dead], the barren womb . . ." (Prov. 30:16). Romans 4:19 indicates that Abraham's body "was as good as dead (since he was about a hundred years old)." Surely that description would also apply to his wife, Sarah.

Genesis separates the godly line from the ungodly line of generations, beginning with Cain and Abel. This separation expresses the theme of the offspring of the woman and the offspring of the serpent. This theme is taken up in the story of Sarah and Hagar, because the offspring from Hagar occurs by a human scheme, and Sarah later comes to regret it.

So the reflections on the story later in Scripture are not just inventing a contrast that did not exist in Genesis. There is a contrast already. And this contrast symbolically echoes the big contrast between divine life coming from above, and earthly life coming by human striving.

In step 1, then, we ask about the significance of the conflict between Sarah and Hagar, and between their two children, within the scope of the book of Genesis. The answer is that they symbolize the conflict between dependence on God's promise and the results of human self-generated striving.

In step 2, we ask about fulfillment. The climactic fulfillment is found in Christ, who is the last Adam. He comes from heaven and is born by a supernatural birth. His birth, or rather his conception and birth, is even more spectacular than the way in which God overcomes instances of barrenness in the Old Testament. Adam is from earth; Christ is from heaven, the offspring of God's promise (1 Cor. 15:45–49; Gal. 3:16).

In step 3, we ask about the application to us. The application is suggested in Galatians 4:21–31. We are to believe in Christ. In union with him, on the basis of his achievement, we become the offspring of "the Jerusalem above" (v. 26).

There is much scholarly discussion about what is going on in Galatians 4:21–31. It would deflect from our main purpose to enter into that discussion. We will be content to say that Galatians 4:21–31 is an instance of typological analysis, in line with the symbolic meaning that exists already in Genesis 16. Galatians 4:24 says, "Now this may be interpreted *allegorically*: these women are two covenants." The word *allegorically* (Greek ἀλληγορούμενα, *allēgoroumena*) means that one can find a second level of meaning. That is indeed true, because the story of Sarah and Hagar has symbolic depth. By commenting on that depth, however, the passage is not endorsing everything that later came to be classified as "allegorical interpretation."

We may summarize our results using Clowney's triangle (fig. 8.3.).

Figure 8.3: Clowney's Triangle for Sarah and Hagar

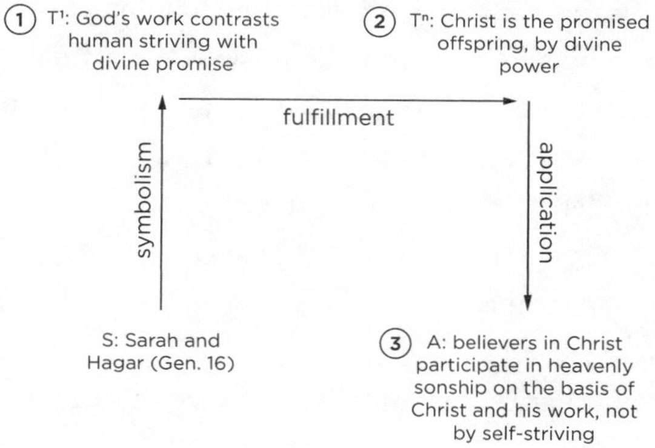

(1) T¹: God's work contrasts human striving with divine promise

(2) Tⁿ: Christ is the promised offspring, by divine power

fulfillment

symbolism

application

S: Sarah and Hagar (Gen. 16)

(3) A: believers in Christ participate in heavenly sonship on the basis of Christ and his work, not by self-striving

Jacob's Ladder

Next we consider Jacob's dream and his reaction, as narrated in Genesis 28:10–22. Does this story have symbolic overtones? It does. The dream features a ladder joining heaven to earth. It symbolizes the path to the full presence of God. God also speaks to Jacob in the dream, and confirms to him the Abrahamic promise. The promise is an expression of blessing that anticipates yet fuller fellowship in the presence of God in the future.

In step 1, we consider the symbolic meaning of the passage within its own context in Genesis. Genesis narrates the early stages of the process of redemption, in which God is working out the generations of the line of promise through Abraham, Isaac, and Jacob. Jacob is one link in this line. The symbolism in the dream expresses aspects of the hope of redemption.

In step 2, we consider how the symbolic meaning points forward toward fulfillment. The fulfillment takes the form of climactic intimacy with God, which God will give to his people who are the spiritual descendants of Jacob. In John 1:51, Jesus alludes to Jacob's ladder:

> And he [Jesus] said to him [Nathanael], "Truly, truly, I say to you, you will see heaven opened, and the angels of God ascending and descending on the Son of Man."

In Genesis 28:12, angels ascend and descend on the ladder. The verse in John 1:51 is then saying that Jesus is the fulfillment of the ladder. The angels ascend and descend on him. He is the path to heaven, as indeed he says in John 14:6: "I am the way, and the truth, and the life. No one comes to the Father except through me."

Step 3 considers the application. The application is that we come to the Father through Jesus, who is the ladder to heaven. We receive through him the intimacy and the blessing and the promise that was earlier given to Jacob.

We may summarize our findings in a diagram using Clowney's triangle (fig. 8.4).

Figure 8.4: Clowney's Triangle for Jacob's Ladder

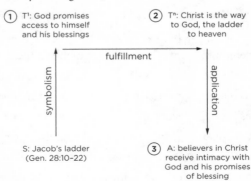

Usefulness of Clowney's Triangle

Not every case involving a type in the Old Testament is equally easy or equally clear. We have used a few relatively clear cases to show how Clowney's triangle works. It is useful in showing what questions to ask. Step 1 is especially useful in focusing our attention on earlier meaning that God communicated to people in Old Testament times. The focus on this available meaning helps to keep us in line with the actual purposes of the Bible passages. We avoid just seeing in a passage whatever truths arise in our imaginations.

9

Underlying Principles for Clowney's Triangle

WHY DOES CLOWNEY'S TRIANGLE work as well as it does? There are some underlying principles concerning the way in which God has planned and worked out our salvation.

Clowney's triangle depends on three basic principles about God's plan and his work in history. Let us explain the principle underlying each one of the three steps.

The Principle Underlying Step 1: God Uses Symbolism to Bring Christ's Redemption to People in the Old Testament.

The underlying principle for step 1 is the principle that God uses symbolism in the Old Testament. Why would he use symbolism?

In the first place, we know that there is only one way of salvation:

Jesus said to him, "I am the way, and the truth, and the life. No one comes to the Father except through me." (John 14:6)

And there is salvation in no one else, for there is no other name under heaven given among men by which we must be saved. (Acts 4:12)

This one way was present in the Old Testament as well as in the New Testament. Everyone who was saved in the Old Testament was saved in the same way—through Christ and his sacrifice, which was still to come. Only so can God "be just and the justifier of the one who has faith in Jesus" (Rom. 3:26).

But it is mysterious how people could be saved when the one true Savior had not yet come into the world. He had not yet actually worked and suffered and died to achieve the forgiveness of sins and present God with perfect righteousness. Christ's work had to have effect *beforehand*. God forgave people on the basis of Christ's work that was still to come.

This forgiveness is evident in the symbolism of animal sacrifice. As Hebrews points out, animal sacrifice was never an adequate basis in and of itself to accomplish forgiveness: "For it is impossible for the blood of bulls and goats to take away sins" (10:4). And yet, in Old Testament times, people *did* receive forgiveness and peace with God. How? The animal sacrifices symbolized beforehand what was to come. The sacrifices *symbolized* forgiveness that was actually to be achieved only through the final sacrifice of Christ.

God set up other symbols as well. The tabernacle of Moses and the temple of Solomon symbolized God dwelling with his people. In both cases, communion with God took place by means of animal sacrifices. The tabernacle and the temple, as physical structures, symbolized the dwelling of God with human beings that took place in reality with the coming of Christ.

These symbols display God's wisdom. In Old Testament times, in God's wisdom, he had to do two things. He had to provide a means by which people in Old Testament times might actually participate in salvation. And he had to do it before the climactic work of Christ had come. God's solution is that the participation takes place through symbolism. Symbolism shows the meaning of the coming work of Christ. At the same time, symbolism shows by its symbolic nature that it is pointing to something *else*, something other than itself. Christ's work is greater than the symbols, and it exists on a plane superior to the symbols. The contrasts between Christ's work and the symbols are actually just as important as the similarities. The symbols have to show their inferiority. In that way they point beyond themselves, and keep people from fixing their hopes *merely* on the symbols and not on the reality to which they point.

A number of texts in the New Testament use the language of "shadow" or "copy" to indicate that the symbols point to something greater:

> Therefore let no one pass judgment on you in questions of food and drink, or with regard to a festival or a new moon or a Sabbath [Old Testament symbolic arrangements]. These are a *shadow* of the things to come, but the *substance* belongs to *Christ*. (Col. 2:16–17)

> They [priests and their gifts] serve a *copy* and *shadow* of the heavenly things. (Heb. 8:5)

> Thus it was necessary for the *copies* of the heavenly things to be purified with these rites, but the heavenly things themselves with better sacrifices than these. For Christ has entered, not into holy places made with hands, which are *copies* of the *true things*, but into heaven itself, now to appear in the presence of God on our behalf. (Heb. 9:23–24)

> For since the law has but a *shadow* of the good things to come instead of the *true form* of these *realities*, it can never, by the same sacrifices that are continually offered every year, make perfect those who draw near. (Heb. 10:1)

The Old Testament is filled with shadows and copies of heavenly things, the things that Christ was to fulfill. It was wise for God to do it that way because these shadows, in their own time, through the work of the Holy Spirit, brought people into contact with the true salvation that Christ was later to achieve.

The Westminster Confession of Faith summarizes this symbolic representation through shadows and copies:

> This covenant [the covenant of grace] was differently administered in the time of the law, and in the time of the gospel: under the law, it was

administered by promises, prophecies, sacrifices, circumcision, the paschal lamb, and other *types* and ordinances delivered to the people of the Jews, all *foresignifying* Christ to come; which were, for that time, sufficient and efficacious, through the operation of the Spirit, to instruct and build up the elect in faith in the promised Messiah, by whom they had full remission of sins, and eternal salvation; and is called the Old Testament.

Under the gospel, when Christ, the *substance*, was exhibited, . . .[1]

The Principle Underlying Step 2: History Leads to Fulfillment in Christ.

The principle underlying step 2 is the principle of progressive revelation. "But when the *fullness* of time had come, God sent forth his Son" (Gal. 4:4). The Father, through the work of the Son, accomplished those things that had been symbolically signified beforehand in types and shadows. The meaning already available to Old Testament people at earlier times is now more fully disclosed through fulfillment in Christ.

The Principle Underlying Step 3: Christ Confers Himself and His Benefits to Believers through the Holy Spirit.

The principle underlying step 3 is that those who believe in Christ are united to him by the Spirit. Through this union they "have every spiritual blessing in the heavenly places" (Eph. 1:3). Therefore, what Christ did has *applications*, both to individual believers and to the church as a corporate body.

---

1   Westminster Confession of Faith (1647), 7.5–6.

PART IV

DEEPENING OUR UNDERSTANDING OF TYPOLOGICAL MEANING

To deepen our understanding of types, we discuss issues about meaning and other kinds of relations between the Old Testament and the New Testament.

10

Symbolism and Theophany

IN EXPLORING THE LARGER CONTEXT for studying types, it helps if we reflect on God's use of symbols. We said in the introduction that a *type* is a symbol specially designed by God to point forward to a fulfillment. Among other things, it is a *symbol*. It is a symbol designed by *God*, not merely by human invention.

Communication

So, what is a symbol? And why does God use symbols? As an aspect of personal fellowship, God communicates verbally to human beings, and human beings communicate in language to other human beings. This communication is, in a very broad sense, "symbolic" communication. Words, clauses, and sentences are "symbolic" in their function. Words, clauses, and sentences "stand for" something. Words can designate objects in the world (the word *horse* can be used to designate a particular horse). But they also can serve to communicate abstract concepts and more complicated views about the world. They can serve practical purposes in organizing human action through questions, commands, requests, and the like. There is a wide range of usage.

In a broad sense, a "sign" is something that "stands for" something else. The something else may be a physical object in the world. But it could also be any kind of meaning. In this sense, all human (and divine!) communication has a sign function and has meaning. This sign function is important. But so far, we have not yet distinguished anything that could be useful in appreciating what might be going on with *types*.

It may help if we distinguish three kinds of relations of signs to their meanings. As an illustration, let us consider a case where firefighters want to warn cars about a fire up ahead. They have three ways of doing it using a *sign*.

First, a sign can relate to its meaning by some kind of resemblance or analogy. The firefighters could put up a road sign that has on it a picture of a flame. The flame *resembles* the fire that is up ahead.

Second, a sign can relate to its meaning by some kind of already-existing system of signs that people have learned. For example, the road sign can have printed words and just say, "Fire ahead," or "Caution! Fire ahead." In this case, the road sign is using the English language as its system of signs. The signs already have meaning because they belong to the English language. This kind of meaning is often described as meaning "by convention." There is no innate resemblance between the sound of the word *fire* and the phenomena of fire. Instead, the association is "conventional" in English. One indication of the presence of convention is that there may be *other*, competing ways of signification, using *other* systems of signs. "Fire" in French is *feu*, in Spanish *fuego*, and in German *Feuer*. There is still some resemblance between the words, in that all begin with *f*. Many words in the languages of Western Europe show some kinship because they belong to the Indo-European family. But we could go to Indonesian, for example, and find that the word for "fire" is *api*. In Mandarin Chinese it is *huǒ*. In all these cases, there is no discernible relationship between the sound and the meaning of the words.

Third, a sign can be related to its meaning through a causal link. We say, "Smoke means fire." The smoke is a causal effect of fire. If there is sufficient smoke, the firefighters might decide that there is no need to put up a road sign. The smoke is already a clear sign to travelers that there is fire up ahead. Anyone who understands the causal link can appreciate the associated meaning.[1]

---

1   Robert Burch, "Charles Sanders Peirce," in *The Stanford Encyclopedia of Philosophy*, ed. Edward N. Zalta (Spring 2021 ed.), https://plato.stanford.edu/archives/spr2021/entries /peirce/, §11, indicates that C. S. Peirce distinguished "icons" (using resemblance),

Thus, there are three kinds of signs: (1) signs that rely on resemblance; (2) signs that rely on convention; and (3) signs that rely on a causal link.

It is the first of these three, meaning by resemblance, on which we will focus. The two other kinds of meaning connection are too broad to help us with typology. To take a particular example: the Old Testament priests *resemble* the final priesthood of Christ in some respects. Of course the two also differ. Some degree of resemblance or analogy belongs to what we want to call "types." Likewise, Noah's flood resembles the final judgment. God's deliverance of Noah resembles his final deliverance of those who belong to Christ. The Passover lamb resembles the work of Christ in dying for us.

Resemblance between Two Levels or Two Areas of Reality

It is convenient to add one more feature to our description of what counts as a "symbol." A symbol not only resembles the meaning about which it speaks; it also speaks about a sphere distinct from the symbol itself.

Let us illustrate with examples. The Old Testament priests are priests. And Christ in the New Testament is our "great high priest" (Heb. 4:14). But the Old Testament priests are on earth, while Christ's priesthood is in heaven (see Heb. 8:4). There is a pronounced difference, which affects the very conception of the meaning of their respective priesthoods.

Noah's flood and the final judgment are both judgments that destroy. But the last judgment is universal and final. It deals with eternal destinies, not only with temporal destinies. So the two judgments belong to two distinct spheres of meaning. They are still parallel. They still resemble each other. But the resemblance crosses over from one sphere of meaning to another.

Heavenly Reality

The book of Hebrews makes it clear that some of the correspondences between the Old Testament and the New involve a change from one

"indices" (using causal connections), and "symbols" (based on "convention"). We are using "symbol" in a manner similar to Peirce's "icons." Peirce may or may not think that these three categories can be sharply distinguished. Our view is that they are more like perspectives. They are partially distinguishable, but not isolatable.

sphere to another. More specifically, the change is a change from earth to heaven, or from heaven to earth, depending on how we look at it:

> They [Old Testament priests] serve a *copy* and *shadow* of the *heavenly things*. For when Moses was about to erect the tent [the Old Testament tabernacle of Ex. 25–40], he was instructed by God, saying, "See that you make everything according to the pattern that was shown you on the mountain." But as it is, Christ has obtained a ministry that is as much *more excellent* than the old as the covenant he mediates is better, . . . (Heb. 8:5–6)

> Thus it was necessary for the *copies* of the heavenly things to be purified with these rites [in the Old Testament], but the *heavenly things themselves* with better sacrifices than these. (9:23)

The Old Testament tabernacle was on earth. It and its furnishing and its rites were symbols of heavenly realities, realities that are more clearly seen now that Christ has accomplished the deliverance to which the symbols pointed. There are, then, two levels: (1) the level of earthly representation in the symbols, and (2) the level of heavenly reality, which has the truths that are being symbolized. The earthly level consists in a "copy and shadow" (8:5).

God's Presence in Heaven

The focus on heaven includes a focus on God's intensive presence in the heavenly sphere. The earthly tabernacle of Moses was only a "copy and shadow," in comparison. God comes to dwell in the tabernacle, to be with the people of Israel. But the earthly presence is a shadow of the heavenly.

Thus we can open a larger vista of symbolism. Earthly realities can symbolize truths about God and his ways. People in Old Testament times have the opportunity to come to know God as he reveals himself in word and deed. He also reveals himself in some special institutions, structures, and events, such as those associated with the tabernacle of

Moses. The temple constructed by Solomon is clearly a continuation of the same system of symbolism.

Theophany

We should pay particular attention to the special appearances of God, called theophanies.[2] Theophanies reveal God. They reveal him in his heavenly glory and holiness. And so they are also connected with symbolism. They often reveal God in symbolic form. They are an enhancement of symbolic dimensions that belong to the relation of God's people to God, within the Old Testament order.

Consider an example. First John 1:5 says that "God is light." When God appears, there may be a bright light as one aspect of his appearing (Acts 9:3; 22:6, 11; 26:13; Rev. 1:16). Physical light symbolizes the purity and splendor of who God is. So light functions as a *symbol* of God's character.

In some theophanies, God appears sitting on a throne (1 Kings 22:19; Isa. 6:1; Dan. 7:9). The throne functions as a physical *symbol* of God's power and control over the universe.

Many times, the use of objects with an added symbolic dimension goes back to the fact that the whole created order reflects the glory of God and displays his character (Isa. 6:3; Rom. 1:20). Physical objects are real and have everyday purposes in human life. God designed them to be a blessing for us. But they may have a symbolic dimension as well, which is activated when they appear in the context of an especially intense presence of God, such as in a theophany, or in the Mosaic tabernacle or Solomon's temple.

---

2 Vern S. Poythress, *Theophany: A Biblical Theology of God's Appearing* (Wheaton, IL: Crossway, 2018).

11

The Nature of Meaning

IN DEALING WITH TYPES, we should also briefly consider issues relating to the nature of meaning. What is meaning? What are we seeking when we talk about the meaning of a particular passage in the Bible?

We must refer readers to other sources for a fuller discussion of meaning.[1] But here we briefly sketch some of the principles to bear in mind.

Meaning and Time

We have seen that the Old Testament priests are types of the priesthood of Christ. When we read an Old Testament passage about the priests, what does it mean? Does it mean only what it meant for someone

---

1 Vern S. Poythress, "Divine Meaning of Scripture," *Westminster Theological Journal* 48 (1986): 241–79, https://frame-poythress.org/divine-meaning-of-scripture/; Vern S. Poythress, "The Presence of God Qualifying Our Notions of Grammatical-Historical Interpretation: Genesis 3:15 as a Test Case," *Journal of the Evangelical Theological Society* 50/1 (2007): 87–103, https://frame-poythress.org/the-presence-of-god-qualifying-our-notions-of-grammatical-historical-interpretation-genesis-315-as-a-test-case/; Vern S. Poythress, *God-Centered Biblical Interpretation* (Phillipsburg, NJ: P&R, 1999); Vern S. Poythress, *Reading the Word of God in the Presence of God: A Handbook for Biblical Interpretation* (Wheaton, IL: Crossway, 2016); Vern S. Poythress, "Dispensing with Merely Human Meaning: Gains and Losses from Focusing on the Human Author, Illustrated by Zephaniah 1:2–3," *Journal of the Evangelical Theological Society* 57/3 (2014): 481–99, https://frame-poythress.org/dispensing-with-merely-human-meaning-gains-and-losses-from-focusing-on-the-human-author-illustrated-by-zephaniah-12-3/; Vern S. Poythress, *In the Beginning Was the Word: Language—A God-Centered Approach* (Wheaton, IL: Crossway, 2009), ch. 7.

reading it when it was first written? Or does it mean all that we can see in it from our present vantage point in history? How we answer the question makes a difference in how we will treat not only the meaning of Old Testament priests but also the meaning of any type in the Old Testament. What is the meaning of Noah's flood, or the bronze serpent, or the Passover lamb, or the Mosaic tabernacle? Does a type mean what it meant originally, or what it means finally, when seen in the light of fulfillment in Christ?

There is something to be learned from both sides here. The meaning at the time that the type was given is a significant starting point and a guide to meaning. But more is involved.

Divine Meaning and Human Meaning

It is important first to affirm that the Bible as a whole, and every book in it, is a product of the joint work of God, the divine author, and a human author whom God raised up. Suppose there had been only a human author, with no special work of the Holy Spirit and no divine inspiration. Then it might seem reasonable to confine the meaning to what the human author intended at the time. He would not have known anything specific about the future coming of Christ and his work.

Suppose, for example, that without special divine guidance a human author wrote a passage like Numbers 21:4–9 about the episode of the bronze serpent. It could be that he recorded it simply as a historical record—such-and-such events happened. He would have known about previous promises of God, such as the promise of the offspring of the woman in Genesis 3:15, the promises to Abraham and his descendants, and the record of the exodus from Egypt. He would then know at least something about a larger pattern of promise and deliverance. But still, everything might be quite vague about the future. He might guess that the bronze serpent and other acts of deliverance might somehow line up by analogy with a future climactic deliverance by the offspring of the woman. But it would be little more than a guess.

If this were our approach, and we were to treat the Old Testament as nothing more than the product of human authors, it would affect our treatment of types. The result for typology would be that anything that appeared to be typological would be typological only in *retrospect*. Once we have events and teachings in the New Testament, we can *look back*. We can see some analogies between Christ and the bronze serpent. But those analogies exist only in retrospect. They are *backward-looking* analogies. They are analogies that are created by us or by the New Testament authors. They are available only after the events and the teachings of the New Testament are before us. The types become types only at the conclusion.

This approach has an attraction—it may seem "safer." It is certainly easier and clearer to wait until we have the New Testament. We can, for example, read what Jesus has to say about the bronze serpent in John 3:14–15. Then we can be on firmer ground in our own interpretation of its meaning. We can say that, in *retrospect*, given the instruction in John 3:14–15, the bronze serpent can be identified as a type. It becomes a type because of what Jesus says about it.

This approach also has extra popularity among biblical scholars because of the dominance of the historical-critical method in universities since the nineteenth century. The historical-critical method tends to *assume*, as a framework for its investigation of the Bible, that God is absent or nonexistent or irrelevant. We have only the human author. If so, it is still possible to talk about typology. But it is a kind of typology that is essentially the invention of human authors in the New Testament (or, sometimes, some of the later human authors of the Old Testament, who are looking back at the past), or an invention of early Jewish and Christian interpreters of the Bible. We can study typology, but only as a series of retrospective human ideas about the past.

But clearly this is a truncated view of typology, because for practical purposes it takes into account only human authors. If there is a divine author, and if the divine author has a plan from the beginning for all of history, everything changes in our viewpoint. God *intended* the Old Testament types from the beginning. They were in his plan even before the events and the records of the events in the Old Testament came into being. God's meaning is preeminent. The human authors whom

God raises up from time to time are commissioned to communicate *his* meaning, not their own (2 Pet. 1:21).

Wholly Divine Meaning

So an alternative approach to typology says that the meaning of any type is what it means for God. It meant that from the beginning. This approach is certainly better than the approach that simply omits divine meaning, for at least three reasons.

First, this approach reckons explicitly with the reality of God. God governs history, so that every event has meaning according to his comprehensive plan. The earlier events really do anticipate later events. When we are genuinely thinking God's thoughts after him, the sense of analogy that we discover between earlier and later events and persons and institutions is not merely a *human* invention, but a divine meaning. God governs not only the events but also the writing of the Old Testament. He is the divine author of the Old Testament and every book in it. So the Old Testament is what *he*, God, says, not merely what the various human authors wrote.

Second, this approach's affirmation of divine meaning, and not the approach through retrospective meaning, is in harmony with what the New Testament says about the Old Testament. As we saw in Romans 15:4 and 1 Corinthians 10:6, 11, the New Testament says not merely that there are analogies in retrospect, but that God caused the Old Testament to be written *with us in mind*, "for our instruction" (Rom. 15:4).

Third, various passages in the New Testament indicate that spiritually sensitive readers of the Old Testament should have had a better understanding of the significance of the events. In the very passage where Jesus mentions the bronze serpent, he rebukes Nicodemus for not understanding better:

> Jesus answered him, "Are you the *teacher* of Israel and yet you do not understand these things?" (John 3:10)

After his resurrection, Jesus talks to his disciples and says something similar to them:

"O *foolish* ones, and *slow of heart* to believe all that the prophets have spoken! Was it not necessary that the Christ should suffer these things and enter into his glory?" And beginning with Moses and all the Prophets, he interpreted to them in all the Scriptures the things concerning himself. (Luke 24:25–27)

Here we confront again the reality of what we have called progressive revelation. The revelation in the Old Testament is already speaking beforehand about Christ and his work. The readers of the Old Testament could have seen that. Yet it is also the case that the New Testament events and words add to the earlier revelation. Not everything was equally clear before the events took place.

Dual Authorship

Each book of the Bible has two authors, one divine and the other human. Both are intimately involved. The involvement of the human author means that we should pay attention to him and his intentions. But the deepest intention of the human author is to be a spokesman of divine communication. So in this way the human intention extends to everything in the divine intention. The human intention is to affirm and convey the divine intention. That includes any aspects that may not yet be fully revealed to the human author. We affirm both divine intention and human intention. But the divine intention has the primacy. That is true because it is the divine intention in inspiration that gets the human author going. And the human author affirms the divine intention even when it exceeds what he understands.[2]

With respect to types, such as the bronze serpent, what is the implication? The bronze serpent means what the divine author intends it to mean, according to his plan. And all of that is affirmed implicitly by the human author, even though he does not understand everything about the fulfillment.

---

2   Poythress, "Divine Meaning of Scripture."

Then and Now

The affirmation of divine intention also provides a platform for dealing with progressive revelation. We should affirm two complementary truths. First, God really did address the people living at the time when his revelation was initially given. The bronze serpent meant something specific to Moses and the people of Israel who saw it. Consequently, we should pay attention to what God intended to say to the people back then and there.

Second, God intended from the beginning to address later generations using the messages included in the canon. We remember Romans 15:4: "for our instruction." Hence it is valid to consider what we can learn from the bronze serpent not only from what the people back then could learn, but also from what can be learned in the light of later revelation, including Jesus's reference to the serpent in John 3:14.

We seem, then, to have two meanings. One is the meaning that God gave to the people then and there. For the events involving the bronze serpent, this meaning would itself have two stages—the first stage when the people look on the bronze serpent in order to be healed; the second stage when the book of Numbers is written, and we have the written word of God instructing the people about the episode.

The second meaning is the meaning in the light of later revelation, including John 3:14. This meaning is richer than the first. It is richer because progressive revelation is indeed *progressive*. Meanings are added. It may be helpful to observe that the meaning we can see is not created out of nothing, so to speak. It is based on comparing the passage in Numbers with what is written in later parts of the canon. Of course we pay special attention to John 3:14, because it specifically alludes to the serpent. But in principle we pay attention to the whole of the Old Testament as well.

Almost all the books of the Old Testament were written later than Numbers. What is written later supplements what is written in Numbers, even when it does not directly allude to a specific passage in Numbers. The rest of the Old Testament provides more instances

THE NATURE OF MEANING 91

of episodes of redemption, more instances of God's judgment on unbelief, more instances of promises looking forward to a greater redemption that will come in Christ. Then we look also at the New Testament, as a further addition to the canon. The whole canon together means more than Numbers. And the meanings belonging to later books interact with the meanings in Numbers to provide a more complete picture.

Progress and Building

We should note three important points. First, God knows the end from the beginning. The entire meaning is known to him from the beginning. It is "there" in God's mind. But it only gradually becomes accessible to *us* who are human. Meaning unfolds over time. That is one of the implications of the idea of progressive revelation.

Second, God never undermines the meaning that he provides in his earlier speech. So the meaning provided to the people in the wilderness is not only valid but also an important starting point for us. The problem with going directly to John 3:14 is not that John 3:14 is not true, but that if we just use it as an "answer," we stop paying attention to what God was saying long ago, in the time of the wilderness and the time of the writing of the book of Numbers. Studying that earlier communication is meaningful and helpful, because it "anchors" the meaning. It helps us not to go off on irresponsible flights of fancy when we search for a fuller meaning.

Third, later revelation *does* add to meaning. But it does so organically. The process is more like the growth of a tree from a seed than like the addition of more marbles into a bag of marbles. The meanings are connected, rather than being like isolated marbles. What is added in terms of depth of meaning will always be compatible with what God communicated earlier, because God is always compatible with himself. He may surprise us, because he is God. We must be ready for that. The proper attitude is one of prayer and study and submission to what is clear. Beyond that, we explore with reverence what is not yet quite so clear to us. In doing so, we receive guidance from later revelation, and in particular from the New Testament, which constitutes a time of climactic fulfillment in Christ.

But even the New Testament is not the complete culmination. God promises that Christ will return, and that he will create "new heavens and a new earth in which righteousness dwells" (2 Pet. 3:13). Meaning will in a sense reach its consummation in this future. We will know more deeply then than we do now. Yet what we do know, and know genuinely now, will not be undermined but rather enhanced by the future revelation in the new heaven and the new earth.

The Implications for Types

There are implications for how we do the study of types. It is the same three points that we already saw.

First, the meaning of a type is fully known by God from the beginning. It is God who makes a type what it is as a type, because it is he who gives it a symbolic meaning, pointing forward to fulfillment.

Second, the meaning of a type is partially revealed at the time when the type is first revealed in history. The meaning includes the meaning that God makes known to the people of the time.

Third, there is more meaning that will be available later, by means of progressive revelation. But that growth in availability is always compatible with the earlier revelation. The meaning of a type is to be found not only in the original passage that discusses it but also in the relation to later passages that throw further light on it.

12

Three Complementary
Perspectives on Meaning

IN ORDER TO ENHANCE FURTHER our understanding of meaning, we now discuss briefly three complementary perspectives on the idea of meaning.[1]

The Particle Perspective

The first perspective on the idea of meaning is the *particle perspective*. The particle perspective views language and meaning as consisting in chunks or "particles." This perspective is also called the "static" perspective, because we focus on what remains the same through time. There are words, clauses, and sentences. These are stable units—particles. If we view meaning as a particle, the meaning of a word, a clause, or a sentence is what we express using that piece of language. The meaning remains stable through the passage of time. We can re-express the same meaning with a different series of words. We paraphrase the earlier expression.

---

1   Kenneth L. Pike, *Linguistic Concepts: An Introduction to Tagmemics* (Lincoln: University of Nebraska Press, 1982), chs. 3–5; Vern S. Poythress, *In the Beginning Was the Word: Language—A God-Centered Approach* (Wheaton, IL: Crossway, 2009), ch. 7; Vern S. Poythress, *Reading the Word of God in the Presence of God: A Handbook for Biblical Interpretation* (Wheaton, IL: Crossway, 2016), 170–73. For roots in the Trinity, see Vern S. Poythress, *Knowing and the Trinity: How Perspectives on Human Knowledge Imitate the Trinity* (Phillipsburg, NJ: P&R, 2018), appendix D.

With respect to types, treating meaning as a particle takes place when we study a particular sentence or paragraph, dealing with a type, and then paraphrase the meaning. We may say, for example, that the meaning of the bronze serpent is that God brings deliverance from death through a cursed object.

The Wave Perspective

The *wave perspective* on language treats language as a process. Language consists in "waves" of communicative processes between people. This perspective is also called the dynamic perspective. Of course, the waves can be analytically broken up into words, clauses, and sentences that can be further inspected. If we do that, we are switching to the particle perspective. But the communication can also be viewed as a process. Over time, the process moves. It travels from one series of sounds and meanings to another series. In rapid speech, the individual pieces may be slurred together so that there is no exact boundary between them.

When we view meaning as a wave, we view it as a process that gradually moves from one person to another. One person gradually sets forth his speech, and another gradually takes it in. He may not fully take it in. So perhaps he asks a question, to clarify. He asks the speaker to slow down.

The word *meaning* in English may itself be one of the difficulties, at least for some people. The word *meaning* makes many people think first of all about fixed chunks. So, to distinguish this new view, we may suggest a new term: *impact. Impact* is the process of conveying meaning. It may, and often does, take time. Even after a speech is complete, the hearer may take time to understand it. (We all know instances where someone gets the point of a joke only after a delay.)

The focus on impact is complementary to the focus on static meaning. Real communication involves both. We cannot really understand impact without understanding the stable meaning that is *making* the impact over time. Conversely, we cannot really understand meaning without ourselves going through a process (an impact) where we come to understand a meaning that we did not understand before.

For types, the value of this perspective is in making us aware that the meaning of a type may develop over time. Because some symbols have a depth that is not immediately understood, it may take time for people to absorb the symbolic depth. Moreover, progressive revelation is about progress in impact. The impact can develop over centuries of time, because more works and words of God are being added.

The Field Perspective

The third perspective on language is the *field perspective*. This perspective considers language as a system of many relations between points. It is also called the relational perspective. So, for example, a word in English, like *horse*, means what it does in relation to a dictionary definition, in relation to near synonyms, and in relation to many contrasting words for other kinds of animals (*dog*, *sheep*, *cow*, etc.).

When we use the field perspective on meaning, we focus on how meanings relate to each other, and how any one meaning is largely determined by its relations to other meanings, including not only linguistic meanings but also meanings out in the world. There is such a thing as a horse. And that is one reason why English has the word *horse*.

Because the word *meaning* suggests a static, fixed entity, we may choose another term to describe the use of the field perspective on the examination of meaning, namely the term *import*. In ordinary English, the word *import* is nearly a synonym for *meaning*. But we are going to use it in order to focus on relations outward to *other* particle-like meanings. We ask ourselves, "What are the implications of this one text when we consider it *in relation to* surrounding texts in the same paragraph, in the same book, and in the entirety of the Bible?" So we may include within the scope of "import" not only the fixed meaning of a single text, but also the multitude of relations between the meaning of one text and many others. Clearly this kind of focus on relations is useful when we are considering the meaning of a single verse of Scripture in relation to the whole book in which it sits.

The field perspective does not compete with the particle perspective or the wave perspective. They are complementary. The field must have particles as endpoints of the relations. And the particles must have relations if they are to mean anything within a larger context. In studying a field, we move from one point to another, from one relation to another. And that movement is a wave movement. So the particle perspective and the wave perspective are there in the background anytime we use the field perspective. The same is true if we use any one of the three perspectives. When we have one perspective in the foreground, the other two are still there in the background. A complete field of relations, if it is complete, is a particle—a single whole. And understanding a field involves a process, a wave.

What are the implications when we consider types? When we deal with types, one of the challenges and difficulties is that types do not have their meanings completely within themselves, so to speak. If, as we have suggested, types are forward-pointing, then the things to which they point are integral to the fullest understanding of the types. Using a term we just introduced, types have *import*. The import goes beyond the meaning of a single passage, if the single passage is considered in isolation from the rest of Scripture. But of course treating a passage in complete isolation is, in the end, artificial. God *designed* Scripture, as his own word, to fit together. Scripture does form an organic whole. It is the word of God permanently recorded for his people. So it is right to consider it *as a whole*. And that means paying attention to the thematic relations and literary relations that one verse has to all the rest. In other words, we consider *import*.

That also implies that we need not artificially bring a huge load of meaning into a single passage or a single type, in *isolation*. The depth of meaning to be found in a type does not arise because of some secret that is inaccessible. It is not like Philo's interpretation of Genesis 6:9. Rather, it becomes known from *relations* of a single passage to others with the same theme. And above all, it becomes accessible when we compare the type with its later fulfillment.

13

The Theme of Mediation

ONE OF THE PRINCIPAL THEMES in the Old Testament is the theme of *mediators* and *mediation*. This theme is integrally connected to types, because many types arise in connection with the role of mediators and mediatorial activities in the Old Testament.

We will briefly survey the theme of mediation in the Old Testament in order to alert readers to its pertinence in considering types.

What Is a Mediator?

For our purposes, we can use a broad definition of *mediator*. A mediator is one who brings God's authority, power, and presence to bear on another.

Most of the time, mediators are personal beings. But in the Old Testament there are also what might be called "mediatorial institutions" or "mediatorial objects." For example, animals that are sacrificed to God as an expression of the divine-human relation are serving as mediatorial objects. They serve to establish, maintain, and mediate the relation of God to the people on whose behalf the sacrifice is offered. The tabernacle is a mediatorial object or institution. It can be called an institution because, besides being a physical structure, it is a space where various rituals are carried out. The purpose of the tabernacle and its spaces and its rituals is to serve as an expression of the relation of God to his people Israel. God says, "And let them make me a sanctuary, that I may dwell in their midst" (Ex. 25:8). God's dwelling in their midst is a manifestation of his *presence*. His presence is *mediated* through the tabernacle.

Mediation in Creation

Even before the fall into sin, God uses *means* in expressing his relation to his creatures. God speaks his word (Gen. 1:3; John 1:1). So in a broad sense, the word of God functions as a mediator between God and man, and also between God and the world to which he speaks.

Genesis 1:2 mentions the presence of the Holy Spirit in the created world. The Spirit *mediates* the presence of God to the world.

When God creates human beings, he instructs them to exercise dominion over the lower creation (Gen. 1:28–30). God has universal dominion. So this dominion by human beings must be a *subordinate* dominion. They will exercise it on behalf of God. They should do it with wisdom from God. In doing so, they are bringing the rule of God and the power of God to bear on the things under their rule. So they exercise a mediatorial role, in a broad sense.

Mediation for a Problem?

At the conclusion of God's acts of creation, he pronounces the completed product "very good" (Gen. 1:31). The mediation that exists is unproblematic mediation, because there is no sin—yet.

In our present context, of course, there is sin. Sin entered the world through Adam and Eve (Gen. 3). Mediation then becomes problematic. In a typical case, when we hear the word *mediator* or *mediation*, we may think first of all of a problem situation. There is a fight; there is a legal dispute. Or, there is a dispute in the workplace between labor and management. If the dispute does not dissolve right away, people may call in a *mediator*. In some legal situations, the parties may be *required* to submit to mediation. The mediator sits between the two parties. He tries to help them resolve the dispute or conflict. He may succeed, or he may not.

So it may seem problematic even to talk about a mediator or mediation in the original situation of creation, in the situation of what is "very good." We just have to remember that "mediation" in this situation does not carry with it the connotations of conflict. We are simply observing that there are channels and means and paths through which God relates to man, or to the lower creation, partly through responsible human care.

The Fall

After the fall into sin, the situation for mankind is very different. Adam and Eve sinned. God cast them out of the garden of Eden (Gen. 3:24). All mankind, "descending from them by ordinary generation," are caught in the web of sin.[1] We are alienated from God; we are guilty; we are subject to death (vv. 19 and 22). We need a mediator in order to have a proper relation to God. We need a mediator to overcome our guilt. We need a mediator to reverse the curse of death. And indeed, in Genesis 3, God promises just such a mediator in "her offspring," the offspring of the woman (v. 15). This promise points to its fulfillment in Christ, who is the offspring of Abraham (Gal. 3:16) and the offspring of the woman.

But what happens until the mediator comes? Every human being is sinful. Every human being needs to be preserved from dying whenever he is confronted by the intense presence of God. Every human being needs preliminary forms of mediation until the time when the final mediator comes.

We may expect, then, that the need for mediation is there all the way through the Old Testament, and into the New Testament. God is holy and man is sinful. The conditions are fundamentally the same, and so also the need for mediation is fundamentally the same.

Examples of Mediators

Let us consider a few instances of mediation. Noah serves as a prophetic mediator. Through him, salvation comes to his wife, his sons, and their wives. Second Peter 2:5 calls Noah "a *herald* of righteousness." It thereby indicates that Noah brought a message of righteousness to the people

---

1   Westminster Confession of Faith (1647), 6.3; Rom. 5:12–21.

around him. In a broad sense, a "prophet" is a person who speaks the word of God to someone else. This role is a mediatorial role, since the person is a channel or mediator of the word of God. Such was Noah.

Abraham also is a prophetic mediator. He receives promises from God that pertain not only to him but also to his descendants. And it is announced that "in you all the families of the earth shall be blessed" (Gen. 12:3). This message from God is eventually recorded in Scripture for the more distant descendants, and for all the families of earth. In this way, Abraham passes the word of God on to others.

Abraham also at one point serves as a *priestly* mediator. One of the functions of priests is to intercede for others. This intercession *mediates* the blessing of God to the people for whom they intercede. Genesis 18:22–33 records that Abraham intercedes for the inhabitants of Sodom and Gomorrah.

Prophets, Kings, and Priests

In the time of Moses, God provides further revelation that explains more thoroughly the offices of prophet (Deut. 13; 18), king (Deut. 17), and priest (e.g., Lev. 8–9). The people who function in each of these three offices are mediators. As we have seen, prophets mediate God to others primarily by mediating the *word* of God. Kings, when they function well, bring the rule of God to bear on people, by executing justice. They mediate the *rule* of God. Priests bring the blessing of God to people. They mediate the *presence* and *blessing* of God.

Throughout the pages of the Old Testament, there are people who are explicitly called prophets, or kings, or priests. They hold an *office*. But the functions of mediation are actually broader. There are people who may receive a message of God only once in their whole life. For example, Rebekah receives a message about Esau and Jacob when the two boys are in her womb (Gen. 25:22–23). This one episode may be unique in her whole life. She is not called a prophetess, because it is only this one message that she receives.

Fathers in a family exercise rule over their families. They are not called "kings," because they are not ruling over a whole nation. Even tribal leaders like those listed in Numbers 2 are not technically "kings," because they are chiefs of only one tribe. But they do serve to rule on God's behalf. So in the broad sense they can be considered as kingly mediators.

In general, people may exercise mediatorial functions in a small way. So besides the narrow, prominent instances of the *offices* of prophet, king, and priest, we find many other instances that might be labeled as displaying more faintly the *function* of a prophet, or a king, or a priest. They deliver the word of God, as prophetic mediators. They exercise the rule of God, as kingly mediators. Or they deliver the presence and blessing of God, as priestly mediators.

Consider another example. Moses himself serves as a mediator in all three aspects. Moses is a mediator of the word of God who speaks to the people of Israel the words that God communicates to him. Moses is a kingly mediator in that he serves as a judge in the early days (Ex. 18), applying the justice of God. Moses is also a priestly mediator. He offers sacrifice, as a priest would do, when he consecrates Aaron and his sons in Leviticus 8.

Pervasiveness of Mediation

Mediation is present implicitly all the way through the Bible. Because God is holy and people are sinful, we absolutely need mediation. God makes it plain that unmediated confrontation with the full presence of God would result in sudden death: "You cannot see my face, for man shall not see me and live" (Ex. 33:20). Sometimes the mediation is obvious and explicit. Moses, as we indicated, is regularly there to mediate between God and the people during the exodus and the wilderness journey. Joshua, his successor, also serves as a mediator. Once Aaron and his sons are appointed as priests, they function as mediators. Joseph mediated God's word to Pharaoh by interpreting his dreams. Abraham mediated God's word concerning his descendants and the families of the earth.

But the *need* for mediation is pervasive. Every time someone is delivered from death, it is a mercy from God. We all deserve death all the time, because death is the wages for sin (Gen. 3:19; Rom. 6:23). We get better than we deserve because of God's mercy. This principle holds for non-Christians as well as Christians. Believers in Christ, and only they, receive the climactic mercy of the gift of eternal life. But everyone who is delivered from death even temporarily is receiving a mercy.

And why do we get mercy when we do not deserve it? Because of mediation. The idea is pictured in Genesis 8:20–22. Noah offers animal sacrifices to the Lord after the flood. The animal sacrifices are mediatorial. The Lord is pleased because of them. They are symbolizing the final sacrifice of Christ. They do not function in isolation, but as pointers that point forward to the sacrifice of Christ. The passage indicates that the Lord is pleased. He is pleased ultimately because of the sacrifice of Christ. Because of the sacrifice of Christ, symbolized beforehand in the animals, the Lord promises not to bring another flood. This promise is a mercy.

It is a mercy that extends not only to godly people like Noah himself but also to ungodly people as well. It is what might be called "common grace." It does not mean that every single individual descended from Noah will be eternally saved. But it *does* mean that all people will receive temporary mercy by being saved from a universal flood. This mercy comes through a mediator. Proximately, the mediators are Noah and the sacrificed animals. Ultimately, these are pointers to Christ, the final mediator.

So it is worthwhile with respect to any passage of Scripture to ask how people receive mercy. Through what channels does the mercy come? It is mediated. Negative judgment also comes through channels, through means. So negative judgment as well as positive mercy is mediated. Negative judgment anticipates or foreshadows the final judgment that comes through Christ (John 5:27).

The Final Mediator

First Timothy 2:5–6 indicates that Jesus is the only mediator:

> For there is one God, and there is *one mediator* between God and men, the man Christ Jesus, who gave himself as a ransom for all, which is the testimony given at the proper time.

Then how is it that there are mediators in the Old Testament? These mediators exist only as shadows of the great mediator. It is only through the final mediation of Christ that the Old Testament mediators are allowed to be mediators at all. We can see this truth if we consider someone like Moses. Moses is a mediator for the people of Israel. But Moses himself is not sinlessly perfect. So he himself needs mediation. God makes this clear when he informs Moses that "you cannot see my face, for man shall not see me and live" (Ex. 33:20). In raising up Moses as a mediator, God is already reckoning with the future, the time when Christ the great mediator will come and expiate the sins of Moses.

In sum, it is always valuable to ask what is happening with respect to mediation. It is a continuing issue throughout the Old Testament. Every instance of mediation is a prefiguration of Christ the great mediator. So every instance of mediation is a *type*. The theme of mediation thus provides a rich resource for discerning and interpreting types in the Old Testament.

Themes Related to Mediation

As a further aid to discerning instances of mediation in the Old Testament, let us consider the themes explored in a recent book on typology by James M. Hamilton Jr.[2] Here is the list that Hamilton offers:

"Part 1: Persons"

Adam-like figures. As Adam-like figures, Hamilton lists not only Adam himself but also Noah, Abraham, Isaac, Jacob, Israel (the nation), David, and finally Christ. These individuals and the nation of Israel are all representative figures through whom blessing (or curse, in the case of Adam) comes to a larger group. They *mediate* the presence and blessing of God.

Priests, prophets, kings. As we observed earlier in this chapter, priests, prophets, and kings mediate the blessing of God, the word of God, and the rule of God respectively.

---

2   James M. Hamilton Jr., *Typology—Understanding the Bible's Promise-Shaped Patterns* (Grand Rapids, MI: Zondervan, 2022). See his table of contents.

The righteous sufferer. As righteous sufferers, Hamilton lists Joseph, Moses, David, and the suffering servant (Isa. 53). The righteous sufferer mediates blessings to others through his suffering. These instances are also instances of a redemptive plot (to be discussed in chapter 22).

"Part 2: Events"

Creation. Hamilton discusses the temple theme in creation. As we observed earlier in this chapter, God's presence in creation is mediated (apart from sin) through various means. On the temple theme, see chapter 7. The tabernacle and the temple in the Old Testament are structures that symbolically mediate the presence of God. They are closely associated with the priesthood and its mediatorial function.

The exodus. The exodus from Egypt is a redemptive plot (see chapter 22), in which God mediates his saving presence to his people Israel.

"Part 3: Institutions"

"Leviticult."[3] The institutions of the Mosaic administration include the temple, the priests and Levites, the law, the covenant, the coming king, the sacrifices, the feasts, and God's presence. All these are mediating institutions.

Marriage. God represents his relation to his people as similar to marriage. He is the husband and Israel is his wife (Isa. 1:21; 54:1–8; 62:5; Ezek. 16; 23; Hosea). Anticipations of the later prophetic material are found already in the Mosaic era (Ex. 34:14–16). Human marriage is not itself a mediatorial institution. But, in a broad sense, it is a type of the mediated relation between God and his people. (See further discussion in chapter 23.)

Conclusion on Hamilton's List

In sum, Hamilton's list of types agrees with the types that can be found by following the theme of mediation.

---

3   The term is Hamilton's (*Typology*, table of contents).

14

Comparing Types with Other Relations between Meanings

WE HAVE TALKED ABOUT the larger framework of understanding God and his plan. It is now appropriate to think more specifically about *types*. What are they? How are they to be distinguished from other kinds of meaning in the Bible?

Definition and Contrast

At the beginning of the book, we defined a *type* as a symbol specially designed by God to point forward to a fulfillment. That is a rough definition. But why single out just *this* kind of communication within the totality of revelation? In considering various passages in the Bible, we have indirectly received some suggestions about why types might be important. Let us briefly consider them.

Types are forward-pointing, and as such they address the challenge of seeing how God designed the Old Testament to be "for our instruction" (Rom. 15:4). How, for example, do we understand Jesus's claim in Luke 24 that the Old Testament is about him?

We can also see that something interesting is going on with some of the examples of types that we have discussed. We have looked at the bronze serpent, at Noah and the flood, at the Old Testament priests, at the Passover lamb, at the tabernacle, at the theme of mediation. All these have import. In the context of the whole Bible, the passages have implications larger than what might appear on the surface.

But are there not other things going on in the Old Testament as well? The Old Testament contains records of history, the history of the people of Israel. It contains poetic songs in the book of Psalms. It contains prophecies.

So let us consider, not types alone, but some other kinds of material. In all these cases, we want to ask three major interpretive questions: (1) What kind of writing is God giving us in a particular place within a particular Old Testament book? (2) How does this material relate forward to Christ and his climactic salvation? (3) How then does it apply to us, as disciples and servants of Christ?

There are many different kinds of writing in the Old Testament. Many books have been written that explore how we read each kind—each genre. Sensitivity to genre helps us to grow in understanding the Old Testament. But, for the purposes of discussing the topic of typology, we want to move to the second question. How does an Old Testament passage relate forward to Christ?

There are several ways.[1] Let us consider them, one at a time.

Analogy

The first kind of relation between passages is a relation of *analogy*. An *analogy* is a similarity or likeness between persons, events, places, circumstances, etc.

"Analogy" is a very flexible category. If we extend it to every kind of analogy, it will be too broad for our purposes. What we have in mind are analogies between two things on the same level, within the same larger field of view. For example, Abraham's faith in God's promises is analogous to the faith that God calls us to have:

> That is why it depends on faith, in order that the promise may rest on grace and be guaranteed to all his offspring—not only to the adherent

---

1   The basic categorization used here is adapted from the classroom teaching of O. Palmer Robertson at Westminster Theological Seminary, circa 1972.

of the law but also to the one who *shares the faith of Abraham*, who is the father of us all, . . . (Rom. 4:16)

. . . just as Abraham "believed God, and it was counted to him as righteousness"? Know then that it is *those of faith* who are the sons of Abraham. (Gal. 3:6–7)

Consider another analogy. There is an obvious analogy between how Isaac and Jacob get their wives. In both cases, the wives are found by a journey back to the land from which Abraham came. There is a sense also in which all the cases where men find wives are analogous to one another. These cases are all on the same level, because the setting is one of normal social customs and expectations about how marriages will be made for the next generation.

These cases of marriage are also analogous to the New Testament teaching that the church is the bride of Christ (Eph. 5:25–27; Rev. 19:7). But now, with Christ and the church, we have made a transition to another level. The language of bride and marriage is being used metaphorically. Instead of applying to normal social relations on earth, it applies to a marriage in heaven, a spiritual union. So this kind of analogy is an analogy between two levels, rather than an analogy between two persons or events on the *same* level.

In our current focus on analogy, we are temporarily leaving this second kind of analogy to one side. We are focusing on analogies between two things that are on the same level. If we need to be explicit, we can call this kind of analogy a *one-level analogy*.

Analogies are one way in which passages in the Old Testament relate forward. The marriage of Isaac has a relation forward to the marriage of Jacob. The early battle of Joshua at Jericho is related to the later battles where the Israelites conquer other cities in Canaan. The Old Testament has relations forward to later parts of the Old Testament, and then also to the New Testament. Men and women continue to have marriages in New Testament times. There continue to be wars.

The New Testament indicates that people in the Old Testament have faith in God's promises. When they exercise faith, they become examples for us, as Hebrews 11 shows. Each instance of faith is analogous to later instances, including instances in our lives today. Our common humanity, our common struggle with sin, and our experience of God's grace along with other believers—all serve in making connections between various events in the Bible. The connections are connections by analogy.

Symbol

A second kind of relation between passages arises when a passage involves a *symbol*. We may define a *symbol* as an earthly representation of divine truth.[2]

A symbol, unlike a one-level analogy, involves two levels. There is the level of the symbol itself, which is earthly or material. Then there is the level of divine truth, the truth symbolized by the symbol. Theophanies provide many examples of symbols. The loud thunder at Mount Sinai symbolizes God's power. The fires at Sinai and in Ezekiel 1 symbolize God's ability to purify his people and to consume evil.

There are other things with a symbolic dimension. The manna from heaven symbolizes God's daily care.[3] The flood of Noah symbolizes God's judgment on human wickedness. The lampstand in the tabernacle symbolizes God's ability to give light to his people.

Symbols activate relations between passages, because a symbol has a relation to every other passage that expresses the same divine truth. So, for example, the passage about the manna in Exodus 16 has a relation not only to other passages that happen to mention manna, but also to passages that express the principles of God's care or that give examples of his care.

Type

We now come to the key word *type*. A *type*, as we are defining the term, is a forward-pointing symbol. It is an earthly representation of divine truth that is also forward-pointing.

---

2   Robertson offers the definition, "A material representation of redemptive truth" (classroom lectures, circa 1972). Symbols typically operate as signs that resemble the thing that they symbolize (see ch. 6).

3   This example comes from Robertson, classroom teaching, illustrating "symbolism," circa 1972.

One example would be the tabernacle. It symbolizes God's dwelling with his people, according to the explanation given in Exodus 25:8–9. Is it forward-pointing? To answer that question takes some reflection. The tabernacle as a symbol of God's presence is analogous to the more intensive form of God's presence in theophany. In fact, after the tabernacle structure is set up, God appears in a cloud, which descends on the tabernacle: "Then the cloud [of theophany] covered the tent of meeting, and the glory of the LORD filled the tabernacle" (Ex. 40:34). The appearances of God in theophany in the Old Testament implicitly look forward to a later, climactic appearance. The implication is that, at some later point in time, when redemption comes to a climax, God will appear and will triumph over all evil. In the meantime, full access to the presence of God is restricted. There are two curtains that separate the inner rooms of the tabernacle from the outside. There are special ceremonies and qualifications that are needed to enter these inner rooms. These restrictions show that a more intense fellowship with God will require something more than the tabernacle offers:

> According to this arrangement [the Mosaic tabernacle], gifts and sacrifices are offered that cannot perfect the conscience of the worshiper, but deal only with food and drink and various washings, regulations for the body imposed until the time of reformation [the time when Christ would come]. (Heb. 9:9–10)

Since the tabernacle is a symbol and is forward-pointing, it is a type.

The design of God. At the beginning of the book, we offered an earlier definition of type: "a symbol specially designed by God to point forward to a fulfillment." This definition includes the further expression "specially designed by God." That expression is a useful reminder. God is the one who gives meaning to types. God gives meaning, for that matter, to all of history. All of history is designed by God.

The word "specially" indicates that God has thought through what he is doing. Even though the meaning of a type is gradually disclosed over a period time—maybe a long period, a period of centuries—God has his design in mind from the beginning. The meaning, when fully available, is a special gift from God.

Time and meaning. Let us consider how symbols and types relate to the idea of progressive revelation. When in history does the meaning of a symbol or of a type come to light?

In our definition of symbol, it was understood that the symbol has its meaning at the time when God originally gives it. The meaning is, of course, first of all meaning in the mind of God, according to the design of God. But it is *also* a meaning that God actually makes known to people, in the nature of the symbol. For example, the manna is a symbol of God's daily care. The people of Israel could see every day that it was a symbol of his care, because they experienced his care as they saw the manna and collected it. In the symbol of the lampstand (Ex. 25:31–40), they could see a reminder that God is the one who furnishes light to his people.

As a general principle, the meaning of a symbol accompanies the symbol from the time when it is initially given to people.

Now what about a type? Since a type is a symbol, it has meaning for people on earth from the time when God originally gives it. But there is something more, because a type is also forward-pointing. It points to a fulfillment. The idea of progressive revelation tells us that the fulfillment will "fill out" the meaning, as well as filling out the work of God. Once the fulfillment is before the people of God, they will be able to see fuller meaning than they saw before. This fullness is closely related to the idea of "import," or meaning residing in relations. The relation between the type and its fulfillment is a relation designed by God as one aspect of his eternal plan. Once the fulfillment comes, people can be instructed by God to see the relation between the fulfillment and the earlier stage, the stage of the original type.

In short, a type has meaning as soon as it appears in history. But the meaning is forward-pointing. It points, then, to a fuller meaning that will be available only when the fulfillment comes to pass. We may also expect that, when the fulfillment comes to pass, God may provide further interpretive messages that help people to see the meaning of the fulfillment more fully, in the light of previous revelation and also in the light of revelation that is just now being provided by God.

Such is true in the New Testament. The New Testament period constitutes a new work of God. Jesus Christ comes to earth. He accomplishes God's plan and accomplishes the redemption of the world. This accomplishment is a new work of God. There are also new *words* of God. Jesus Christ, during his earthly life, teaches the people. And then he commissions his apostles and other disciples to spread the news of the gospel to the ends of the earth. As part of this ministry, the New Testament is written. It provides more words that interpret the deeds. The *meaning* of Christ's work is further explained. These New Testament meanings relate organically to the earlier meanings found in types.

We observed earlier that the Old Testament priests are types of the priesthood of Christ. The priests symbolize the need for a mediator to offer gifts and sacrifices to God, to obtain forgiveness of sins and fellowship with God. The symbolic meaning is there when the priests are established as priests. The priests are forward-pointing symbols, pointing to the fulfillment in Christ's priesthood. Christ's priesthood is richer than the Old Testament priests. He is on another level. He is the priest who actually accomplishes the forgiveness of sins through his own death, once and for all (Heb. 4:14–10:39). So his priesthood, and the interpretation of its meaning in the pages of the New Testament, *adds* to the meaning of priesthood in the Old Testament. The meaning that was already known to people in Old Testament times still exists. But there is an organic growth. There is progressive revelation.

Prophecy

Our next category is *prophecy*. *Prophecy* can be defined as "verbal or enacted prediction."[4] Verbal predictions occur when prophets predict near-future events (Isa. 7:8) or far-future events such as the coming of the Messiah (9:6–7). *Enacted* prediction describes a situation where a prophet acts out a series of actions, and these actions depict future

---

4   Robertson, classroom teaching, circa 1972.

events. A classic case occurs when the Lord tells Jeremiah to make a yoke and put it on his neck. It is a symbol of the fact that the smaller nations are going to have to submit to the rule of Nebuchadnezzar, king of Babylon (Jer. 27). Usually, these enacted predictions are also explained verbally. So enacted prediction becomes a reinforcement of an accompanying verbal prediction.

Prediction has an obvious relation to the events that it predicts. The relation is straightforward. The point about this whole category is that it represents a different *kind* of relation than what we have seen before, with analogy, symbol, and type.

We should make one further note. The prophets whom God raised up in the Old Testament were spokesmen for God. A prophet can be defined as a person who speaks the word of God (Ex. 7:1). Whatever God commissions the prophet to say, he says. So the *contents* of what he says could be whatever God determines. *Sometimes* the contents are predictions of the future. The predictions may be straight predictions, such as Isaiah's predictions concerning the Messiah (e.g., Isa. 9:6–7; 11:1–10; 53:1–12). They may be *conditional* predictions, according to which the events will come out differently depending on whether the people repent (Jer. 18:7–10).

Old Testament prophets may also speak hortatory messages, or messages in which God evaluates past deeds, or in which he recalls records of the past. So our use of "prophecy" to denote prediction differs in meaning from the meaning "what a prophet says." It is nevertheless convenient to have *some* word to label the instances when we deal with direct predictions in the Bible.

Various Relations

So now we have at least four categories describing various kinds of relations that God's word may have to later words and events: analogy, symbol, type, and prophecy. It is useful to have all four. It reminds us that the way in which the Old Testament relates to the New, the way in which the earlier relates to the later, is multifaceted. There is more than one way in which relations exist. Our task as readers is to take into account this richness. We should not try to force everything into one mold, so that everything is treated as if it were a one-level analogy, or everything is treated as a symbol.

If we stand back and look at the complete set of categories, we can see that we are dealing with several intersecting criteria. One of the questions is whether the passage presents us with only one level of meaning, or two. In other words, is there a symbolic dimension, using a symbol to express divine truth? A second question is whether the passage is forward-pointing. Then, if it is forward-pointing, does it point forward by means of straightforward prediction, or only indirectly, through some hint of a future? If we put all these features together, we obtain a table that classifies the four different categories. (See table 14.1.)

Table 14.1: Distinctive Features of Four Categories of Old Testament Passages

Category	One-Level	Two-Level	Forward-Pointing?
Analogy	✓		
Symbol		✓	Maybe
Type		✓	✓ (indirectly)
Prophecy	✓	✓	✓ (directly)

By our definition, prophecies are directly predictive. But they could accomplish the prediction in two distinct ways. A "prophecy" could include either one-level meaning or two-level meaning. In fact, both occur in the Old Testament. Some Old Testament predictions are straightforward predictions, like the prediction of the coming of the Messiah in Isaiah 9:6–7. Other predictions, however, use symbols. Ezekiel 40–47 describes a vision (40:2) of a temple. A temple is a structure with a symbolic dimension. It signifies God's dwelling with his people. So it can be debated (and it *is* debated) as to whether Ezekiel is predicting a future temple of stone, or predicting the fulfillment of the symbol in a future "temple" that will bring to realization the second level of *meaning* of the physical temple of Solomon.

We can produce another table, which classifies passages according to two dimensions. A passage will fall into one of two distinct columns according to whether it has one-level meaning or two-level meaning. And then the same passage will fall into one of three distinct rows, depending on whether it is not forward-pointing, indirectly forward-pointing, or directly forward-pointing (in a direct prediction). (See table 14.2.)

Table 14.2: Various Kinds of Relations—Clarified

	Two-Level Meaning	One-Level Meaning
Not forward-pointing	Symbol (but not a type)	Analogy (on a single level)
Indirectly forward-pointing	Type (and also a symbol)	
Directly predictive	Prophecy (symbolic)	Prophecy (not symbolic)

Table 14.2 has one empty space, the space for one-level meaning that is indirectly forward-pointing. This combination is not so easy to find. A direct prediction can have one level of meaning. It directly describes a future event. In that case, it is what we have labeled as "prophecy." But how could a passage be *indirectly* predictive? It could be if it has a second level of meaning, and if this second level indicates in some way that there is a greater future realization. Without a second level of meaning, a passage does not have sufficient resources in meaning to generate an indirectly forward-pointing meaning that is obvious. There might still be a forward-pointing aspect, but it would be faint. For example, we have observed earlier that, according to Hebrews 11, the instances of faith in the Old Testament are analogous to the faith that Christians are supposed to exercise. Does Abraham's faith "point forward" to Christian faith? It is not so obvious that it does. But in a sense, because all of history is unified by the plan of God, and because God brings developments in history that lead to greater manifestations of his plan, we can infer that Abraham's faith might look forward to greater instances of faith. But this forward-pointing aspect is not obvious.

Note also that our definition of "symbol" is inclusive. A symbol is a symbol by virtue of having two-level meaning. It could be either forward-pointing or not. If it is forward-pointing, it is not only a symbol but also a type. If it is not forward-pointing, then it is merely a symbol and not a type.

Many prophecies, such as Ezekiel 40–47, use symbols. Table 14.2, by including two distinct entries for prophecy, affirms this possibility.

15

Analogies, Symbols, Types, and Prophecies as Perspectives

ALTOGETHER, WE HAVE FOUR DISTINCT CATEGORIES for ways in which the Old Testament relates to the New Testament: analogies, symbols, types, and prophecies. It is not hard to find examples in each of the four categories. But is it always easy to see, for a particular example, *which* category it falls under? In fact, it is not always easy. In this chapter, we explore ways in which the four categories overlap, rather than functioning as cleanly separated, discrete boxes.

Fuzzy Boundaries

Consider the distinction between a symbol and a type. A type, we say, is a symbol that is forward-pointing. So how do we tell whether a symbol is forward-pointing? For some symbols, like the tabernacle, it seems safe to say that they are forward-pointing. The explanation of the tabernacle in Exodus makes it reasonably clear that the tabernacle is a structure that is useful *along the way*, within the history of redemption. And sure enough, when we come to the time of Solomon, when the people are settled in the land, the tabernacle is replaced by Solomon's temple.

What about Noah's flood? It seems to point forward to final judgment. But the signals of that meaning may be less obvious within the immediate context of Genesis 6–9.

What about other symbols in the Old Testament? The laws about uncleanness after childbirth in Leviticus 12 seem to have a symbolic dimension, because the concept of uncleanness is used by God as a symbol for the contrast between his holiness and sinful contamination. But are these laws forward-pointing? How much evidence does it take, and what kind of evidence, in order for us to conclude that they are forward-pointing?

Such evidence is a matter of degree, not a black-and-white contrast between full and obvious evidence on the one hand and absolutely no evidence on the other hand. That being the case, it seems that the line between a non-forward-pointing symbol and a type is a fuzzy one. There are things that sit comfortably on one side of the line, like the tabernacle. There are things that sit comfortably on the other side of the line, like the laws for childbirth. But we cannot guarantee beforehand that there will be no cases in the middle, cases that seem to straddle the line between the two categories.

The Universality of God's Plan

Moreover, we know that God's plan is a universal and unified plan, encompassing all of history. Every event in history has meaning. And all of it is headed forward toward the consummation, when all things will be summed up in Christ (Eph. 1:10). In the broadest sense, *everything* is forward-pointing, when we look at it against the background of the general teaching of the Bible about the nature of history.

So now, if we expand the meaning of *type* to include instances of this broadest form of pointing forward, *all* symbols become types. The two categories—symbol and type—coalesce. Not only so, but every event whatsoever becomes "forward-pointing," because that is the nature of history, according to the plan of God.

Prophecy versus Indirect Prediction

Let us consider now the difference between prophecy and indirect prediction. We have defined prophecy as verbal or enacted prediction of the future. Types do point forward to the future, but the *way* in which they point forward is different. Their symbolic meanings will be fulfilled in the future. But a type is already a symbol when it is first given. So a more straightforward examination of a type would typically concentrate on the meaning of the type when it is initially given. The future is in view only *indirectly*.

Could we call a type an "indirect prediction"? Possibly. The word *prediction* might seem to be not quite right. The word may promise too much—it may sound as if a type is necessarily a rather full or complete description of the future. But that is seldom true. A type functions like a shadow (Col. 2:17; Heb. 8:5; 10:1). It does not immediately disclose all the features of the thing it foreshadows. For example, Old Testament priests do not immediately teach everything about the priesthood of Christ that we could gather from reading all of Hebrews. The shadow is less full than the thing of which it is a shadow. So we might want to say that a type "hints" at the future, or "anticipates" or "foreshadows" the future. It does not give us a maximally specific prediction.

However, whether a prediction is specific is a matter of degree. A verbal prediction never gives us all the details about a future event. Neither, for that matter, does a verbal description by someone who actually saw or participated in an event. There are always more details belonging to the event itself.

Moreover, some prophecies in the Bible are not as specific as we might want them to be. Some are only rather general in content. God says enough so that people may have hope, or so that they may be warned to repent. But the nature of progressive revelation, as *progressive*, implies that the fulfillment is going to fill out dimensions that have not been fully explained beforehand.

For these reasons, we cannot treat types and prophecies as if they were sharply distinguishable on the basis of whether their content is sufficiently specific.

But we can still distinguish them as to whether their predictive thrust is direct or indirect. Prophecies are direct prediction, while types are indirectly predictive. We have a workable distinction between them.

But the distinction is not as weighty as we might think. It has to do with the *form* or *genre* of a text, not so much with its content. In content, both prophecies and types point forward. So could we not "stretch" the term *prophecy* and call types "indirect prophecies"?[1]

Something similar to this approach is actually found at one point in the Gospels. Matthew 11:13–14 says,

> For all the Prophets and the Law prophesied until John, and if you are willing to accept it, he is Elijah who is to come.

Jesus is speaking here about John the Baptist, whom he has identified as a prophet (v. 9). John appears on the scene at the point of transition between the Old Testament prophets and the new kingdom of God that comes with Jesus. He stands on the brink of the climactic time. He says, "Repent, for the kingdom of heaven is at hand" (Matt. 3:2). He is predicting the kingdom of heaven. Likewise, the Old Testament prophets predicted it. So it is easy to see that "all the Prophets . . . prophesied until John" (11:13). What is more striking is that Jesus says in this same verse that "the *Law* prophesied." The "Law" is the first five books of the Old Testament, Genesis through Deuteronomy. These books do have some scattered predictions. But that is not their dominant content. They have "law." They also have quite a bit of the history of the patriarchs and the nation of Israel. So how does this material "prophesy"? It does so *indirectly*, just as we have seen. It depicts beforehand the era of climactic salvation. But the depiction takes place partly by types, not just by direct prediction. Matthew 11:13 has expanded the word *prophesy* to include this kind of indirect prediction. We may conclude that every type is *also* a "prophecy," in an expanded sense.

---

1   Patrick Fairbairn, *The Typology of Scripture: Viewed in Connection with the Whole Series of . . . The Divine Dispensations* (New York and London: Funk & Wagnalls, 1911), 1.1.2.52, calls types "*prophetic symbols*" (emphasis original). See also 1.1.5.106. "From the general resemblance between type and prophecy, we are prepared to expect that they may sometimes run into each other" (1.1.5.107).

We are here using "prophecy" as a perspective. It is as if we were saying, "Treat all the Law in a way that *sees* it as functionally like prophecy, like direct prediction." That is legitimate, because God's plan is comprehensive. Everything has a forward-pointing aspect to it, though it may be subtle and less obvious.

Analogies versus Types

Finally, we may consider the distinction between analogies and types. Is there a clear-cut distinction between the two? There is at least a rough distinction between *symbols and types* on the one hand and *analogies* on the other hand. Symbols and types operate with two distinct levels of meaning. Analogies operate on a single level.

So on the surface there is a straightforward distinction between analogies and types. We can illustrate this distinction with any number of examples. The bronze serpent in Numbers 21:4–9 is not a flesh-and-blood serpent, but a symbol of a serpent. There are two levels, the symbols of the serpents and the serpents themselves. If we just compare one flesh-and-blood serpent to another, we have only one level. There are images of cherubim woven into the curtain of the tabernacle, and images of two cherubim attached to the cover of the ark (Ex. 26:31; 25:16–20). These are images of cherubim, not the real thing. The real thing is the awesome angelic beings who are called "cherubim" or "living creatures," and who are positioned around God's throne (Ezek. 10:20). So there are two levels: the images of the cherubim and then the cherubim themselves.

At times the distinction between levels is more subtle. The animal sacrifices in the Old Testament are real sacrifices, not just pictures of sacrifices. But they are not on the same level as the final sacrifice of Christ. The priests in the Old Testament are real priests and real human beings. Christ is comparable to them in being truly human. But his priesthood is on a second level, the heavenly level (Heb. 9:23–28).

The instances with the bronze serpent, the cherubim, the animal sacrifices, and the priests all have two levels of meaning. But is such a difference in levels always this clear? In fact, the idea of two levels is not defined with infinite precision. When do two cases count as two levels? The Old Testament prophets were prophets, and Christ is a prophet (Heb. 1:1-2). Because of the nature of progressive revelation and the nature of climactic fulfillment in Christ, the fulfillments associated with Christ and his work and his words and his people are bound to *exceed* what was displayed in the Old Testament. How much excess, and what kind of excess, counts as a second level? And how do we decide when we are dealing with only one level? We might say that Isaiah was a greater prophet than Noah ("a herald of righteousness," 2 Pet. 2:5) because of the extent and profundity of his prophecies. But is Isaiah on a second level? Most people would probably say no. But almost any difference at all might conceivably be treated as a difference in "level," if we are so inclined. So the idea of two levels is not as precise as it might at first appear to be.

Healing through the Bronze Serpent

Consider another example. By the provision and power of God, looking at the bronze serpent resulted in healing and rescue from physical death. A cursed thing, an image of a serpent, reversed the curse of death. The work of Christ is analogous to this reversal of the curse. Christ was lifted up on the cross, bearing the curse of sin, in order to heal us and rescue us from eternal death. Eternal death is a second level, in comparison with physical death. Eternal life is a second level, in comparison with temporary life on earth. There are clearly two levels. But what about when Christ healed a person like the centurion's slave, who was at the point of death (Luke 7:1–10)? Is that healing on the same level as the healing through the bronze serpent?

It depends on how one looks at it. Both instances of healing are physical healing. Both are temporary. Both symbolically *signify* God's power to bring eternal healing. So we could say that they are on the same level. At the same time, Christ's miracles of healing belong to *Christ*, who is the final Savior. They belong to the redemptive era of the coming of the kingdom of God, which is the climactic era in comparison with the Old Testament. So we have reason to stress these differences and to say that Christ's healing, though focused on the body, is still on a second level. The final healing of the body that takes place in the resurrection of the dead is also a bodily healing, but we can easily say that it is on a second level, because it is comprehensive and permanent.

In sum, there are intermediate cases between one-level comparisons and two-level comparisons. The distinction between one-level and two-level meanings is not perfectly precise.

Broad Analogy versus Narrow Analogy

We should also remember that in ordinary language the words *analogy* and *analogous* can be used more broadly. If we use the word *analogous* loosely, we may say that Christ is analogous to the Old Testament priests. The cherubim are analogous to the pictures of the cherubim. But when we defined *analogy* in chapter 14, we decided to restrict it to one-level analogy. That was our decision, in order to distinguish one-level analogy from the two-level structures of meaning that we encounter with symbols and types. The possibility of a broader kind of analogy is nevertheless important. It shows us that we could, if we wished, broaden our concept of analogy until it becomes a perspective. We *view* all relations between the Old Testament passages and their fulfillments as if they were analogies. And they are *indeed* instances of analogy, in a broad sense, because a fulfillment of an Old Testament passage can hardly count as a fulfillment at all unless there are *some* similarities between the fulfillment and the earlier passage. Those similarities exist in the midst of other features that are differences. If two things are partly similar and partly different, they are—broadly speaking—analogous.

In sum, we can use the term *analogy* either more broadly or more narrowly. In a narrow sense, it designates a comparison between two things on the same level ("one-level analogy"). In this use of the word *analogy*, an analogy is distinct from a symbol or a type, both of which have two levels. But we can also use the term *analogy* more broadly, in which case it encompasses symbols and types. Symbols and types rely on *analogies* between the two levels of meaning.

Escalation

The result is that sometimes we might consider a particular analogy as either a one-level relation between meanings or a two-level relation, depending on what is our focus, and depending on what degree of difference we require in order for us to say that we have two levels.

We can also return to the point that the saving work of Christ *exceeds* God's works of deliverance that came in earlier eras. Fulfillment is *escalated*[2] in comparison with earlier events. So we might easily argue that *all* the events and persons in the New Testament era act within a framework of a second level, in comparison with the Old Testament.

One of our earlier examples of analogy was the example of faith. The saints catalogued in Hebrews 11 had faith in God. We, as followers of Christ, are also supposed to exercise faith (Heb. 11:39–12:16). Is this faith on the "same level" as that of the Old Testament saints? From one point of view, yes. It is faith in God and in God's promises in all the cases. But from another point of view, New Testament faith is heightened, because God invites us to contemplate directly the realities of eternal salvation, rather than to see salvation through Old Testament foreshadowings. Galatians 3:23 says, "Now before *faith* came, we were held captive under the law, . . ." How do we make sense of the expression, "before faith came"? In the previous paragraphs, Galatians holds up the faith of Abraham as a model or example. Clearly there was "faith" of a sort for Enoch and Noah and Abraham and Isaac and many others. But it was not *this* faith: faith in the crucified and risen Christ (3:1). Is New Testament faith escalated, as compared to Old Testament faith? In a sense, yes.

So how do we classify an instance of analogy between a person or event in the Old Testament and a parallel in the New Testament? Is the analogy a one-level analogy or a two-level instance of a type? Either the concept of type or the concept of analogy can be expanded into a perspective. Every relation is an analogical relation, when analogy

---

2   The terminology of "escalation" comes from G. K. Beale, *Handbook on the New Testament Use of the Old Testament* (Grand Rapids, MI: Baker, 2012), 14, 19.

becomes a perspective. And every relation becomes a typological relation, if our concept of "type" becomes a perspective on all of history.

Are Distinctions Worthless?

So what do we do with the distinctions that we introduced in chapter 14: analogy, symbol, type, and prophecy? Are they valid distinctions? They are useful distinctions for the purpose of making us aware of the variety of ways in which the Old Testament relates forward to the New Testament. But their usefulness is compatible with two complementary observations. First, any one of the four categories can be stretched or expanded into a perspective on all of history. Second, the boundaries between categories are not perfectly sharp. There are gray areas. The difference between prediction and nonprediction is not sharp, and people may sometimes disagree, depending on how they look at the situation and what they notice and emphasize. The situation is similar for the difference between one-level and two-level meaning, and for the difference between forward-pointing and non-forward-pointing meanings.

We must be careful not to overstate the difficulties and the complexities. The lack of a *sharp* boundary is not the same as having no boundary at all. Some instances in the Old Testament are clearly types. Some instances are clearly symbols. We can work confidently with these cases. We are *not* saying that there are no clear-cut cases. We are only saying that not *everything* is so clear-cut.

It might seem frustrating not to have neat, precise, perfectly controllable categories. But in one way it is actually an advantage. Being aware of limitations may encourage us to pay maximal attention to everything in the Bible, rather than simply subjecting each case to a general formula ("this is an analogy; this is a symbol; this is a type") and then ceasing to notice anything else—ceasing to probe for further riches and further nuances.

16

Allegorization

WE SHOULD NOW INTRODUCE another category label, *allegorization*, to describe an illegitimate kind of interpretation. For the purposes of this book, let us stipulate that the term *allegorization* means finding extra symbolic meaning through accidental, incidental, or artificial relationships.[1]

We need a clarification. Our use of the word *allegorization* should not be confused with what Galatians 4:21–31 does in discussing the implications of the story of Sarah and Hagar. Galatians 4:24 comments, "Now this [the story of Sarah and Hagar and their two sons] may be interpreted allegorically." English translations of verse 24 may include the word *allegory* (KJV) or *allegorically* (ESV) or *figuratively* (NIV). Galatians 4:24 makes sense because the background passage about Sarah and Hagar has more than one level of meaning (see chapter 8). Our own view is that it is an instance of typological interpretation. It is *not* an artificial imposition of extra meanings, as we are defining a wrongful kind of allegorization for our purposes here.

The Challenge of Illegitimate Interpretations

We offer our definition of allegorization as an aid to distinguishing between legitimate and illegitimate cases of typological interpretation.

---

1   O. Palmer Robertson, classroom teaching at Westminster Theological Seminary, circa 1972, spoke simply of "accidental, incidental, or artificial relationships."

Types, as we have seen, involve symbolic meaning. There are two levels of meaning. But how are these two levels related, and how do we properly discern the meaning on the second level? A symbol represents and symbolizes some divine truth. But what truth? In the history of biblical interpretation, some interpreters have attributed to passages a second level of meaning without adequate grounds.

An Example from Matthew 2:11

In chapter 2 we mentioned Philo's interpretation of Genesis 6:9. Consider another example. One person told me that the gold, frankincense, and myrrh—the three gifts from the wise men in Matthew 2:11—stand for the Father, the Son, and the Holy Spirit. Is this true?

Divine truth includes the truth that God is three persons: the Father, the Son, and the Holy Spirit. The question is not whether that is true, but whether the truth is symbolized in Matthew 2:11. There is indeed a relationship between the truth about the Trinity and the verse in Matthew. There are three persons in the Trinity. There are three gifts from the wise men. The number three occurs naturally in both contexts. But the relation between the two contexts is superficial; it is artificial. We might just as well get out three apples or three tennis balls and say that a group of three apples or three tennis balls stands for the persons of the Trinity. Such an interpretation is an example of *allegorization*. It finds symbolic meanings. And the meanings may be expressions of divine truth. But the truth is actually to be found in other places—in passages that actually teach that there is one God, and that each of the three persons is God, and that the persons are distinct from each other.

Dangers from Allegorization

The dangers from allegorization should be obvious. The same procedures that might allow us to derive the Trinity from a list of three gifts would allow us to derive a "quadrinity" from any biblical list of four items (e.g., Mark 12:30). Unbiblical, heterodox doctrines as well as orthodox doctrines can be the result, once we remove restraints on how we find symbolic meaning.

A second danger, less obvious, is that once we find a symbolic meaning, even though it is not right, we stop looking carefully at the passage we have been studying. We may in fact *miss* a symbolic dimension that is actually there because we have already imported a symbolic meaning that is *not* there.

This effect actually takes place with Matthew 2:11. The Gospel of Matthew is quite interested in fulfillment. One of the refrains in Matthew is that "this took place to fulfill what the Lord had spoken by the prophet" (1:22), and similar expressions. Matthew 2:11 is thematically parallel to Isaiah 60:6, where Isaiah prophesies about the nations bringing gifts celebrating salvation: "They [the nations, not Israel] shall bring gold and frankincense, and shall bring good news, the praises of the LORD." There is a rich relation between the meanings of Isaiah 60:6 and Matthew 2:11. Matthew 2:11 is not the complete fulfillment, since Isaiah is, in context, prophesying in a broader way about salvation that includes the coming of God to both Israel and the nations. This salvation comes more fully after the day of Pentecost, when the message of Christ begins to go out to other languages and nations. But the coming of the wise men is certainly an anticipation of that later day. So it can be viewed as setting in motion the coming fulfillment. Matthew 2:11 wants us to see that the gifts of the wise men are one step in fulfilling the prophecy in Isaiah 60:6.

But if we stop with the idea that the trio of gifts is a sign of the Trinity, we miss the actual meaning found in the relation between Matthew 2:11 and Isaiah 60:6.

The point, then, is that once a person has read in an artificial meaning, it tends to discourage him from noticing the real meaning. It is a loss, rather than a gain.

Thus, we use the term *allegorization* for misuses of the Bible. Allegorization can superficially look like legitimate typological interpretation. The difference is that, in the case of allegorization, the meanings that are set forth do not come from the passage itself, nor from its relation to its fulfillment.

Allegory

While *allegorization* is an illegitimate kind of interpretation, however, *allegory* itself can be a rich source of biblical truth. An *allegory* is a fictional narrative with a second level of meaning. Features within the narrative—characters, events, speeches, or props—symbolically signify something else, in another realm of meaning.

John Bunyan's *Pilgrim's Progress* is often cited as a classical case of allegory. The protagonist, Christian, goes on a journey and confronts various challenges. The journey as a whole is a symbol for the progress of the Christian life. Opponents whom Christian meets signify various obstacles and temptations in the Christian life. Helpers signify aids to the Christian life. There is thus an extensive correspondence between two levels of meaning. The first, obvious level is the level of physical movement and meetings with various other characters. The second level is the level of meaning with respect to lessons for Christian living.

Sometimes allegory is defined more broadly. If we like, we could drop the requirement that it be a narrative. Or we could drop the requirement that it be fictional. But if it is nonfictional, the *point* of the story must still be found on the second level. From the standpoint of the author, the point is not at all whether the events really happened in time and space, but rather that they signify something else—a second level of meaning.

Notable Comparisons

So what should we say about allegories? The first thing to note is that there is nothing the matter with an allegory. It is one way that people can choose to communicate meaning. The Bible itself contains some allegories. One of the early instances is found in Jotham's story in Judges 9 about talking trees (vv. 8–15). Both Jotham and his listeners know that trees do not talk. Jotham is making up the story. It is a fictional story, and everyone knows that it is fictional. After the story is finished, he goes on to comment about the treachery of Abimelech in killing Gideon's sons. He thereby indicates directly that the story has a second level of meaning. The trees stand for actual living people, and the dialogues among the trees stand for the thoughts of people. This story is clearly an allegory. It is a story, it is fictional, and it has a second level of meaning.

Likewise, the parable of Nathan in 2 Samuel 12 and many of Jesus's parables are instances of allegory. Many cases of allegory, like John Bunyan's, use a fictional form to communicate principles and doctrine that are already known through other means. Nathan and Jesus, by contrast, introduce ideas that are not fully known beforehand. Both Nathan and Jesus aim to convict their hearers, to get them to judge themselves by comparison with the story. There are extra complexities and dimensions to these parables. But these extra elements do not change the fact that the stories are allegories. They may be *more* than allegories, but they are at least allegories.[2]

The result is that *allegory* must be carefully distinguished from *allegorization*. An allegory is a recognized literary device. Allegorization is a bad method of interpretation, in which unrelated meanings get carried into a text. To treat an allegory *as* an allegory, or to treat a type *as* a type, is common sense. It recognizes meanings that the author has

---

2 Unfortunately, New Testament scholarship traveled for awhile in a confusing direction by claiming that Jesus's parables were *not* allegories. Allegedly, a parable has one point while an allegory has a series of discrete points. But this way of trying to establish a distinction is not helpful. For one thing, it is disconnected from the already-established meaning of *allegory* in literary analysis. Allegories often make one main point by means of several smaller points acting together. Bunyan's *Pilgrim's Progress*, for example, has one main point: the necessity of perseverance, watchfulness, and dependence on God for the "journey" of the Christian life. It communicates this one main point by means of many particular episodes. Each episode has its own main point, which it makes by means of a series of correspondences between the two levels of meaning.

Similarly, Jesus's parable about the lost sheep in Luke 15:3–6 makes a single main point: the propriety of rescuing sinners. This main point is established by means of a series of correspondences between shepherds, sheep, lostness, and friends of the shepherd on the one hand, and Jesus himself, the people of Israel, the "sinners," and the angels on the other hand (vv. 7, 10). (See Madeleine Boucher, *The Mysterious Parable: A Literary Study* [Washington: Catholic Biblical Association of America, 1977].)

It is sometimes suggested that in an allegory, every detail has two levels of meaning. But such an additional requirement is artificial. Classical cases of allegory may have many points of correspondence. But some details may just be there to add color.

put there. To import unrelated meanings is irresponsible, whether in the case of an allegory or a type or any other kind of textual representation.

There is nevertheless a kind of suggestive relation between the concept of allegory and the concept of allegorization. We could try to capture something of the relation by saying that the procedure of allegorization treats—or tends to treat—the whole Bible as if it were all allegories. Everything in the Bible is treated as if it had a second level of meaning, even when there is in fact no second level.

Some passages do have a second level of meaning. But others do not. To treat Jotham's allegory as an allegory is not wrong, because that is what it is. But it is a mistake to treat Genesis 1 as allegory, because that is not what it is. Genesis 1 is nonfiction, for one thing. And the focus is not on a second level of meaning, but on God's creative action bringing visible things into existence.

Both Jotham's allegory and the types in the Old Testament have two levels of meaning. It is not allegorization to recognize that they have a second level, symbolized by a first, more "earthy," level. But with these passages, as with any other passage, there still remains a danger of importing meanings that do not really belong. For example, someone could misconstrue Jotham's allegory by claiming that it is "really about" the general principle of friendship, or about the trees symbolizing virtues, or the trees symbolizing schools of philosophy, or some other extraneous meaning. One could misconstrue the meaning of Old Testament priests by claiming that the Levitical priests stand for mental virtues, while the false priests set up by Jeroboam stand for mental vices.

The important issue, then, is whether an interpretation is importing meanings that do not belong. That issue cannot be decided merely by appealing to labels. We must look at each passage and try to assess its meaning fairly. If it discloses a second level of meaning, well and good. If it does not, then we refrain from pretending that it does.

If a passage *does* have a second level of meaning, we still need to be careful. Our goal is not to drag in a meaning that does not belong. We are seeking to understand what meaning is symbolically signified by the passage itself, within its historical and literary setting. The value of step 1 in Clowney's triangle comes in at this point. Step 1 investigates symbolic meaning that is associated with a given passage at the time when God gives it to his people. We do that kind of analysis before trying to relate the passage to meanings found later on in progressive revelation, especially in the New Testament.

PART V

ENRICHMENT OF CLOWNEY'S TRIANGLE

We explore some additional steps that may help to enrich further our understanding of a passage that has types.

17

Enhancements to Clowney's Triangle

IN A WAY, THE MOST VALUABLE CONTRIBUTION of Clowney's triangle to our discussion of biblical typology lies in its first step. It tells us to pay attention to the meaning that God gave earlier in history. When that step is done well, it lays the ground for step 2, in which we determine the antitype or fulfillment. And then in step 3 we consider the applications.

To deepen our understanding of what is going on in a type, we may consider adding still further steps. They are less central to the process of finding the main meaning of a type. But they are still useful. We will consider them briefly, one at a time, and apply each of the steps to the tabernacle, as an example.

Step 4: Surplus in Fulfillment

Step 4 consists in asking about how the fulfillment surpasses the earlier shadow or type that points to it. We focus not on the similarities between the type and its antitype, but on their differences.

We have talked about types as "foreshadowing" or "prefiguring" fulfillment. Both of these expressions hint at the fact that the reality is greater than the shadow and greater than the prefiguration. This surplus in the fulfillment is already anticipated when God first provides a type. A type points forward to *climactic* fulfillment, as it comes in the first coming of Christ or the second coming. Our appreciation can grow if we notice the ways in which the fulfillment involves an escalation[1] or enlargement or enhancement of the meaning, both in the richness of ideas communicated and in the richness of the events themselves. The work of God in Christ surpasses the earlier works of redemption. And the verbal revelation explaining the work of Christ surpasses in richness the earlier explanations, which prophetically foresee what is to come.

So in step 4 we ask both how the antitype—that is, the later persons and events, especially the work of Christ—surpasses the type, and how the meanings belonging to the antitype add to, rather than simply repeat, earlier revelations. (See fig. 17.1.)

Figure 17.1: Step 4: Surplus in Fulfillment

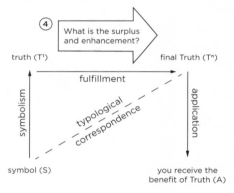

Step 4 for the Tabernacle

How does step 4 apply to the tabernacle? Christ is the final dwelling place of God, the fulfillment of the tabernacle. He is the antitype. He exceeds the tabernacle in several respects. He is a person, with a human nature, not just a physical building structure. He combines in himself all the aspects of fellowship and communion with God that were symbolically represented in the tabernacle. He is the reality, not just a symbol. He comes from heaven, presenting us directly with the

---

1   G. K. Beale, *Handbook on the New Testament Use of the Old Testament* (Grand Rapids, MI: Baker, 2012), 19.

heavenly reality of God, not just an imitation of it (John 3:31; Heb. 8:5; 9:24; 10:1; etc.). He brings permanent access to God and permanent release from sin, guilt, and shame. (See fig. 17.2.)

Figure 17.2: Step 4 for the Tabernacle

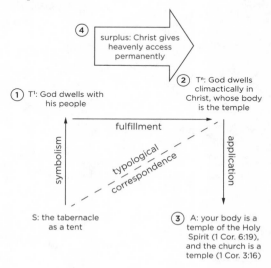

Step 5: Noticing More in the Type

Step 5 consists in further studying a type in order to notice hints that we might not have noticed in step 1, when we considered the meaning of the type in its original setting. In the light of the fulfillment, we ask whether there were further features in the type itself, which may have seemed to be unimportant details, but which become more clearly significant when we compare them with the fulfillment. The details were there, and they had meaning, but it was subtle. (See fig. 17.3.)

Step 5 for the Tabernacle

How do we apply step 5 to the tabernacle? The tabernacle is constructed after a heavenly pattern, according to Exodus 25:40. This connection to heaven turns out to be even more significant when we observe that Christ is sent from heaven, and speaks about having come down from heaven (John 6:38, 42). The imagery of the tabernacle as a tent in which God dwells anticipates the promise of dwelling in God's house in heaven, in the place that Jesus prepares (John 14:1–3). (See fig. 17.4.)

Figure 17.3: Step 5: Meaning in Details in a Type

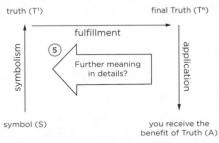

Figure 17.4: Step 5 for the Tabernacle

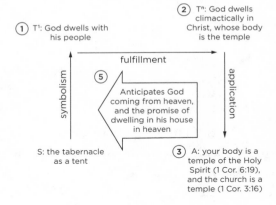

Step 6: From Creation to Consummation

Step 6 consists in asking how the truths expressed in a type and its antitype have roots in creation and how they find expression in the consummation. Step 6 invites us to travel backward in time to the point of creation, and also forward in time to the consummation. A type has symbolic meaning at the time when God originally gives it. But does it have predecessors and anticipations that were there even earlier in time? And if it does, do the predecessors include something that God did during the six days of creation? These are questions worth asking. The potential for symbolic meaning often has roots in the potential for symbolic meaning possessed by created objects and aspects of the created order.

Step 6 consists in two substeps: one looking backward to creation, and the other looking forward to the consummation. (See fig. 17.5.)

Figure 17.5: Step 6: Roots in Creation and Expression in the Consummation

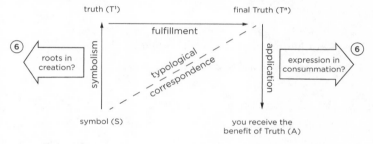

Step 6 for the Tabernacle

A. Creation. How do we apply step 6 to the tabernacle? Going back to creation, we ask whether there is a symbolism for a dwelling place for God in the creation record in Genesis 1–2.

There are two aspects there. The first is that the garden of Eden, before the fall, is a place for fellowship between God and man. But when God specifically comes and meets with Adam and Eve after the fall (Gen. 3:8–24), he bars the way to the garden of Eden and the tree of life by placing cherubim to guard it (v. 24). This procedure shows that the garden of Eden is being treated as a holy place. As we saw earlier in discussing the lampstand in the tabernacle, the lampstand symbolizes the tree of life, which is in the garden. Later Scripture confirms the idea that the garden is a holy place. Ezekiel 28:14 alludes to the garden of Eden as "the *holy* mountain of God."

The second aspect is the presence of the Holy Spirit in Genesis 1:2. This special presence of God suggests that the entire structure of heaven and earth is designed to be a dwelling place of God. This idea too is confirmed by later Scripture:

> But will God indeed dwell on the earth? Behold, *heaven and the highest heaven* cannot contain you; how much less this house that I have built! (1 Kings 8:27)

> Thus says the LORD:
> "*Heaven* is my throne,
>   and the earth is my footstool;
> what is the house that you would build for me,
>   and what is the place of my rest?" (Isa. 66:1)

The garden of Eden is then a localized expression of what God has done in the structure of the cosmos as a whole. The universe itself and the garden of Eden then function as creational backgrounds for the tabernacle in Exodus 25.

B. Consummation. We also need to move forward and ask whether there is a further expression of the tabernacle theme in the consummation.

Once again, there are two aspects. The first is the localized expression of the presence of God in the holy city of Jerusalem. Jerusalem is shaped like a perfect cube (Rev. 21:16), the same shape as the Most Holy Place in the tabernacle.

Second, the entire cosmos is filled with the presence of God. No sun or moon are needed (21:23). We may summarize these aspects of the consummation with information placed to the left and to the right of Clowney's triangle (fig. 17.6).

Step 7: Distinctive Atmosphere for Distinct Stages of Redemptive History

Step 7 consists in paying attention to the distinctions between type and antitype, and other stages in the history of redemption, in order to try to appreciate how a particular meaning fits into its own stage in the history of redemption. The focus here is not on the differences between type and antitype (step 4) as such, but on how those differences are appropriate within the overall plan of God.

Figure 17.6: Step 6 for the Tabernacle

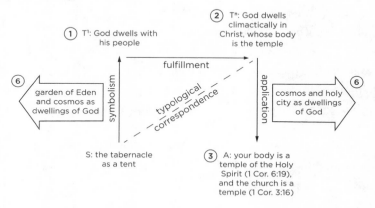

Step 7 could be included in the diagram for Clowney's triangle as a remark off to one side or below the triangle. But it may be best represented in a diagram if we draw a timeline from left (creation) to right (consummation) and think about distinctive stages in the history of redemption. We have already talked about the basic outline of creation, fall, redemption, and consummation (chapter 4). There are further time divisions or distinctive stages within the history of redemption. Each instance of a type or a theological theme fits into its own place in the work of the history of redemption. The symbolism of types in the Old Testament is suitable to the overall symbolic and foreshadowing character of God's acts of redemption within that stage of history.

So we depict step 7 as a question about the timeline of redemptive history (fig. 17.7).

Step 7 for the Tabernacle

We can now apply step 7 to the tabernacle. The tabernacle belongs to the redemptive stage when the people of Israel are in the wilderness.

For a time, the tabernacle also exists after the conquest under Joshua, but it is eventually superseded by Solomon's temple.

The fact that the tabernacle is a tent fits the circumstances of the time. It must be portable, because the people of Israel are moving their encampments. God is with them, and his presence is moving with them. The people of Israel are living in tents, and their living is supposed to imitate God's living in holiness (Lev. 19:2).

The tabernacle is a symbolic structure. It reflects God's heavenly dwelling. This presence of symbolism harmonizes with the whole redemptive stage in which they are living, in the wilderness. The Mosaic era has symbols that are shadows and prefigurations of the reality that is to come in Christ (Heb. 8:5).

We may compare the tabernacle to earlier and later representations of the dwelling place of God. In the garden of Eden before the fall, God dwelt with Adam and Eve. There was no house structure. There were no barriers in the form of curtains or veils, because there was no sin to overcome. Adam and Eve were naked, and were not yet living in houses or tents.

In Genesis 28 God gives Jacob a vision of a ladder reaching to heaven (vv. 10–15). When Jacob awakens, he realizes that he has experienced the unique presence of God, and he calls the place "the house of God" (v. 17). The message and promise of God remain with Jacob, as a kind of presence. But the dream itself is transitory. It is appropriate that there is not yet a permanent physical structure in the form of a house or tent.

When Christ comes, his own body and his human nature are the permanent dwelling place of God (John 1:14; 2:21). Since God is personal, and since Christ as the Redeemer takes on human nature, the dwelling of God takes human form in his human nature.

At the consummation, the glory of God fills the universe. This final filling is the fitting endpoint. It is manifested in the fact that the whole universe has become the dwelling of God.

The distinct manifestations of the theme of the dwelling of God have variations in tune with the various stages of history. (See fig. 17.8.)

Figure 17.7: Step 7: Distinctions Based on Stages

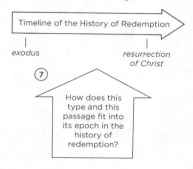

Figure 17.8: Step 7 for the Tabernacle

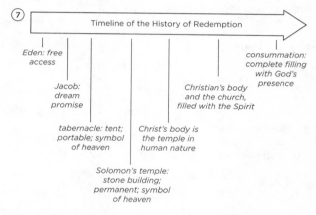

Step 8: Benefits for Old Testament Saints

Finally, step 8 asks about how Christ's benefits are applied beforehand to saints in the Old Testament.[2] We know that Christ is the exclusive mediator and the exclusive way to God (1 Tim. 2:5; John 14:6). So if the saints in the Old Testament receive benefits from God—and they do—it must be through the mediation of Christ. The types in the Old Testament are one way that God uses to depict the message of redemption beforehand. As Old Testament saints believe in God and

---

2   I am grateful to Timothy P. Yates for pointing out that this step can be added.

his promises, as depicted in the types, they are saved and they receive the benefits of Christ's work beforehand. As we saw in chapter 9, the Westminster Confession of Faith summarizes this bestowal of benefits:

> This covenant [the covenant of grace, which is the exposition of God's one way of salvation in Christ] was differently administered in the time of the law, and in the time of the gospel: under the law, it was administered by promises, prophecies, sacrifices, circumcision, the paschal lamb, and other types [!] and ordinances delivered to the people of the Jews, all foresignifying Christ to come; which were, for that time, sufficient and efficacious, through the operation of the Spirit, to instruct and build up the elect in faith in the promised Messiah, by whom they had full remission of sins, and eternal salvation; . . .[3]

In step 8 we focus again on the original setting of the type. We ask how Christ and his benefits come to be applied to the people who receive the type. (See fig. 17.9.)

Step 8 for the Tabernacle

Now we may illustrate how step 8 applies to a case like the tabernacle.

The tabernacle ordinances included communication from God to Israel, as God spoke through the Ten Commandments and spoke from above the mercy seat (Ex. 25:22). The animal sacrifices prefigured the forgiveness of sins. The priesthood prefigured the work of Christ as final high priest. Through the meanings of these ordinances, the people of Israel could in faith believe in God's word and in his mercy, and trust in the promise of final redemption still to come in the person of Christ. (See fig. 17.10.)

Benefits

Steps 4 through 8 help us to appreciate further the richness in the plan of God in progressive revelation and in the centrality of Christ. By asking

---

3   Westminster Confession of Faith (1647), 7.5.

the distinct kinds of questions found in these steps, we may notice biblical themes and thematic relations that we failed to notice before.

Figure 17.9: Step 8: Application of Christ's Work through a Type

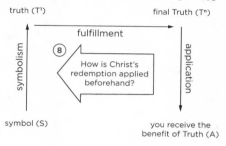

Figure 17.10: Step 8 for the Tabernacle

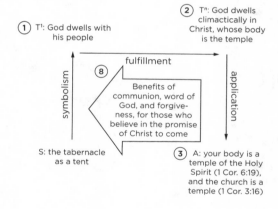

18

Multifaceted Meaning

WE SHOULD NOTE that the relations in meaning between types and the rest of redemptive history are multifaceted.

Multifaceted Relations for the Tabernacle

The tabernacle as a type points forward to Christ as the antitype. The relation between type and antitype is the main relation to which people pay attention. But relations in meaning extend in other directions as well. The tabernacle is related backward to creation and forward to the consummation. It is related upward to God's dwelling in heaven. It is related outward to the tents of Israelite families. As a holy people, they in their tents are supposed to imitate the holy tent of God.

The tabernacle is related forward to Christ as the antitype. But the truths manifested in Christ are then imitated in individual believers and in the church as the corporate body of Christ. The individual's body is a temple of the Holy Spirit (1 Cor. 6:19). And the church is the temple of the Holy Spirit (1 Cor. 3:16).

We may summarize all of these relations in a single diagram, with the tabernacle itself in the center. (See fig. 18.1.)

Multifaceted Relations for David and Goliath

We may follow similar reasoning in analyzing the story of David and Goliath in 1 Samuel 17. The fight between David and Goliath has symbolic dimensions. The ancient Near Eastern cultures thought that the gods could enter into a military conflict and help to give victory to their favored party. Goliath invokes this context when he "cursed David by his gods" (v. 43). David understands that the battle is not an ordinary one, because Goliath "has defied the armies of the living God" (v. 36). He says to Goliath, "The LORD will deliver you into my hand" (v. 46).

Figure 18.1: Multifaceted Relations for the Tabernacle

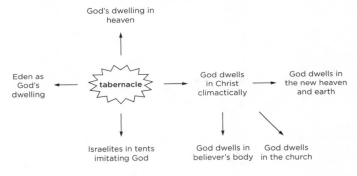

So the earthly battle points upward to the heavenly battle between God and his enemies. The enemies include false gods, behind whom are demons.

The earthly battle also points outward to the people of Israel as a whole. If David wins, the whole army wins, and the people of Israel are delivered from oppression by the Philistines.

The battle against evil also points backward. The battle against evil began with the serpent's temptation in the garden of Eden. It continues when Pharaoh oppresses the people of Israel and attempts to fight them when they leave Egypt. In this respect, David is a kind of Adam-like figure whose victory over Goliath will also deliver others whom he represents.

David has been anointed to be the future king of Israel (1 Sam. 16:1, 12–13). In functioning like a king, David is a mediatorial figure, pointing forward to Christ.

Christ defeats Satan in the climactic battle when he dies and rises again (Col. 2:15; Heb. 2:14–15).

In Christ, the battle against evil also becomes ours. Ephesians 6:10–20 indicates that we are to fight "against the cosmic powers over this present darkness" (v. 12).

The final defeat of Satan and his agents comes in connection with the second coming (Rev. 19:11–19; 20:7–10). We may summarize all these thematic connections in a single diagram (fig. 18.2).

Figure 18.2: Multifaceted Relations for David's Fight with Goliath

Benefits

Cases like these illustrate the fact that there is more in the plan of God than simply a lineup of similarities between a type and its antitype. There is a larger context of the history of redemption.

This context is itself Christ-centered. Consider the various relations that David's fight with Goliath sustains with other people and events. Adam as the head of the human race is himself a type of Christ. The defeat of Pharaoh at the Red Sea is a benefit that comes to the people after they have sacrificed the Passover lamb, which signifies Christ beforehand. The fight against supernatural evil by Christians in our era is empowered by the armor that they receive from Christ. The consummation to which we look forward is a consummation filled with the glory of Christ. Thus there is an organic unity belonging to the connections that David's defeat of Goliath has with the rest of history.

19

Boundaries for Typological Interpretation

CAN WE GO TOO FAR with typological interpretation? What are the boundaries?

Compatibility and Harmony with Earlier Meaning

The first boundary for typological interpretation is the one inherent in Clowney's triangle. It involves the first, vertical leg of the triangle. The first leg tells us that we should inquire about the meaning of a symbol at the time when it is given. That is our starting point.

So we should be bound by the meaning that God makes publicly available at the time when he provides a particular book of the Bible, and at the time when he does a particular redemptive act. Yes, the progress of revelation in the history of redemption implies a potential progress in understanding. We may understand more deeply and more thoroughly some of the implications of earlier events and earlier texts, when we see them in the light of later developments. But God is always consistent with himself. The progress should never be allowed to undermine, contradict, or displace the meanings that God made available earlier. The earlier meaning, as it is found in the first leg of Clowney's triangle, offers an important boundary or limitation, reining in imagination and speculation.

No New Doctrine

A second limit is that no new doctrine should be inferred on the basis of typological reasoning. Types may underline and confirm doctrines that are openly taught in the New Testament. But a type in the Old Testament should not be used to craft a new doctrine that is not clearly found in the New Testament. For that matter, neither should a type that is found in the works of Jesus on earth serve as the basis for a new doctrine that is not set forth clearly in the New Testament. The works of Jesus on earth, prior to his crucifixion and resurrection, do represent a stage in the fulfillment of Old Testament promises. But they remain, in a sense, preliminary to the great, climactic work of death and resurrection. The fullest exposition of the meaning of these climactic events lies in the New Testament letters, the sermons in Acts, and the book of Revelation.

Why not allow a new doctrine to be built on a type? There are several reasons. The central reason lies in the nature of progressive revelation. Revelation is progressive over time. The later revelation enhances, deepens, and further explicates what has been revealed or taught earlier. To create new doctrines from old texts is to reverse this divinely designed flow of history. It is to claim to find *more* riches and more explication in what is earlier rather than what is later.

The transition from earlier to later in progressive revelation is not only a transition from partial to fuller content. It is also a transition from shadow to reality: "These [Old Testament ordinances] are a shadow of the things to come, but the substance belongs to Christ" (Col. 2:17). Retreating to the shadow, in order to find fullness there, undermines the reality that fullness of life is found in Christ. As Colossians 2:19 warns, the introduction of secret teaching means "not holding fast to the Head [Christ], from whom the whole body, nourished and knit together through its joints and ligaments, grows with a growth that is from God."

Once Christ appears on earth, we can say that the reality has indeed come. But it still takes time for him to complete his work on earth. The meaning of that work is not fully disclosed until after it is accomplished.

This principle of fullness in Christ goes together with warnings against claims to secret teachings. In the New Testament, after the day of Pentecost, Christ is openly and freely and clearly proclaimed. The message of the gospel, the message about Christ, is not a secret message available only to people who are a specially qualified spiritual elite. Rather, it is open to the whole world:

> We refuse to practice cunning or to tamper with God's word, but by *the open statement of the truth* we would commend ourselves to everyone's conscience in the sight of God. And even if our gospel is veiled, it is veiled to those who are perishing. In their case the god of this world has blinded the minds of the unbelievers, to keep them from seeing the light of the gospel of the glory of Christ, who is the image of God. For what we proclaim is not ourselves, but Jesus Christ as Lord, with ourselves as your servants for Jesus' sake. For God, who said, "Let light shine out of darkness," has shone in our hearts to give the light of the knowledge of the glory of God in the face of Jesus Christ. (2 Cor. 4:2–6)

> We have *spoken freely* to you, Corinthians; . . . (2 Cor. 6:11)

The Peril of Desiring Secrets

The warning against pursuing secrets is particularly important, because in all forms of religion there lurks a dangerous temptation to nourish spiritual pride. In religion, people seek secrets that make the person who has them feel superior to the common kind of human being. Secrets that are supposedly derived from typology have the same potential as any kind of religious secret.

No New Predictions for the Future

A third limitation is that predictions for the future should not be based on typological interpretation. Typological interpretation is, if you will, backward-looking interpretation. It sees further significance in a type by use of later revelation concerning the fulfillment of the type. But such interpretation is properly guided only if we have the fulfillment to which the type points.

We may put it another way. Typological interpretation always involves, among other things, interpretation of *symbols*. There is a second level of meaning in a symbol. The presence of a second level of meaning gives us grounds for seeking what this meaning is. But having a second level of meaning is more complicated than having just one level. There is more potential for misunderstanding. In particular, there is potential for us to let our imagination run wild and impose a meaning created by our imagination, rather than submit ourselves to a meaning that is already there. As an example, consider God's promise to David that his descendants will be a line of kings, leading to the Messiah (2 Sam. 7:12–16). If we just interpret the passage with our own preformed idea of kingship, and what kingship symbolizes about the final rule of God, we might think that the promise was incompatible with a suffering Messiah. But David himself suffered. We have to go to other passages in the Old Testament, such as Isaiah 53, and then also to the fulfillment in Christ, in order to know the details of what kind of kingship the Messiah represents.

Meaning is already there, for any symbol found in Scripture. But it is a more subtle challenge for interpretation than if we just had everything bluntly blurted out. The meaning that God gave at an earlier time is, of course, a guide to later fulfillment. But because of the progressive nature of revelation, we cannot safely postulate what will be the details of the fulfillment until the fulfillment comes.

For many biblical types and symbols, the fulfillment has already come, in Christ. That fulfillment gives a solid basis for typological interpretation that shows how the earlier symbol points to the fulfillment. But the situation is different when we are dealing with events still in the future, such as the events surrounding the second coming of Christ, the resurrection of the dead, and the final judgment. We know that these events are indeed going to come, because the Bible talks openly about them, especially in the New Testament. But because they are still future, we must respect the limitations of our present knowledge.

We should not pretend to *add* to our knowledge of the future, based on typological meaning.

The types can indeed confirm what God says in direct predictions about the future. But we do not have sufficient insight from the symbolism to add any details to the predictions. For example, Moses as a prophet of God is a type, pointing forward to Christ as the great and final prophet. Christ is the final prophet both in his first coming and in his second coming. At his second coming, he will destroy his enemies by the sword of his mouth (Rev. 19:15, 21). In this destruction, he will act as the final prophet. We know it will happen because Revelation 19 predicts it. But we would not be justified in adding details as to exactly how he will do it, by using the parallels with Moses.

20

Maxims for Typological Interpretation

WE MAY NOW SUMMARIZE the results from previous chapters by presenting a series of maxims. A "maxim" is a little like a proverb. It is a short summary. It is a generality. But it may have exceptions. It needs to be used within a larger context of understanding. It is not independent of the other maxims. The maxims are intended to be useful summaries of the larger discussion in which we have engaged in the rest of the book:

- The Bible is the word of God, who is infinitely wise. Each part of the Bible is to be interpreted in the light of the whole Bible.
- God designed each part of the Bible to address the people to whom it was originally given. The meaning available to the original recipients is the starting point for relations in meaning to earlier and later revelation.
- Revelation is progressive.
- Revelation and redemption come to a climax in Christ and his work.
- History has a design according to God's plan. There are distinctive phases—creation, fall, redemption, consummation. Each passage in the Bible needs to be seen in the light of its place in the history of redemption.
- People, things, and institutions with a mediatorial function are types of Christ the final mediator.

- Types are always symbols. According to the first, vertical leg of Clowney's triangle, we begin by asking what the symbol symbolizes within its own place in history.
- As a second step, we move forward in history from the meaning of the symbol in its own time to the fulfillment in Christ and his work.
- As a third step, we ask how the fulfillment in Christ results in applications to his people, both individually and corporately (the church).
- A type is never equal to its fulfillment (the antitype). The fulfillment is richer than the type and exceeds the meaning of the type. We need to seek out the ways in which the fulfillment is superior.
- We should note the correspondences between the type and the antitype. But we should not limit ourselves to a list of similarities between the two. Symbolism in the Bible is often multifaceted. So we should note thematic connections that may exist in other dimensions, such as a relation backward to a theme in creation, or forward to a theme in the consummation.
- In proclamation, if we are explaining a passage that has a type in it, we expound the fulfillment (antitype) in relation to the type; we avoid expounding the antitype *instead of* the type (so that the type in effect disappears). If we want to expound the antitype by itself, we should just choose a New Testament passage that directly teaches about Christ and his people.
- The people of God need, not just information about types, but communion with God. The information needs to serve communion.
- We should pay attention to the limitations of typological interpretation, as indicated in the previous chapter: (1) build on meaning that God gave his people at the earlier time; (2) no new doctrine; and (3) no new predictions.

PART VI

THE PRACTICE
OF TYPOLOGICAL
INTERPRETATION

We consider some challenges in dealing with various kinds of
biblical material: the Mosaic administration; redemptive plots;
creation; the earthly life of Jesus.

21

Types in the Mosaic Administration

IN CHAPTER 7, WE PRESENTED some examples of types within the tabernacle. We can multiply examples of this kind. The tabernacle, along with the priesthood, the sacrifices, the festivals, and the leaders (Moses, Joshua, elders, judges), give us symbolic pictures of aspects of God's kingdom. God's reign over Israel is mediated by the institutions in the Mosaic administration. These mediatorial functions foreshadow the final mediation of Christ.

One of the helps in interpreting details in this part of the Bible is to see the details in the light of the larger picture. We ask, "What is God saying and what is God doing in the entire process?" He takes the people of Israel to be his own special people:

> "You yourselves have seen what I did to the Egyptians, and how I bore you on eagles' wings and brought you to myself. Now therefore, if you will indeed obey my voice and keep my covenant, you shall be my treasured possession among all peoples, for all the earth is mine; and you shall be to me a kingdom of priests and a holy nation." These are the words that you shall speak to the people of Israel. (Ex. 19:4–6)

This covenantal relation between God and his people anticipates the covenantal relation in the New Testament, mediated through Christ. God's rule over the people of Israel anticipates his rule over the New

Testament people of God, through Christ the King. If we examine how the details fit into this broader picture, we have a good start in assessing the typological meaning of the details.[1]

1   For further examples, we refer readers to Vern S. Poythress, *The Shadow of Christ in the Law of Moses* (repr., Phillipsburg, NJ: P&R, 1995); and Patrick Fairbairn, *The Typology of Scripture: Viewed in Connection with the Whole Series of . . . The Divine Dispensations* (New York and London: Funk & Wagnalls, 1911).

22

Types in Redemptive Plots

ONE FORM OF TYPOLOGICAL SYMBOLISM to which we need to be alert is the dynamic symbolism of redemption. Christ is the only Redeemer. He is "the way, and the truth, and the life" (John 14:6). Though Christ's redemption is unique, episodes of redemption in the Old Testament foreshadow and anticipate his climactic work.

Plots of Deliverance

Many stories in the Old Testament are stories of *deliverance*. The deliverance can be deliverance from physical threats of various kinds. God delivers people from famine, from disease, from homelessness, from barrenness, from war, from death, from prison (Ps. 107). The plots of deliverance have a particular shape. There is an initial difficulty or threat. The threat may grow in intensity. There is a tense confrontation with the threat. The threat is overcome and the people enjoy deliverance. These acts of God's grace foreshadow the final deliverance that Christ has accomplished in his death and resurrection. The many small cases of deliverance are temporary. The people get a reprieve from some threat. But ultimately death will still overtake them. This temporary quality is true even concerning the spectacular cases in which someone is raised from the dead. The widow of Zarephath's son in 1 Kings 17:17–24, the Shunammite's son in 2 Kings 4:18–37, the dead man in 2 Kings 13:21, the daughter of Jairus in Matthew 9:18–26 and

Mark 5:21–43, and Lazarus in John 11 will, later in their lives, eventually succumb to death. All the temporary deliverances are less than the full thing. They are types.

Tragic (Anti-Redemptive) Plots

In the Bible, in addition to redemptive plots, we also have "tragic" plots whose endings are grim. Individuals or groups fall into sins, and the sins spiral downward to a disastrous ending. We may call these episodes "anti-redemptive plots." They still point in an inverted way to the necessity of redemption. And they have a thematic connection to the life of Christ, because his substitutionary death takes the form of an anti-redemptive plot. He became our sin-bearer and identified with sin (2 Cor. 5:21; 1 Pet. 2:24). That is why he suffered the punishment of death. But of course in his case, the plot is also a redemptive plot. Because of his obedience, he was raised from the dead (Phil. 2:8–11). It follows that the life of Christ represents the climactic case of both a redemptive plot and an anti-redemptive plot.

In secular literary analysis of ordinary stories, people speak of "comic" and "tragic" plots. The comic plots have a happy ending, while the tragic plots have a grim, disastrous ending. Literary analysis usually focuses on fictional plots. But fiction imitates life. In life itself, there are comic and tragic plots. These plots reflect, on a small scale, the great issues of life and death, success and failure. Any instance of failure or death is a reminder that we live in a fallen world. And the longing for happy endings exists because, in spite of their rebellion, people cannot escape a longing for eternity.[1] The story of redemption in Christ is the central story for all of history. It took place in time and space. Other human stories are dependent on this central story. That is why we can see analogies between plots—what we call redemptive plots and anti-redemptive plots.

---

1   See Vern S. Poythress, *In the Beginning Was the Word: Language—A God-Centered Approach* (Wheaton, IL: Crossway, 2009), part 4.

Using Clowney's Triangle for Redemptive
and Anti-Redemptive Plots

Clowney's triangle is applicable to both redemptive and anti-redemptive plots. With the first leg of the triangle, we ask about the meaning of a particular plot within its own immediate historical and literary context. A redemptive plot already has the meaning of deliverance within its own time frame. We are not inventing anything. People have longed for deliverance in every epoch of history since the fall. They can see the need. Deliverances that happen to other people symbolize the general need for a greater deliverance that will finally overcome the curse of death.

Likewise, anti-redemptive, tragic plots already have a tragic meaning within their own immediate time frame.

The second, horizontal leg of Clowney's triangle tells us to move forward in the history of redemption. We move forward to the great redemption in Christ. Thus, our treatment of redemptive and anti-redemptive plots is in harmony with the principles of Clowney's triangle.

Application to Us

We may also note that there is an application to us who are believers in Christ. We are united to Christ. And so we participate in his deliverance. Spiritually, we are raised from the dead, as Ephesians 2:4–6 indicates:

> But God, being rich in mercy, because of the great love with which he loved us, even when we were dead in our trespasses, made us alive together with Christ—by grace you have been saved—and raised us up with him and seated us with him in the heavenly places in Christ Jesus, . . .

The full accomplishment of our deliverance is still future, in the resurrection of the body (John 5:28–29).

Let us illustrate redemptive plots with a number of examples.

Noah and the Flood

The story of Noah's flood can serve as one example. The threat of the flood is made known to Noah. Noah builds the ark. Through the ark, Noah and his family are saved. The whole sequence constitutes a redemptive plot. God saves Noah and his family from the flood.

As we saw in our earlier discussion of Noah (chapter 2), this deliverance from the flood is a type, pointing to the climactic deliverance that Christ accomplishes. He delivers us from eternal death.

The Bronze Serpent

The story of the bronze serpent in Numbers 21:4–9 shows us another case of a redemptive plot. The threat is the threat of death from the bites of the serpents. God instructs Moses to make a bronze serpent and put it on a pole. The people receive deliverance from death by looking at the serpent on the pole. The difficulty that the people experience is the threat of death. God delivers them by means of the serpent. This deliverance, as we saw (chapter 3), is a type of Christ's deliverance (John 3:14–15).

David Defeating Goliath

Another instance of a redemptive plot is found in 1 Samuel 17, where David defeats Goliath. The initial difficulty is the threat from the Philistines. The Philistines threaten to defeat the Israelite army and make them slaves. God through David delivers them and defeats the Philistines, the enemy of God and his people. This defeat is a type of the defeat of Satan and his agents, which Christ accomplished (Heb. 2:14–15; Col. 2:15).

The Fall of Adam and Eve (Gen. 3)

The fall of Adam and Eve, recorded in Genesis 3, constitutes an antiredemptive plot. The initial difficulty is the temptation from the serpent. Adam and Eve succumb to the temptation, rather than resisting it. As a result, they suffer a curse (though, in the mercy of God, that is not the end of the story). The narrative has three main stages: the initial difficulty, the defeat of Adam and Eve, and the consequent punishment (curse and expulsion from the garden of Eden). This anti-redemptive plot is a type of the coming final judgment of the wicked (Rev. 20:11–15). It is also fulfilled in Christ himself, because as a substitute he dies for our sins, a death due to the curse of God (Gal. 3:13).

In sum, attention to the form of plots of deliverance enables us to identify types in the form of redemptive and anti-redemptive plots.

Rise and Fall of Tension, according to John Beekman

If we like, we can elaborate more fully on the structure of redemptive and anti-redemptive plots. John Beekman has provided a series of useful labels for distinct elements in how plots develop.[2] We provide here a slightly modified form of his definitions:

SETTING. The Setting is composed of statements about static facts, location, time, circumstances, or movement in location. Usually such information comes at the very beginning of a new episode.

PRELIMINARY INCIDENTS. Preliminary Incidents are events (not descriptions of static states of affairs) relevant to what follows, but before the problem or tension has been introduced into the episode.

OCCASIONING INCIDENT. The Occasioning Incident is the event that introduces notable conflict or tension. In the nature of the case, there is seldom more than one such incident.

COMPLICATION. Complication is an event increasing tension, making a solution (apparently) more difficult. There can be more than one paragraph devoted to Complications of various kinds. (Unlike the Occasioning Incident, Complications can and often do occur more than once in a single episode.)

---

2 John Beekman, "Toward an Understanding of Narrative Structure" (Dallas: Summer Institute of Linguistics, 1978).

CLIMAX. Climax is the incident of maximum conflict or tension. It is where, in a melodrama, one would expect the music to play the loudest.

RESOLUTION. Resolution is the event or events that solve the problem, release the tension, and unravel the tangles—or at least they contribute toward the solution.

ADDITIONAL INCIDENTS. An Additional Incident is a further event that is a consequence of the Climax or Resolution but is not a significant part of the Climax or Resolution itself.

COMMENTARY. A Commentary contains the narrator's comments on, evaluation of, or moral for the story. Unlike Additional Incidents, it does not contain events continuing the straight line of the narrative.

Variations on Beekman's Labels

We may note, by way of further explanation, that not all of these elements need to occur in every plot. Some of them, like the Preliminary Incidents and Additional Incidents, may be absent in simple stories. Some stories may break off without a clear ending. Some may start in the middle, as it were, without a clear-cut Occasioning Incident. The framework must be adapted to the nature of the particular story being investigated. The framework is nevertheless useful because it highlights the importance of tension and the importance of the striving to overcome a difficulty.

The Resolution

If the Resolution is favorable to the main participants, we have a redemptive plot. If it is unfavorable, we have a tragic plot, that is, an anti-redemptive plot. Awareness of the significance of the rise and fall of tension is useful in identifying the theme of deliverance. Sometimes people receive deliverance from extreme tension, such as death or the threat of death. At other times, the tension is much less. But if there is any tension at all, we can see that there is some analogy with the big plot of redemption—redemption achieved in Christ.[3]

3   Further discussion can be found in a number of places: Poythress, *In the Beginning Was the Word*, chs. 24–29; Vern S. Poythress, *The Miracles of Jesus: How the Savior's Mighty Acts Serve as Signs of Redemption* (Wheaton IL: Crossway, 2016); Vern S. Poythress, *Reading the Word of God in the Presence of God: A Handbook for Biblical Interpretation* (Wheaton, IL: Crossway, 2016), 276–79.

23

Types in Creation

WE NOW TURN TO CONSIDER TYPES IN CREATION. We consider primarily the main record of creation in Genesis 1–2. But other passages in the Bible reflect on creation. These passages sometimes bring out analogies between creation and redemption. But we have a more specific question: Are there *types* in creation?[1]

Adam as a Type

Certain passages in the New Testament indicate that Adam was a type of Christ. Romans 5:14 says that Adam "was a *type* of the one who was to come." The word *type* as used here does not have its later technical meaning (see appendix B). It means an example or an instance of a pattern. But the larger discussion in Romans 5:12–21 clearly indicates that Adam, like Christ, was a representative for a larger group of people. Adam was a representative for the human race, that is, for Eve and for all who descended from Adam by ordinary generation. Christ is a representative for all who are united to him by the Spirit. Romans 5:12–21 indicates that there are striking parallels between the two. First Corinthians 15:44–49 also discusses analogies between Adam and Christ.

---

1 Compare Patrick Fairbairn, *The Typology of Scripture: Viewed in Connection with the Whole Series of . . . The Divine Dispensations* (New York and London: Funk & Wagnalls, 1911), 1.1.4 (ch. 4).

It is clear also that Christ surpasses Adam. He is not on the same level. So there is a symbolic dimension to Adam.

But was the symbolic dimension already there in Genesis? Or is it visible only later, once Christ has come into the world and has taken on human nature? As usual, we have to deal with progressive revelation. Because revelation is progressive, not everything in the meaning of the history of redemption is going to be available in a clear and obvious way at the earlier stages. But is there at least a hint of the symbolic dimension of Adam already in Genesis?

Several features in Genesis encourage us to answer yes. For one thing, the episodes after Adam's fall indicate that the effects of sin and death spread out to the whole human race. Sin increases until the time of Noah, and death pervades. Adam is representative of the later sin.

In addition, there is the promise of the "offspring" of the woman in Genesis 3:15. This offspring will reverse the curse that Adam brought in. Genesis 3:15 promises a redemptive mediator. There is a redemptive plot, according to which this mediator will achieve victory over the serpent. So Genesis 3:15 includes an antithetical parallel between Adam and the curse on the one hand, and the offspring of the woman and the blessing on the other hand. The two are linked. Thus, Genesis 3:15 indicates that what happened in Adam symbolizes in reverse what will happen with the offspring of the woman. This offspring, ultimately, is Christ (Gal. 3:16; Heb. 2:14–15).

The symbolic depth of the story of Adam is also suggested in the role of the serpent. Is the serpent just a snake and nothing more? No, the serpent has a supernatural ability to speak. And what he speaks is supernatural in origin—it is cleverly evil. So the narrative hints that underneath the surface there is a supernatural conflict between the goodness of God and the evil of whatever is empowering the serpent's words. Thus the reactions of Adam and Eve have depth to them. They are engaged in a deep spiritual battle. Unfortunately, they lost the battle. But, as Genesis 3:15 reminds us, their loss was not the end of the story. It is reversed in God's plan of redemption.

The Marriage of Adam and Eve

Once we realize that Adam was a type of Christ, we can open the door to recognizing other types. The marriage between Adam and Eve symbolizes the marriage of Christ and the church, according to Ephesians 5:22–33. In particular, consider verses 29–32:

> [29] For no one ever hated his own flesh, but nourishes and cherishes it, just as Christ does the church, [30] because we are members of his body. [31] "Therefore a man shall leave his father and mother and hold fast to his wife, and the two shall become one flesh." [32] This mystery is profound, and I am saying that it refers to Christ and the church.

Verse 31 is a quotation from Genesis 2:24, which is about the union of Adam and Eve. Ephesians 5:29–33 compares the union of Adam and Eve with the union between Christ and the church. This comparison suggests that the union of Adam and Eve is a *type* for Christ and the church.

How do we evaluate this idea? Once again, it is important to use the principles in Clowney's triangle. We first ask about the meaning of Genesis 2 in its own historical and literary context. Does it have symbolic dimensions?

Genesis 2 is a nonfiction prose narrative.[2] It is not fiction. It does not just invent a story in order to make a theological point. But there are nevertheless larger theological themes. We cannot consider all of them, but we may note that the key quoted verse, verse 24, articulates a general pattern, not merely what happens in the case of Adam and Eve as individuals. Adam and Eve, as the first husband and wife, represent a larger pattern that is to hold in all cases of marriage.

In addition, we know from Genesis 1:26–27 that Adam and Eve are made in the image of God. They are male and female, whereas God is not a biological, sexual being. But because they are made in his image, they are going to reflect on the level of creation some aspects

---

2   Vern S. Poythress, *Interpreting Eden: A Guide to Faithfully Reading and Understanding Genesis 1–3* (Wheaton, IL: Crossway, 2019), ch. 6.

of his character. In particular, the personal relation of intimacy that God has with human beings is to be reflected in the intimacy between husband and wife. So the union between husband and wife already has a symbolic dimension. It is reflective of the covenantal union between God and human beings.

The events recorded in Genesis 2 are early in history. Genesis as a complete book comes later. It fits together with Exodus and the other books of Moses (Leviticus, Numbers, and Deuteronomy). Fairly early in Israelite history, God indicates that he is like a husband to Israel, and Israel is like his wife (Ex. 34:14–16). This analogy links the whole institution of marriage to the covenantal relation between God and his people. Later passages like Hosea and Ezekiel 16 and 23 develop further the comparison with marriage. So the text in Genesis 2 is intended by God to be seen in an analogical relation to the union between God and his people. And this union in Old Testament times points forward to the climactic union between God and his people that takes place in Christ.

Creation Anticipating Redemption

It appears, then, that there are types pointing to Christ in the record of creation in Genesis 1–2. But we must be careful. In his comprehensive plan, God knows every event that is to take place in all times. But we must beware of the idea that redemption is intrinsically needed to complete creation. Redemption enters into the picture only because there is a fall into sin. We must not ignore the distinction between creation and the fall.[3]

If Adam and Eve had resisted the temptation of the serpent, there would have been further development. They would have had children. They would still have had the task assigned by God in Genesis 1:28, to "fill the earth and subdue it." But this development would have taken place with no need for redemption. There would also not have been the need for Christ to take on human nature in order to be our substitute and our sin-bearer. Christ became the *last* Adam only because the *first* Adam, that is, the first man, failed; he succumbed to sin.

---

3   Fairbairn, *Typology of Scripture*, 1.1.4.86.

Thus, the parallel worked out in Romans 5:12–21 and 1 Corinthians 15:44–49 between Christ and Adam makes sense only because of the special redemptive role that Christ took on himself. Likewise, the marriage of Christ and the church, depicted in Ephesians 5:22–33, is a marriage that involves redemption. Ephesians 5:26 says that Christ "cleansed her [the church] by the washing of water with the word. . . ." From what did he cleanse her? From sin.

As a matter of historical record, Adam and Eve did sin. Christ did undertake to redeem his chosen ones from their sin. But those future events were not built into the order of creation itself. Adam and Eve did make a genuine choice. And it could have been otherwise, if the plan of God had been otherwise.

So does the role of Adam as representative of the human race point forward to the role of Christ as the last Adam? There is definitely a relation between the two. The relation is worked out in Romans 5:12–21 and 1 Corinthians 15:44–49. But the relation is not a necessity built into the original order of creation itself.

I would suggest that the same is true concerning other aspects in creation that later serve as symbols of redemption. The symbolism is proper symbolism. It is not artificial. But it never implies that sin is built into the original creation itself.

Legitimate Ties between Creation and Redemption

We can see the legitimacy of a relation between creation and redemption when we notice that redemption is sometimes depicted in the Bible as re-creation. It is *new* creation. Second Corinthians 5:17 says, "[I]f anyone is in Christ, he is a new *creation.*" Romans 8:18–24 indicates that the new creation repairs the ways in which the original creation has been damaged by the fall. Revelation 21:1 speaks of "a new heaven and a new earth," in obvious parallel with "the first heaven and the first earth" that "had passed away." Once the fall into sin has taken place, and once it is clear that God has undertaken to provide redemption, this redemption will have many parallels with unfallen creation. The parallels include the parallels between Christ and Adam, as we have observed.

We can speak of these parallels as "types," if we want to use the word *type* in a more extended way. But when we introduced the word *type* earlier, one of the features was that it was forward-pointing. Creation points forward in many ways to its completion in the consummation. But before the fall into sin, it cannot yet unambiguously point forward to the details of the exact route by which the consummation is reached. That route, according to the plan of God, includes sin and redemption, neither of which is *necessitated* by the structure of prefall creation itself.[4]

In dealing with the parallel between Christ and Adam, we have tried to proceed in this very way. Adam is the representative head of the race. His headship dimly reflects God's own headship over creation. We may also say that the eternal Son of God, the second person of the Trinity, is one who as the Word of God executes the plan of God the Father. So he exercises the rule of God, and he is head over creation and over all humanity. To put it another way, Adam, as the created image of God, is created after the pattern of the Son of God, who is eternally the divine image of God (Col. 1:15; Heb. 1:3). But the specific character of Christ as the last Adam belongs to him because he has taken on human nature for the sake of our salvation. That final aspect is not built into prefall creation.

Similar truths hold with respect to the parallel between Eve and the church. From the beginning, even before sin entered, marriage symbolizes the union of God with his people. It reflects the eternal union between persons of the Trinity. But the specific role of Christ in Ephesians 5:22–33 has respect to redemption.

The Creation out of Nothing

Let us now consider other aspects in Genesis 1–2 that have a symbolic dimension.

---

4   Fairbairn, *Typology of Scripture*, 1.1.4 (ch. 4), has an extended discussion. I agree with Fairbairn in maintaining that the incarnation took place on account of sin. Conceptually, the incarnation is to be carefully distinguished from the role of the eternal Word, the eternal Son, in the work of creation and in all of God's providential rule.

God's work of creating out of nothing in Genesis 1:1 manifests his absoluteness and his all-sufficiency. It thus has a symbolic dimension. His absoluteness and all-sufficiency are also displayed in his acts of re-creation, as Romans 4:17 reminds us: ". . . the God in whom he [Abraham] believed, who gives life to the dead [redemptively] and calls into existence the things that do not exist." The expression "calls into existence the things that do not exist" echoes the original acts of God in Genesis 1, including the initial, most spectacular act of creating the heavens and the earth with no preexisting material.

The link between creation out of nothing and the redemptive re-creation in Romans 4:17 is based on the fact that redemption is a kind of new creation (2 Cor. 5:17; Col. 1:15–20). But, as we have stressed before, the analogy between the two does not imply that redemption is built into the original acts of creation.

Day 1: The Creation of Light

God created the light on day 1 (Gen. 1:3). The created light reflects the character of God, who "is light" (1 John 1:5). When Jesus comes into the world, he is "the light of the world" (John 8:12). The focus in John 8:12 is on redemptive light. He delivers people from walking in the darkness of sin: "Whoever follows me will not walk in darkness, but will have the light of life" (v. 12). But John 1:4–9 indicates that there is a broader background, namely that the Word—even before the incarnation—is light. That is true in the context of creation (v. 3).

As usual, the redemptive meaning of light builds on the meaning of light in creation (Gen. 1:3). But the two are distinguishable. God's nature and his glory are displayed in the world, even apart from redemption.

Day 1: God Created by Speaking

God created light by speaking, by saying, "Let there be light." And there was light (Gen. 1:3). This power of God in speaking has its deepest root in the eternal Word, as expounded in John 1:1. So we may say that God's speech in Genesis 1:3 is a type of the Word, who will manifest himself more fully in the progress of revelation. The same holds for the other instances where God speaks in Genesis 1.

Day 1: God Evaluated What Is Good

Genesis 1:4 says that "God saw that it was good." This record reflects God's authority in evaluation. His evaluations will be revealed more fully in the progress of revelation. In the final judgment, God will be the Judge. So we may say that this one instance of evaluation is a type of God the Judge, and that fulfillment comes in the person of Christ, who executes the judgment of the Father (John 5:22).

Day 1: God Separated the Light from the Darkness (Gen. 1:4)

In this and other acts of separation in Genesis 1, God manifests his ability to make distinctions and to determine the multifaceted diversity in the world. The authority to separate reflects the divine authority of God himself in his absoluteness. The diversity in the world reflects on the level of the creature the original diversity among the persons of the Trinity. Both of these manifestations anticipate further displays of God's character in the progress of revelation.

Day 3: God Created Living Plants and Trees

God has life in himself. His life is reflected in the created order when he created living things that reproduce (Gen. 1:11–12). The climactic manifestation of the life of God is found in Jesus Christ, who says, "I am . . . the life" (John 11:25; 14:6).

The Remaining Days of Creation

We may proceed in a similar manner through the rest of the record in Genesis 1 concerning the days of creation. When God created, he manifested aspects of his own character. Those aspects are climactically manifested in Christ. So we should not be surprised that later parts of the Bible take up elements from creation and use them in metaphors and prophecies concerning the coming of God in redemption and in consummation. For example, Jeremiah 31:35–37 and 33:20–21 draw attention to an element in creation—the faithfulness of God in maintaining the fixed order of day and night. This element in creation is parallel to an element in redemption—God's faithfulness to his promises of the new covenant and the covenant with David. Genesis 22:17 and Jeremiah 33:22 mention elements in creation—the vastness of the host of heaven and the sands of the seas. These are compared to an element in redemption—the multitude of the offspring of Abraham and David.

In all the links between creation and redemption, we also distinguish between the two. God displays his nature in both creation and redemption.

24

Types in the Earthly Life of Jesus

THE OVERALL PLAN OF GOD INCLUDES progress in redemption over a long span of time. Within the overall history, the Old Testament prepares the way for the coming of Christ. Then, when Christ comes, redemption is accomplished. In a sense, redemption *does* come to people within the epochs of the Old Testament. But it comes by way of shadows and anticipations of the great redemption to come. People can experience eternal salvation, but only by participating beforehand, in a quite mysterious manner, in the fruits of the work of Christ, who is still to come.

The Change in Epoch with the New Testament

All of these things of a preliminary nature, belonging to the Old Testament, change when Christ comes on the scene. When he comes, the shadows and types and preliminary pictures of redemption have served their role. They are made obsolete because the reality, namely Christ himself, has come.

So, naively, we might expect that within the life of Christ on earth, there will be no more types. There will simply be the reality of who he is.

Yes, the reality has come. "And the Word became flesh and dwelt among us," as John 1:14 says. But during his earthly life, Christ's work on earth still has to come to its own climax. Jesus speaks about an "hour" that has not yet come (2:4). It is the "hour" of his crucifixion, death, and resurrection.

Jesus gives words and works miracles during his earthly ministry. But these remain still on the "unrealized" side of redemption, from the standpoint of the climactic work of crucifixion, death, and resurrection. So we find that Jesus's words and deeds point forward to that climactic work. In this respect, they serve as "types" in a broad sense. For example, Jesus's feeding of the 5,000, as recorded in John 6:1–14, is interpreted by him as a pointer to the fact that he is "the bread of life" (v. 35). He will give his flesh and his blood to be eaten and drunk (v. 53). This giving takes place in his sacrificial death. He promises eternal life to those who eat and drink, and the eternal life becomes theirs because Jesus has eternal life in his resurrection from the dead. On this basis, we can fill out Clowney's triangle as applied to the feeding of the 5,000 (see fig. 24.1).

Figure 24.1: Clowney's Triangle Applied to the Feeding of the 5,000

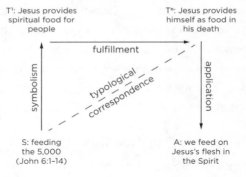

Clowney's Triangle Applied to the Miracles of Jesus

In a similar way, other miracles of Jesus have a typological function. Clowney's triangle can accordingly be used to analyze them, just as we used it to analyze Old Testament types.[1]

---

1   For a fuller exploration of this analysis, see Vern S. Poythress, *The Miracles of Jesus: How the Savior's Mighty Acts Serve as Signs of Redemption* (Wheaton, IL: Crossway, 2016).

PART VII

INTERPRETATION
OF ANALOGIES

*We consider how to adapt Clowney's triangle to instances of analogy
without a clear-cut structure of two levels of meaning.*

25

Analogies as Similar to Types

NOW WE TURN TO CONSIDER how we deal with analogies that we find in the Bible. Let us begin with a particular case of analogy, found in Hebrews 11. Hebrews 11 discusses a considerable number of Old Testament personages. The common theme is faith. All these people exercised faith. The faith of any one person is analogous to the faith of the other people. It is analogous also to the faith that *we* should have as Christians. The succeeding passage in Hebrews 12:1–2 explicitly mentions "our faith." Our faith is to be encouraged by "so great a cloud of witnesses," an allusion to the preceding chapter.

There are in fact many cases of analogical connections between the Old and New Testaments. How do we take them into account in our study of the Old Testament?

Analogy versus Typology

In chapter 14, we considered several distinct categories of connections: analogy, symbolism, typology, and prophecy. The term *analogy* can be used very broadly. But we used it to designate connections that were one-level connections. Such a one-level structure contrasts with the two-level structure that exists with symbolism and with types.

The theme of faith in Hebrews 11 seems to be a case of a one-level structure. All the instances of faith are on the same level. All are analogous to each other. All of them are also analogous to Christian faith.

Christian faith is fundamentally human faith in God and his promises. Because of progressive revelation, Christian faith exists within a fuller context of revelation. Christian faith is faith in Christ who has come. Old Testament faith was faith in Christ who was to come in the future. Christian faith is faith in Christ who has been raised from the dead and is now enthroned. Yet there is a decided continuity with saving faith in the Old Testament. So it is right to see an analogy among all the instances of saving faith.

Analogy and Typology as Perspectives

But there is more that can be said. As we saw in chapter 15, analogy and typology are not rigidly separated from each other. Each can serve as a perspective on the entirety of the history of redemption. We can confirm this perspectival possibility by looking at the nature of faith in the New Testament. There is a deepening of the understanding of the nature of faith that takes place in the New Testament, because Christ as the object of faith is more fully revealed. His work on earth has been accomplished, and faith can look back on that work.

We may also observe that Jesus Christ took on human nature. He became fully human. He himself had to trust in God. His trust is unique, however, not only because he alone is a perfect human being but also because he is our representative. There are key differences. We have faith in Christ; Christ did not have faith in himself, but in the Father.

Our faith is empowered by the Holy Spirit, who is the Spirit of Christ. The Spirit conforms us to the pattern of Christ (2 Cor. 3:18). We must acknowledge the uniqueness of Christ. But we also acknowledge that there are aspects in which our faith should imitate the trust that Christ exhibited as a man on earth.

Adapting Clowney's Triangle

If analogies and types are similar to each other in some respects, it leads us to ask whether Clowney's triangle can be adapted for use with analogies. Can we create a triangle to use for analogies, in addition to Clowney's triangle for types?

Yes, we can, as we shall see. But we confront a difficulty right away when we consider how we might replace the first, vertical leg of Clowney's triangle. Recall that the vertical leg represents the transition from a symbol to the meaning of the symbol. (See fig. 25.1, reproducing fig. 6.1.)

Figure 25.1: Clowney's Triangle

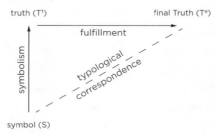

The symbol S is at the bottom, and the vertical leg goes from there to $T1$, "truth-one," which is its meaning. But this transition from S to $T1$ depends on there being a symbol, which has two levels of meaning—the symbol itself, and then the truth it symbolizes. If we do not have a symbol within a passage, it seems that we have no proper starting point.

The First Leg of the Triangle for Analogy

But let us consider, what is the main contribution of the vertical leg of Clowney's triangle? It tells us to pay attention to the meaning of the symbol within its immediate historical and literary context. This attention is important as a first step. It contrasts with the tendency of some interpreters to want to leap directly to a consideration of an antitype and a fulfillment. It says, "Not so fast. First, think about the meaning when God originally gave the symbol."

This principle of attending to the immediate context is always helpful. It does not apply *only* to situations that involve symbols. So we can use the same idea in modified form, in order to deal with relations of analogy. In our modified triangle, the first leg consists in asking, What is the meaning of a passage, or what is the meaning of a person or event within the passage, within its original context? That is useful. It applies to every passage. But how could it help us to begin to see a relation of analogy with *other* passages?

We can begin a process of thinking about relations by first asking what general principle or pattern or truth is exemplified in our starting passage. There may be more than one such pattern. But a significant clue can come from the immediately neighboring passages, and from the book of the Bible in which the passage is found. Are there prominent themes that run through the book? Are any of these themes exemplified in our passage? Does the passage share some theme or themes with neighboring passages?

There will often be such themes. So we can try to make a transition from the particular case that occurs in our passage to the general pattern.[1] That transition is the first leg of our triangle. (See fig. 25.2.) The triangle as a whole, once it is complete, will be called *the triangle for analogy*.

Figure 25.2: The First Leg of the Triangle for Analogy

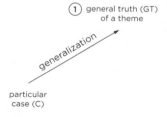

The leg is drawn at an angle in order to suggest that the principle, the general truth (GT), will have further manifestations along a historical timeline (in the figure, time is pictured as proceeding from the left to the right).

The Faith of Noah (Heb. 11:7)

As a particular example, let us consider the passage in Genesis 6:9–19 about Noah. We have already seen that Noah functions as a type of Christ (chapter 2). But we can still consider other dimensions of the passage. In

---

1   This step is similar to what Walter Kaiser has called "principlizing" (Walter C. Kaiser Jr. and Moisés Silva, *Introduction to Biblical Hermeneutics: The Search for Meaning*, rev. and expanded ed. [Grand Rapids, MI: Zondervan, 2007], 91–93).

particular, we can consider how Noah was a man of faith (Heb. 11:7). In Genesis 6:17, God told Noah that he was going to send a flood. Noah had to believe what God said. He had to obey God by beginning to build the ark. In this response, Noah is similar to other people of faith in Genesis. Hebrews 11 lists some of the other ones—Abel, Enoch, Abraham, Sarah, Isaac, Jacob, and Joseph. Within Genesis itself, the positive, believing response of these people contrasts with the unbelief of others, such as Cain, Lamech, Noah's contemporaries, the builders of the tower of Babel, and the citizens of Sodom and Gomorrah. Our attention to faith is in agreement with one of the themes of Genesis. The general principle is that people should have faith in God and that God repeatedly has mercy and saves those who have faith in him. We can represent this meaning in Genesis 6:9–19 using the first leg of our triangle for analogy (see fig. 25.3).

Figure 25.3: The First Leg of the Triangle for Analogy, for Noah

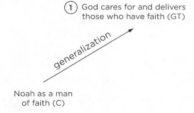

The Second Leg of the Triangle for Analogy

Now we are ready for our second step. In Clowney's triangle, the second step is represented by the horizontal leg of the triangle. This leg represents the unfolding of the history of redemption. Is there something analogous when we are dealing with analogy? Yes, the history of redemption is still a controlling context. The general principle that we have found at an earlier point in the history of redemption may be expected to be embodied climactically when Christ comes, at the climax of the history of redemption.

So we can draw a second leg of the triangle. This leg descends from the general principle to the particular embodiment in Christ. (See fig. 25.4.)

Figure 25.4: The Second Leg of the Triangle for Analogy

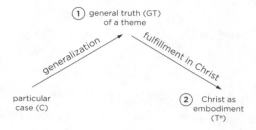

The Second Leg of the Triangle for Analogy, in the Case of Noah's Faith

Let us think how this leg works in the case where we start with Noah's faith. We know that when Christ comes, he comes as incarnate. He takes on human nature. According to his human nature, he too is supposed to live with faith in God. And out of his faith will flow obedience. God delivered Noah; he will also deliver Christ, who trusts in the Father. And so it happens. Christ trusts in God even when confronted with the agony of the cross. His trust and his obedience are perfect (Heb. 4:15). This trust and obedience are climactic. But because he is fully human, we may also say that in his humanity he is fully in line with the other instances of faith that we see in the Old Testament. Though Christ is unique, he is also an embodiment of faith. (See fig. 25.5.)

Figure 25.5: The Second Leg of the Triangle for Analogy, for Noah

The relation between the initial case (C) of Noah and the embodiment in Christ (T^n) is a relation of *analogy*. (See fig. 25.6.)

Figure 25.6: The Relation of Analogy

Multiple Instances of Analogy

The history of redemption may show complex forms of development. We have said that we look for fulfillment in Christ, as the climactic mediator of salvation. But there may be earlier instances of parallels. As Hebrews 11 points out, Noah as a man of faith is parallel to many examples in the Old Testament of people who exercised faith. If we look for a climactic fulfillment in Christ, that need not mean that we ignore parallels that occur either earlier or later in the Old Testament.

The same possibility of multiple instances occurs when we consider types. For example, we discussed earlier (chapter 23) the fact that Adam is a type of Christ. The theme of offspring of the woman, first mentioned in Genesis 3:15, has its fulfillment in Christ. But there are instances within the Old Testament that we could describe as "partial fulfillments" or "analogical fulfillments," related to the promise in Genesis 3:15. Noah, Abraham, Moses, and David are to some degree "Adamic" figures. All of them are offspring of the woman in a broad sense, offspring in the line of promise. But none of them is the ultimate deliverer.[2]

The Third Step: Application

For Clowney's triangle, there is also a third step, the step of application. In the case of the triangle for analogy, this third step will work similarly to how it worked with types. Application can be represented by the

---

2   G. K. Beale, *Handbook on the New Testament Use of the Old Testament* (Grand Rapids, MI: Baker, 2012), 21–22.

text marked (3) in figure 25.7. This text is placed to the right of the text marked (2) representing Christ's embodiment of the truth. In the diagram as a whole, developments in time go from left to right. We to whom the truth applies are in the history of redemption at a point later in time than the Old Testament and later than the earthly life of Christ. (See fig. 25.7.)

Figure 25.7: Application in the Triangle for Analogy

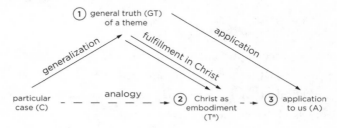

In this diagram we have included a double arrow, rather than a single arrow, moving from the general truth (GT) to fulfillment in Christ (T^n). This double arrow represents the fact that Christ is the supreme embodiment of the truth.

The Third Step of Application, in the Case of Noah's Faith

It is through Christ that we have the power to live a new life. That includes the power to trust in him and in God the Father. So we can represent in a diagram what application is like in the case of the analogy involving Noah and his faith. (See fig. 25.8.)

Figure 25.8: Application in the Triangle for Analogy, for Noah's Faith

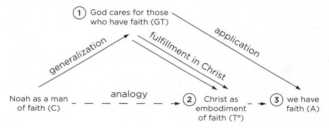

Comparing Clowney's Triangle and the Triangle for Analogy

So how do Clowney's triangle and the triangle for analogy compare? We might say that the triangle for analogy is the result of tipping Clowney's triangle toward the right. In addition, there is a little bit of squishing. Step 2 is represented by the movement on the horizontal line in Clowney's triangle. By comparison, in the triangle for analogy, step 2 becomes movement on a line that travels downward from a general truth (GT) to fulfillment in Christ (T^n).

To some degree, the three steps do correspond when we compare the two triangles. The first step focuses on meaning at the time that God gives an initial revelation. The second step focuses on the line of the history of redemption, and how progressive revelation moves forward to come to fulfillment in Christ. The third step focuses on application to us.

The differences arise primarily because, in the case of analogy, there is no longer a clear case of two levels of meaning. The movement from symbol S to truth $T1$ within Clowney's triangle is not fully parallel to the movement from a particular case C to a general truth GT within the triangle for analogy. The general truth is a generalization. But it does not belong to a distinct realm of thought.

Nevertheless, there is some benefit in picturing the general truth as residing on a higher plane. The general truth belongs, in a sense, to all times. It hovers above any particular time. The particular cases—represented by a lower level—belong to particular times. The initial particular case C belongs to its own location in time within the Old Testament era. Fulfillment Tn belongs to the time of Christ's work. Application A belongs to our own location in time. Since one of the main differences is the difference in location in time, we represent the three cases by putting them all on the same horizontal level.

A Fuzzy Boundary between Analogy and Type

The parallels between Clowney's triangle and the triangle for analogy provide help when we deal with cases of a fuzzy boundary. In chapter 15 we argued that though we can make a rough distinction between an analogy and a type, the distinction is indeed a rough one. The boundaries are fuzzy. Both the category of analogy and the category of type can easily be "stretched" into a perspective on the whole of revelation.

Suppose we are dealing with a textual passage that seems to be of an intermediate kind. It seems to be halfway between a clear-cut case of a type and a clear-cut case of an analogy. What do we do? We can use either triangle as we wish—either Clowney's triangle or the triangle for analogy. If we do the three steps, we should come out more or less with the same results, whichever model we use.

This parallel between the two triangles also helps us to appreciate how either analogy or type can serve as a perspective. If we use analogy as a perspective, then we see everything using a reasoning process with the triangle for analogy. Clowney's triangle becomes a kind of specialized variant form of the triangle for analogy. Conversely, suppose that we use the idea of a type as a universal perspective. Then we see everything through the reasoning process represented in Clowney's triangle. The triangle for analogy becomes a kind of specialized variant form of Clowney's triangle.

If we like, we can emphasize the similarity between the two triangles by deliberately reconfiguring the triangle for analogy, to make it the same shape as the triangle for types. The result is figure 25.9.

Figure 25.9: Reshaping the Triangle for Analogy

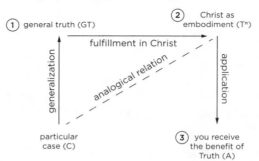

This reconfigured triangle has the advantage of better highlighting the centrality of Christ. The two configurations in figures 25.7 and 25.9

have the same meaning. In subsequent chapters, we will use the configuration of figure 25.9.

Because the two triangles may be treated as variants of each other, the additional steps 4–8, discussed in chapter 17, can all be extended to apply to the triangle for analogy.

26

Using the Triangle for Analogy

LET US NOW CONSIDER a few examples of how to use the triangle for analogy.

God Bringing Good out of Evil (Gen. 50:20)

We may begin with Genesis 50:20. After the death of Jacob their father, Joseph indicates to his brothers his attitude toward their earlier wrongdoing:

> As for you, you meant evil against me, but God meant it for good, to bring it about that many people should be kept alive, as they are today.

Joseph's brothers "meant evil" when they sold him to the Ishmaelite traders (Gen. 37:28), but God brought good out of it. Joseph is speaking about a particular episode from the past. But, given the knowledge of God assumed in the book of Genesis, one of the implications is that God has the wisdom and power to do a similar thing in other cases.

The rest of Genesis shows that God is committed to his promise of salvation, given initially in Genesis 3:15. He cares for his people again and again, in the course of time. And there are cases where he brings good out of evil.

For example, God confuses the languages at Babel, and that confusion is on the face of it a curse. God has brought evil upon them because their plans were evil. But out of this curse it develops that the people are "dispersed," which is in accord with God's good purpose that human beings should "fill the earth" (Gen. 1:28).

Jacob is involved in scheming when he buys Esau's birthright (Gen. 25:32–34), and when he later deceives his father, Isaac (27:18–29), and obtains the blessing. In the midst of these sinful actions, God is sovereignly working to bring blessing, that is, goodness, to Jacob as the chosen son.

The episode with Judah and Tamar is not free from sin. But God uses it to bring to birth the next descendant in the promised line, leading to Christ the King (Matt. 1:3).

We may therefore conclude that the particular case in Genesis 50:20 is an instance of a larger pattern. There is a general truth (GT) that God brings good out of evil. Arriving at this general truth is the first step in the triangle for analogy.

The second step is to ask how this general truth plays out in the history of redemption. In particular, how is this general truth manifested at the climax of redemption, in the life of Christ? The answer is plain. The crucifixion of Christ is an act by the hands of unjust men. It is evil. But God uses it to accomplish good, namely the salvation of all those who belong to Christ:

> [T]his Jesus, delivered up according to the definite plan and foreknowledge of God, you crucified and killed by the hands of lawless men. God raised him up, loosing the pangs of death, because it was not possible for him to be held by it. (Acts 2:23–24)

The third step is to apply the truth to ourselves. There are many instances in each of our lives when God brings good out of evil. But the preeminent case is salvation itself. Our sins, which are evil, are washed away by the substitution of Christ, by the blood of Christ. God brings good, namely our salvation, out of evil, namely our sins.

> For our sake he [God] made him [Christ] to be sin who knew no sin, so that in him we might become the righteousness of God. (2 Cor. 5:21)

We may summarize all three steps together by means of the triangle for analogy (fig. 26.1).

Figure 26.1: The Triangle for Analogy for Genesis 50:20

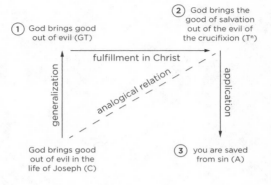

① God brings good
   out of evil (GT)

② God brings the
   good of salvation
   out of the evil of
   the crucifixion (T^n)

generalization

fulfillment in Christ

analogical relation

application

God brings good
out of evil in the
life of Joseph (C)

③ you are saved
   from sin (A)

Joseph Resisting Temptation (Gen. 39:6–13)

As a second case, let us consider Genesis 39:6–13, where Joseph resists temptation coming from Potiphar's wife. His resistance to temptation and his loyalty to God (v. 9) are positive examples among a great many negative and mixed examples in the book of Genesis. One thinks particularly of the temptation of Adam and Eve in Genesis 3. Each situation of temptation is analogous to the other situations.

So, as the first step in the triangle for analogy, we move from the particular case, namely the temptation of Joseph, to the general principle. The general truth is that God tells us to resist temptation and to show loyalty to him in situations of temptation. It is also true that the responses vary. Some people do show loyalty to God; others cave in to temptation.

What about the second step in the triangle for analogy? We move from the general truth (GT) to fulfillment in Christ. Christ was perfectly loyal to God the Father throughout his whole earthly life. We may point particularly to his resistance when tempted by the devil in the wilderness (Matt. 4:1–11), and his loyalty in the garden of Gethsemane and on the cross.

Finally, in step 3, we apply the general truth to ourselves. We are to be loyal to God and resist temptation in the power of the Spirit of Christ.

We may summarize the entire analysis using the triangle for analogy (fig. 26.2).

Figure 26.2: The Triangle for Analogy for Joseph's Refusal (Gen. 39:6–13)

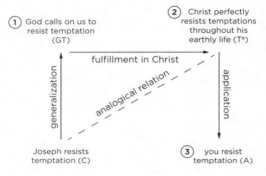

Cases of analogy could easily be multiplied. Human nature is the same everywhere. Cases in human experience often suggest analogies. In many cases, it is fairly easy to proceed.

Jacob's Vow (Gen. 28:18–22)

We will turn to two cases that are somewhat more challenging. The first is the case of Jacob's vow, recorded in Genesis 28:18–22. What do we do with it?

Step 1 is to search for a general pattern. Records of vows occur here and there in the Old Testament. It is clear that people in the ancient Near East were familiar with the idea of vow. More than one place in the Old Testament contains more general instructions regulating how vows are to be carried out (e.g., Lev. 22:21–23; Num. 6; Deut. 12:11; Eccl. 5:4–5). So our passage is included under the general topic of vows.

But the topic can become more specific if we pay attention to the details of Genesis 28:18–22 and its context in the life of Jacob. Jacob makes his vow in response to the promise of God given in verses 13–15. The promise is a unilateral promise of favor to Jacob, including a promise to be with him and to keep him: "I am with you and will keep you wherever you go" (v. 15). It includes a renewal of the promise of the land of Canaan, a promise already made to his father, Isaac, and his grandfather, Abraham. This line of promise extends onward until it is fulfilled in Christ, who is the great heir in the line of Abraham. So the passage could be explored for typological connections. Jacob as the offspring of Abraham symbolizes the final, exalted offspring.

Instead, let us stick with the theme of Jacob's vow. That vow can be the starting point for connections by analogy.

One challenging point here is that Jacob repeatedly shows himself to be a schemer and a manipulator. God promises Jacob his favor. But in making the vow, is Jacob trying to manipulate God? Earlier, he bargained with Esau, and later on he will bargain with Laban. In Genesis 28, is he trying to bargain with God? A tension runs through Jacob's life, between two interacting themes. On the one hand, God promises to bless Jacob out of his free favor. On the other hand, Jacob tries to achieve the goals by manipulation. When Jacob makes the vow, which is it? Is he simply expressing his heartfelt gratitude for free grace? Or is he trying to manipulate God? The text does not give us a clear answer. Maybe it is some of both. That is part of the challenge of dealing with the life of Jacob. Jacob is not a perfect saint. He is a mixed character.

So we could treat his vow either through the theme of gratitude for grace, or the theme of attempts to manipulate God. The intersection of the two themes is interesting, partly because Christians are not completely free from the second path, the path of attempting to manipulate God. We have to learn progressively that the grace of God is indeed free.

How do we express these insights within the triangle for analogy? Step 1 consists in discerning the general truth (GT), that people respond to God both in genuine gratitude and in attempts to manipulate him in order to gain favor. Step 2 consists in discerning fulfillment in Christ. Christ is the perfect man, who is full of genuine gratitude and does not manipulate his Father. Step 3 consists in application. We as Christians learn progressively, again and again, to believe in God's free favor in Christ, and to repent from the tendency to try to manipulate. We may summarize these insights using the triangle for analogy (fig. 26.3).

Figure 26.3: The Triangle for Analogy for Jacob's Vow (Gen. 28:18–22)

The Sons of Ham (Gen. 10:6)

Let us consider another case, namely the passage about the division of the nations in Genesis 10. We focus on a single verse: "The sons of Ham: Cush, Egypt, Put, and Canaan" (v. 6). Can we use the triangle for analogy to understand the significance of this verse?

In step 1, we ask what general truth is exemplified in this case. The whole chapter, Genesis 10, is about the origin of the various nations, who are descended from Noah. The general truth is that, by God's providence, he brings about the differentiation of the human race into a variety of nations, as Noah's sons have children and they in turn have children. This focus on the nations is a significant theme, because the promise made to Abram is that in him "all the families of the earth shall be blessed" (12:3). The division into nations also has a thematic connection with the scattering of people that took place after the tower of Babel (11:9), and the original plan of God that the descendants of Adam would "fill the earth" (1:28; see 9:7).

In step 2, we ask how the general truth comes to fulfillment in Christ. Christ, as we know, is the offspring of Abraham (Gal. 3:16) and the offspring of the woman (Gen. 3:15). It is in Christ that the nations will be blessed:

> . . . so that in Christ Jesus the blessing of Abraham might come to the Gentiles [the nations], so that we might receive the promised Spirit through faith. (Gal. 3:14)

The Great Commission in Matthew 28:18–20 also explicitly includes a mention of the inclusion of the nations:

> Go therefore and make disciples of *all nations*, baptizing them in the name of the Father and of the Son and of the Holy Spirit, . . . (v. 19)

In mentioning these verses, we have already anticipated step 3, because the inclusion of the nations in the blessing of Abraham is a fruit of Christ's work. He is the Son and the heir, and in him we become sons and heirs (Gal. 3:26–4:7).

Among all nations are the nations listed in Genesis 10:6. Genesis 10:6, in context, indicates that God brought about the division of nations and that this division exists within the context of the fundamental unity of the human race. We are all descendants of Adam and also descendants of Noah. God knows about all these nations, including the specific ones mentioned in verse 6. To these nations, among others, the gospel goes out, according to the command of God given in the Great Commission. People from among these nations come to faith in Christ and are saved by Christ (Acts 10:43–48). They become part of the great multitude of the saved people depicted in Revelation 7:9–12 and 21:3, 24.

These truths may be summarized using the triangle for analogy (fig. 26:4).

Figure 26.4: The Triangle for Analogy for the Sons of Ham (Gen. 10:6)

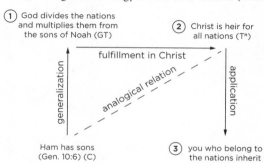

Wide Use of Analogy

The use of analogy in the case of more challenging passages, like the sons of Ham in Genesis 10:6, indicates the potential for its wide use. All such uses are naturally to be guided by (1) the immediate literary context (such as Gen. 10); (2) the context of the book of the Bible, including its major themes (Genesis, with its theme of the nations); and (3) the Bible's teaching about God's overall plan for the history of redemption, including its teaching about the centrality of Christ (Luke 24:25–27, 44–49; 2 Cor. 1:20; Heb. 1:1–3).

27

Analogies for the Attributes of God

WE SAW IN THE PREVIOUS CHAPTER that the use of analogy can be quite broad. Encouraged by this breadth, let us consider how analogies operate with respect to the attributes of God.[1]

Analogies Based on an Attribute of God

Analogies exist between any two events, both of which display the same attribute of God. The two events are analogous precisely because they have in common the display of the same particular attribute.

For example, a number of passages in Genesis display the mighty power of God. The acts of creation in Genesis 1 display his power. The act of bringing the flood of Noah displays his power (Gen. 7–8). The judgment on Sodom and Gomorrah displays his power (19:24–25). All these events, broadly speaking, are analogous to one another in that they display the power of God. We can extend our list of passages beyond Genesis and into the other books of the Bible. Many passages display God's power.

---

1 The idea for this chapter stems from interactions with Timothy P. Yates, China Reformed Theological Seminary, Taipei, Taiwan. See especially Yates's framework of lex Christi (Vern S. Poythress, "Introducing the Law of Christ [Lex Christi]: A Fruitful Framework for Theology and Life," version 1.0, https://frame-poythress.org/introducing-the-law -of-christ-lex-christi-a-fruitful-framework-for-theology-and-life/, accessed September 2, 2021; T. P. Yates, "Adapting Westminster Standards' Moral Law Motif to Integrate Systematic Theology, Apologetics, and Pastoral Practice" [thesis, North-West University, 2021]; T. P. Yates, http://www.bethoumyvision.net/).

God displays his mercy in Genesis. The initial noteworthy display of mercy comes right after the fall into sin in Genesis 3:6. God could have destroyed Adam and Eve on the spot. But in his mercy he does not. He does judge them and speak about painful consequences of their sin (vv. 16–19). But he also makes a promise of redemption (v. 15) and clothes them (v. 21). He has mercy on Noah and his family. He has mercy in calling Abram (12:1). He has mercy in rescuing Abram and Sarai in Egypt (12:10–20). And so on throughout the book of Genesis and the rest of the Bible.

God displays his ability to speak whenever he does speak. In Genesis 1, he brings things into existence by speaking. He speaks about the task of mankind (1:28–30). He speaks to Adam about the tree of the knowledge of good and evil (2:16–17). He speaks to the serpent, to Eve, and to Adam after the fall (3:15–19). And so on.

God displays his justice in events in which he executes justice. The pronouncements against sin in Genesis 3:15–19 are in this category. So also with the pronouncements against Sodom and Gomorrah and the judgment that befalls them.

God's wisdom is on display in any number of passages that talk about wisdom—especially those that indicate that wisdom comes from God.

Using the Triangle for Analogy with Respect to an Attribute of God

If we choose a particular attribute of God, all the passages that display this attribute are analogous to each other. They are similar to each other because they display the same attribute. They are also different from each other because they display this attribute in different ways, with different details.

Because we are dealing with cases of analogy, it is appropriate to apply the triangle for analogy. Let us consider how the process works with the display of the power of God in his acts of creation in Genesis 1. We focus on a particular case, namely the creation of light in Genesis 1:3.

In step 1, we ask ourselves what general truth is exemplified by the particular case on which we are focusing. The general truth is that God is all-powerful and that he accomplishes what he determines to accomplish.

In step 2, we ask how this general truth unfolds in the history of redemption, and then in particular how it is fulfilled in Christ. The answer is that Christ during his earthly life performed many miracles, exhibiting the work of God's power. The most climactic miracle of all comes at the end of his earthly life, when he is raised from the dead. Christ's resurrection lays the foundation for the whole new world to come (Rom. 8:18–25). It is like the foundation stone for the new heaven and the new earth (Rev. 21:1). It is as earthshaking in its own way as the original creation of the original heaven and earth in Genesis 1.

Finally, in step 3, we ask how the general truth about God's power applies to us. God's power is on display every day even in ordinary things. We pray, "Give us this day our daily bread." And he does (Acts 14:17). The most spectacular case for an individual believer is his new birth through the Holy Spirit (John 3:3, 5). In it, the individual becomes a new creation (2 Cor. 5:17). He is raised to new spiritual life (Eph. 2:6; Col. 3:1).

We may summarize these thoughts using the triangle for analogy (fig. 27.1).

Figure 27.1: The Triangle for Analogy, for the Power of God in Creation

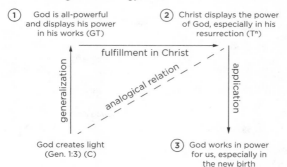

Christ as Central in the Manifestation of God

God's power is displayed from one end of history to the other. So is it right to single out the manifestation of God's power in the life of Christ? The New Testament indicates in various ways that the manifestation of God in Christ is climactic and definitive:

For the law was given through Moses; *grace* and *truth* came through Jesus Christ. No one has ever seen God; the only God, who is at the Father's side, he has *made him known*. (John 1:17–18)

Philip said to him, "Lord, show us the Father, and it is enough for us." Jesus said to him, "Have I been with you so long, and you still do not know me, Philip? Whoever has seen me has seen the Father. How can you say, 'Show us the Father'?" (John 14:8–9)

For in him the whole fullness of deity dwells bodily, . . . (Col. 2:9)

Long ago, at many times and in many ways, God spoke to our fathers by the prophets, but in these last days he has spoken to us by his Son, whom he appointed the heir of all things, through whom also he created the world. He is the radiance of the glory of God and the exact imprint of his nature, and he upholds the universe by the word of his power. (Heb. 1:1–3a)

So, yes, all the attributes of God are found in him and are definitively manifested in him.

The Presence of God

God is omnipresent. He is present at all times and at all places. Since God is indivisible, *all* of him is present. He is present in all his attributes. One attribute cannot actually be separated and neatly cordoned off from the rest. His power is a merciful and just and wise power. His wisdom is a powerful and just wisdom. And so on.

So every location and every point in time and every event in all those places displays all the attributes of God, not just one or a few. But that means that every event is analogous to every other event. Events are analogous because they display the same attributes of God. If so, have we not made the idea of analogy so broad that it is useless?

No, we should not wipe out all distinctions. Some events display some attributes of God more prominently. Consider God's works in creation. The works of God in creating the world display his power in an obvious manner. They also display his wisdom, but this display is less obvious. They display his eternity, but that is even less obvious. So it still makes sense for us to focus on more prominent displays of God's attributes. When we do, it also makes sense for us to link them by analogy with the display of God's attributes in Christ and in his life, death, and resurrection.[2] That is what fig. 27.1 represents.

The Attributes of God and *Lex Christi*

The study of the attributes of God can be further integrated into the texture of systematic theology and the texture of biblical themes using the framework of *lex Christi* developed by T. P. Yates.[3] This framework views the Ten Commandments as reflective of the attributes of God. It singles out ten attributes of God, one underlying each of the Ten Commandments. (See table 27.1.)[4]

Table 27.1: The Ten Commandments Reflecting Attributes of God

Summary of the Commandments	Attributes of God
1. do not have other gods	supreme
2. do not bow to images	holy
3. do not use God's name in vain	blessed
4. keep the sabbath	dynamic
5. honor parents	harmonious
6. do not murder	living
7. do not commit adultery	intimate
8. do not steal	giving, generous
9. do not falsely witness	truthful
10. do not covet	contented

2 See the use of the theme of the resurrection of Christ in Vern S. Poythress, *The Mystery of the Trinity: A Trinitarian Approach to the Attributes of God* (Phillipsburg, NJ: P&R, 2020).
3 Poythress, "Introducing the Law of Christ."
4 Poythress, "Introducing the Law of Christ," 1.

Some of the entries in table 27.1 need further explanation. The first commandment does not need much explanation. If God alone is to be God, he is supreme and absolute. The second commandment is associated with holiness, which is less obvious. In the Bible, the holiness of God is a prime reason why he must be approached in a particular way, the way that he himself prescribes. Serving idols is a false path to accessing the sphere of the holy.

The third commandment is associated with God's being blessed, partly because of Numbers 6:23–27. Israel as the people of God receives God's blessing when the priests "put my name upon the people of Israel" (v. 27).

The fourth commandment is about imitating God's pattern of work and rest. This pattern is a temporal pattern, a pattern of dynamic activity. God works dynamically, and rests on the seventh day, as we see in the pattern of creation established in Genesis 1:1–2:3. The sabbath commandment specifies that human beings are supposed to imitate this dynamic pattern.

The fifth commandment tells us to honor father and mother. But the principle extends outward to enjoin us to give what is due to people in all interpersonal relations. We are supposed to live in harmony with our neighbors. Such harmony reflects the original harmony among the persons of the Trinity.

The sixth through the tenth commandments are more easily associated with a specific attribute of God. The main step is to understand that what is prohibited is the opposite of what God himself represents. The opposite of bringing death by murder is preserving and enhancing life. So the sixth commandment is closely linked with life as an attribute of God. God is the living God. The opposite of adultery is proper intimacy. The original intimacy is the intimacy of the persons of the Trinity. The opposite of theft is preserving property and being generous—giving. God is the original giver. The opposite of false witness is telling the truth. God is the origin of all truth. The opposite of coveting is being contented.

It should be noted that, because all of God's attributes belong together, each attribute functions like a perspective on the whole of God. Each attribute qualifies every other attribute. Consequently, all the attributes are present all through history.

Any one of the ten attributes listed in the second column of table 27.1 can be used as a theme in examining the Bible. For example, let us start with the attribute "supreme," associated with the first commandment. All the passages that display God as supreme are linked together by the common theme. They are all analogous to each other. We can apply to them the framework of the triangle for analogy.

All ten attributes are meant to be embodied and exemplified at a creaturely level in human beings. That is one implication of the Ten Commandments, as they are directed to human beings. Christ perfectly fulfills all ten commandments, and that goes together with his being a perfect manifestation of the attributes of God. As we are conformed by the Holy Spirit to the image of Christ, we begin to reflect his attributes in our lives. This reflection is a form of application.

In short, starting with the ten attributes of God, we can work out how they appear within the framework of the triangle for analogy. As an example, we consider the second case, focusing on God's attribute of being holy. God himself is holy; that truth underlies the second commandment. The general principle (GT) is that God is holy in himself and in all his works. The manifestation in Christ is that Christ is the Holy One of God (John 6:69). In union with Christ, we become holy and are called to walk in holiness (1 Pet. 1:14–16). (See fig. 27.2.)

Similar reasoning applies for each of the attributes of God associated with each of the Ten Commandments.

Figure 27.2: The Triangle for Analogy, for *Lex Christi*, "Holy"

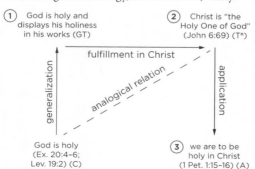

28

Analogies for the Trinity

IN THE PREVIOUS CHAPTER we considered how passages could be analogous to each other by displaying the same attribute of God. We may now ask whether they can be analogous to each other by displaying or reflecting the Trinity.

Traces of the Trinity

Various authors have discussed in what ways the Trinity might have displays or reflections in various features within creation and the created order. There is even a term, *vestigia trinitatis,* "traces of the Trinity," to designate what might be there.

In considering reflections of the Trinity, we must be careful. The Bible makes it clear that God is distinct from the world. God is the Creator, and the world is his creation. Pantheism, which says that God is identical with the world, is a blasphemous error, because it gives to the world the honor that belongs only to the Creator. The world displays that God is the Creator, according to Romans 1:18–23. But the world is not identical with God. God is infinite and the world is finite.

So when we consider the possibility of reflections of the Trinity, we mean to look at displays in the world that reflect the Trinity in patterns of three. But these reflections always include the truth that the world is itself finite. It displays its infinite Creator as one who is infinitely greater than anything in the world.

If there are traces of the Trinity, the places or locations or events in which these traces occur will be analogous to each other in a broad way. And the traces themselves may be analogous to the original that they "trace," namely the Trinity itself.

It would take a whole book to explore possible traces of the Trinity. We cannot do it here. But we can refer to a book that at least begins the exploration: *Knowing and the Trinity*.[1] Any of the triads in this book could be a starting point for exploring analogies. Each particular case of a triad points to the general truth represented in the triad.

Let us illustrate using a particular case.

The Triad for Lordship

The triad for lordship consists in three attributes of God: authority, control, and presence.[2] John Frame originally introduced it and uses it widely.[3] Frame argues that the three attributes correlate meaningfully with the three persons of the Trinity.[4] We may say that the three, taken together, are analogous to the three persons of the Trinity, and that they reflect the Trinity. God the Father is preeminently the source of *authority*. He has planned the course of history. God the Son is preeminently the one who executes the plan of the Father. In doing so, he exercises *control* over the world. God the Holy Spirit is preeminently the one who applies God's plan by his presence in the world, and his special presence to each individual believer and to the church. So the Holy Spirit is preeminently associated with the *presence* of God in the world.

At the same time, all of the persons of the Trinity work together. All participate in the plan (authority), in the execution (control), and in God's presence in the world (presence). They do so by indwelling each

---

1   Vern S. Poythress, *Knowing and the Trinity: How Perspectives in Human Knowledge Imitate the Trinity* (Phillipsburg, NJ: P&R, 2018).

2   Poythress, *Knowing and the Trinity*, ch. 14.

3   John M. Frame, *The Doctrine of the Knowledge of God* (Phillipsburg, NJ: Presbyterian & Reformed, 1987), 15–18; John M. Frame, "A Primer on Perspectivalism," 2008, http://frame-poythress.org/a-primer-on-perspectivalism-revised-2008/, accessed September 2, 2021; Poythress, *Knowing and the Trinity*, ch. 14.

4   Frame, "Primer on Perspectivalism," §2; Poythress, *Knowing and the Trinity*, ch. 14.

other. Though one person may have a particularly preeminent role in a particular act of God, the others are not absent. This harmony among the persons is in turn reflected in the harmony of the three attributes: authority, control, and presence. Each attribute is always present with the other two attributes (and of course with other attributes of God as well).

Now, each event where God works in history displays the three attributes. Each event is a particular case. Each case exemplifies the common theme of the triad, which reflects the Trinity.

Using the Triangle for Analogy, Applied to the Triad for Lordship

We can use the triangle for analogy to talk about the instances of the triad for lordship. One instance expressing lordship is the Ten Commandments. They express divine authority, in being commandments from the Lord. They express divine control, particularly in the historical prologue (". . . who brought you out of the land of Egypt," Ex. 20:2) and in the blessings and curses that are attached (vv. 5–7, 12). They express divine presence, because God is present to his people when he speaks at Mount Sinai (19:3–25; 20:18–21). This expression of lordship is a particular case (C), the starting point for the triangle for analogy.

Step 1 asks what general truth is exemplified in the particular case. The general truth is that God is the Lord, who has authority, control, and presence. This general truth also reflects at a deeper level the fact that the one God is Father, Son, and Holy Spirit.

In step 2, we ask how the general truth comes to fulfillment in Christ. Christ, as the climactic manifestation of God on earth, displays the authority, the control, and the presence of God.

In step 3, we ask how the general truth applies to us. One way is that, through Christ, God's authority, control, and presence come to bear on us in our salvation.

We may summarize all these thoughts using the triangle for analogy (fig. 28.1).

Figure 28.1: The Triangle for Analogy, for the Triad for Lordship

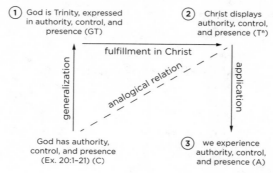

Using the Triangle for Analogy for Other Triads

Similarly, we may see a multitude of cases where God reflects his Trinitarian nature in specific exemplifications of specific perspectival triads. This principle applies to all the triads in *Knowing and the Trinity*. There is a rich spectrum of manifestations of God, and therefore also a rich spectrum of analogies.

29

The Extent of Analogies

THE PRECEDING TWO CHAPTERS show that the process of finding and appreciating analogies can be extended quite broadly. A broad extent for exploring analogies is possible because analogies can sometimes be quite striking, while at other times they can still be there even though they are faint or more subtle.

Clear Cases of Analogy

Consider the analogy between two cases in which God displays mercy. He displays mercy to Adam and Eve in not immediately destroying them, and in giving them the promise of a Redeemer (Gen. 3:15). He shows mercy to Noah and his family, when everyone around them is swept away by the flood. These are dramatic cases of mercy. We see the connection fairly easily, once it is pointed out to us. Or consider two cases in which God brings good out of evil. He brings good out of Jacob's scheming. And he brings good out of the evil actions of the brothers in selling Joseph into slavery. Once we notice the general theme of God bringing good out of evil, it becomes reasonable to see an analogy between the two specific cases.

Fainter Cases

But not all cases are this striking. Some of the other examples may not appear to be as strong as the ones above. The analogies may be fainter when we deal with some attributes of God, and some of the cases exemplifying the attributes of God, because the attributes of God are displayed throughout creation and throughout the history of God's actions (Rom. 1:20–21).

Consider a case of a less obvious analogy. God's infinite power is displayed in the miracles of Jesus. It is particularly striking when Jesus controls nature in a spectacular way, as he does when he stills the storm in Matthew 8:23–27. God also displays his power when he takes care of the sparrows and the hairs on our head:

> Are not two sparrows sold for a penny? And not one of them will fall to the ground apart from your Father. But even the hairs of your head are all numbered. Fear not, therefore; you are of more value than many sparrows. (Matt. 10:29–31)

But we would not be so likely to notice God's display of power in sparrows if Jesus had not specifically drawn our attention to it. So is the stilling of the storm analogous to the falling of a sparrow or the coming out of a hair on our head? Yes, they are analogous, because they display the power of God. But the analogy is faint, rather than striking.

One aspect of the nature of analogy is that an analogy can be either more or less striking; it can be either more or less faint. Each case of analogy between two cases includes both similarities and differences. Merriam-Webster's online dictionary provides the following two definitions of analogy:

> 1a : a comparison of two otherwise unlike things based on resemblance of a particular aspect
> 1b : resemblance in some particulars between things otherwise unlike : similarity[1]

1   *Merriam-Webster Dictionary*, online, https://www.merriam-webster.com/dictionary/analogy, accessed September 2, 2021.

Both definitions combine a mention of similarity with a mention of difference. The similarity is described as "resemblance" or "similarity," while the difference is indicated with the phrase "otherwise unlike." This combination is appropriate. If there are no similarities, the two cases are not really analogous, but just contrasting. If there are no differences, the two cases are identical.

A Spectrum for Analogy

But clearly both the similarities and the differences may be matters of degree. Two cases may be more or less similar. If they are very similar, the analogy is striking. If they are only loosely or faintly similar, the analogy is faint.

The consequence is that there is a spectrum of analogies, some more striking, some more faint. There is no firm cut-off point at which we suddenly declare that analogy has disappeared altogether and yet what we have left still displays some kinds of similarities.

Now, when we apply this idea of a spectrum to the cases with an attribute of God or with a trace of the Trinity, it means there may be subtle or faint analogies as well as ones that are more striking. God has crafted it this way. In principle, the same kind of spectrum can crop up when we deal with still other cases of analogy in the Bible, cases united by a single broad theme.

Communication That Deals with Analogies

In dealing with this challenge, we need a sense of proportion when we read the Bible and respond to it. We need to avoid claiming that an analogy is striking and prominent if it is not. Conversely, we need to avoid claiming that there is no analogy just because what we find is fainter or less prominent.

In proclaiming the message of the Bible and in sharing our insights with others, the same sense of proportion needs to be active. We can mention an insight without regarding it as all-important. In typical cases of Christian public proclamation, one of the constraints is a limitation in time. A second constraint is a constraint to major on majors in order to make sure that the people who hear us learn the main things they need to know, not just interesting tidbits that are not the main point. Moreover, Christian public proclamation needs attention to persuasiveness. It is easier to persuade people about a prominent, striking analogy than about a faint analogy. It is easier to see that God's power is displayed in the stilling of the storm than in the falling of a sparrow. God himself has designed analogies to be on a spectrum. We respect that by having a sense of proportion in our own communication.

My point in this chapter, however, is a complementary point. It concerns the riches of who God is, and then, subordinately, the riches that belong to his word, the Bible. The Bible's meaning is not exhausted when we devote ourselves (rightly) to its main points. This richness of the Bible particularly shows itself when, in the triad of meaning, impact, and import, we focus on import—the relational aspect of meaning. There are a multitude of relations in meaning in the Bible as a whole. The stilling of the storm is related to the falling of a sparrow. We never come to a complete end. There are also faint strands of analogy that run in different directions than what we have already explored, and what we may think we have mastered.

The same observations continue to hold when we explore general revelation. The Bible is God's word, his key instruction to us. By his design, it has a central role in our lives. But it talks about the world. It has implications for how we think about the world as a whole, and the details within it. God is present in every nook and cranny in the world. He is present with all his attributes. He is present as the Trinitarian God. And so the Bible invites us to *notice* his presence. "[T]he whole earth is full of his glory!" (Isa. 6:3). The Bible invites us to see the imprint of God's presence everywhere (Rom. 1:20). But we are supposed to do so with a sense of proportion, as we have observed.

Conclusion

THIS BOOK IS DESIGNED TO BE AN INTRODUCTION to exploration of types and analogies in the Bible. In order to treat types and analogies judiciously, we need the grace of God. We need humility. We need the fruit of the Holy Spirit in our lives (Gal. 5:22–23).

We also have to apply ourselves to paying attention to the Bible as a whole, and to its parts. Growing in understanding the Bible is the work of a lifetime. It is *our* work, but even more, it is the work of the Holy Spirit within us. It is appropriate here at the end of the book, as well as at its beginning, to have the reminder that the Holy Spirit is the gift of Christ, from the Father, for those who belong to Christ (Acts 2:33). So understanding the Bible begins with putting your faith in Christ for your own salvation.

This book has also attempted to bring to light some particular principles:

- God is a majestic and awesome God.
- The Bible is the word of God, with his truthfulness.
- God has a plan for history, and he rules over all.
- Christ is at the center of history; he is the one who accomplishes salvation and reveals God climactically.
- We need God's redemption in order to understand the Bible.
- Revelation is progressive.
- We should pay attention to what God meant and communicated to the original recipients of a particular book of the Bible.

Further implications that we find ("import") should build on
this meaning.

- We should pay attention to the historical context and literary
  context of any one passage in the Bible, and not treat it as if it
  were isolated.
- We should pay attention to the texture of the history of redemption and the larger purposes of God.
- Clowney's triangle is useful as a reminder to do typological
  analysis in two main steps, not in a leap that directly postulates
  a typological meaning.
- The triangle for analogy is useful as a reminder to analyze
  analogies in two main steps, not in a leap that directly postulates fulfillment in Christ or application to us.
- God is always richer than what we have already discovered.
- We should be humble and patient in participating in the gradual
  process of growing in understanding what God says in the Bible.

May the Lord continue to instruct his people, individually and corporately, for the sake of the glory of his name!

APPENDICES

Appendix A

Patrick Fairbairn's Principles for Typology

PATRICK FAIRBAIRN'S BOOK *The Typology of Scripture* is a classic work with a thorough discussion of many aspects of typology. Here we briefly summarize and comment on the five main principles that Fairbairn lists for typological interpretation.[1] They overlap with some of the principles represented in Clowney's triangle for typology.

(For the sake of smoother exposition, we have rearranged the order of Fairbairn's five principles.)

1. We should *"be careful to make ourselves acquainted with the truths or ideas exhibited in the types, considered merely as providential transactions or religious institutions."*[2]

This principle would seem to be the most fundamental, even though Fairbairn lists it third. What Fairbairn has in mind here is parallel to Clowney's triangle, step 1. Fairbairn's principle advises us to look at

---

1 Patrick Fairbairn, *The Typology of Scripture: Viewed in Connection with the Whole Series of . . . The Divine Dispensations* (New York and London: Funk & Wagnalls, 1911), 1.1.6.140–67, "The Interpretation of Particular Types—Specific Principles and Directions."

2 Fairbairn, *Typology of Scripture*, 1.1.6.150, emphasis original. In Fairbairn's original order, this is principle 3.

the "truths or ideas" that a type exhibits within its own historical and literary time frame. Fairbairn further clarifies:

> That they [types] had a moral, political, or religious end to serve for *the time then present*, so far from interfering with their destination to typify the spiritual things of the Gospel, forms the very ground and substance of their typical bearing. Hence their character in the one respect, the more immediate [their own time frame], may justly be regarded as the essential key to their character in respect to what was more remote [their antitypes].[3]

2. "[W]e must be guided, *not so much by any knowledge possessed, or supposed to be possessed, by the ancient worshippers concerning their prospective fulfilment, as from the light furnished by their realization in the great facts and revelations of the Gospel.*"[4]

This principle might seem to be in tension with principle 1 above, but in fact it is complementary. It has two purposes. One purpose, a more negative one, is to discourage speculations about how much and how clearly the "ancient worshippers" in general understood the detailed shape of the coming fulfillment or antitype. Through the ages of church history, some interpreters have been inclined to imagine that some of the ancients had a rather full vision or grasp of what Christ would come to do. And theoretically this might be the case, if the Holy Spirit gave them a private special revelation. At the other extreme, some interpreters have been inclined to imagine that the ancients had little if any notion of what was to come. And if they were spiritually dull, such might be the case. But we must pay attention to the Old Testament texts. We should not rely on speculation about extra visions or insights from the Holy Spirit that might go beyond the meaning of the text. Neither should we rely

---

3   Fairbairn, *Typology of Scripture*, 1.1.6.151, emphasis added.
4   Fairbairn, *Typology of Scripture*, 1.1.6.145, emphasis original. In Fairbairn's original order, this is principle 2.

on speculation that would say that the ancient readers understood almost nothing.

The second, more positive purpose of this principle is to remind us of progressive revelation. In the light of the New Testament and the gospel, we can have more knowledge than the ancients. So this principle of Fairbairn's is related to step 2 in Clowney's triangle, according to which we reckon with the progress of redemption and the progress of revelation.

3. A "symbol . . . has properly *but one radical meaning, yet the fundamental idea or principle exhibited in it may often be capable of more than one application to the realities of the Gospel.*"[5]

This principle is an implication of the principle we listed first, the principle telling us to pay attention to the immediate historical context (step 1 of Clowney's triangle). In the original biblical context, a text or a symbol has a unified meaning. This unity is what Fairbairn has in mind with the expression "one radical meaning." This unity ought not to be undermined by an overactive imagination in typological interpretation. Fairbairn is careful to qualify his principle in two respects. First, he notes that some types exhibit in themselves some complexity. For example, the flood of Noah is both a judgment on the wicked and a means of salvation for Noah and his family. Second, Fairbairn notes that in many cases there may be more than one application. Christ is the fulfillment of many Old Testament types—in a broad sense, of all Old Testament types. And this fulfillment has applications both to individual believers and to the church, by virtue of their being united to Christ. The existence of such applications is not in tension with the unity of fulfillment. Fairbairn also allows that fulfillment can take place in two stages, in Christ's first coming and in his second coming. Fairbairn's principle for applications, given above, is closely related to step 3 in Clowney's triangle.

---

5   Fairbairn, *Typology of Scripture*, 1.1.6.154, emphasis original. In Fairbairn's original order, this is principle 4.

4. *"[D]ue regard must be had to the essential difference between the nature of type and antitype."*[6]

This principle underlines the fact that there is genuine progress in redemption, and that the antitype displays superiority to the type. It is related both to step 2 of Clowney's triangle and to step 4, which we added and explained in chapter 17.

5. *"[N]othing is to be regarded as typical of the good things under the Gospel which was itself of a forbidden and sinful nature."*[7]

This principle is a more specific implication of principle 1 above, which is similar to step 1 in Clowney's triangle. The "forbidden and sinful nature" of the thing belongs to the meaning available in the original text in the Old Testament. Such a meaning would be completely canceled and undermined if we claim to find fulfillment in "the good things under the Gospel." Step 1 in Clowney's triangle says that we must pay attention to the original meaning, and find our guidance from it.

We might have hoped that this principle 5 would not have to be separately enumerated, since it is a natural implication of step 1 of Clowney's triangle. But Fairbairn gives examples where it has been violated.

Fairbairn clarifies this prohibition by saying that there can be evil things that are types of further, later evil. Evil things in the Old Testament may find fulfillment in climactic forms of evil that oppose the kingdom of Christ.[8] There are types of the antichrist.

We might further qualify his prohibition by observing that evil is often a counterfeit of the good. The antithesis of the evil to the good shows up the good for what it is, by way of contrast. Consider, for

---

6   Fairbairn, *Typology of Scripture*, 1.1.6.158, emphasis original. In Fairbairn's original order, this is principle 5.
7   Fairbairn, *Typology of Scripture*, 1.1.6.141, emphasis original. In Fairbairn's original order, this is principle 1.
8   Fairbairn, *Typology of Scripture*, 1.1.6.145.

example, the triad of Satan, the beast, and the false prophet in Revelation (16:13). They form a kind of counterfeit of the Trinity.[9] The evil kings in the history of Israel and Judah show the opposite of what the coming messianic King will be.

---

9   Vern S. Poythress, *The Returning King: A Guide to the Book of Revelation* (Phillipsburg, NJ: P&R, 2000), 16–25; Vern S. Poythress, "Counterfeiting in the Book of Revelation as a Perspective on Non-Christian Culture," *Journal of the Evangelical Theological Society* 40/3 (1997): 411–18.

Appendix B

The Terminology for a "Type"

WHAT IS A "TYPE"? Is this key word found in the New Testament?

Some Occurrences of "Type" in the New Testament

One of the New Testament passages about Adam uses the word *type* as a key word:

> Yet death reigned from Adam to Moses, even over those whose sinning was not like the transgression of Adam, who was a *type* of the one who was to come. (Rom. 5:14)

The word *type* in the English Standard Version (ESV) corresponds to the Greek word τύπος (transliterated *typos* or *tupos*) in the original.

What does it mean that Adam was a "type"? Romans 5:12–21 indicates that there are many structural parallels—and contrasts—between the disobedience of Adam and the obedience of Christ. Adam corresponds in these respects to Christ, who is "the one who was to come" (v. 14).

We find a similar idea of correspondence in another verse, 1 Peter 3:21, which discusses Noah's flood:

> Baptism, which *corresponds* to this [Noah's flood], now saves you, not as a removal of dirt from the body but as an appeal to God for a good conscience, through the resurrection of Jesus Christ, . . .

The Greek word underlying the idea of correspondence is the word ἀντίτυπον (*antitypon*), which is etymologically related to the English word *antitype*. Baptism is called an "antitype." It corresponds to the flood. The *type* would be the flood, and baptism would be the thing to which the type points, the thing that corresponds to it.

Other New Testament Uses of "Type" or Similar Words

Passages like these two may seem promising. So we might investigate all the other passages in the New Testament that use similar Greek words—"type," "antitype," or "typically" (τύπος, ἀντίτυπος, τυπικῶς, ὑποτύπωσις). We find a spectrum of uses of the key word "type" (τύπος):

> *mark, trace, copy, image, statue, form, figure, pattern, text, content, design, example.*[1]

Out of a total of fourteen or fifteen occurrences in the New Testament, the standard lexicon recognizes two or three occurrences that approach the more technical meaning of "type": Romans 5:14, 1 Corinthians 10:6, and 1 Corinthians 10:11.[2]

When we look at all the cases, we can see that the Greek word (τύπος) is an ordinary word, rather than a word with specialized, technical meaning.[3] The uses cluster in the general area of meaning represented by a "pattern" and an "expression/copy/image/example of

---

1   A sample, taken from Frederick William Danker, ed., *A Greek-English Lexicon of the New Testament and Other Early Christian Literature*, 3rd ed. (Chicago: University of Chicago Press, 2000), under τύπος (*typos*).

2   Danker, *Greek-English Lexicon*, τύπος, 6c. First Corinthians 10:11 is listed as a *possible* case, depending on which of two text-critical alternative readings is chosen. The preferred reading is τυπικῶς (*typikōs*), not τύποι (*typoi*), but the meaning is similar in either case. Expanding the search to include the Greek word ἀντίτυπος (*antitypos*) turns up two more cases (Heb. 9:24 and 1 Pet. 3:21) but does not substantially change the situation.

3   Patrick Fairbairn, *The Typology of Scripture: Viewed in Connection with the Whole Series of . . . The Divine Dispensations* (New York and London: Funk & Wagnalls, 1911), 1.1.2.42–43; David L. Baker, *Two Testaments, One Bible: A Study of Some Modern Solutions to the Theological Problem of the Relationship between the Old and New Testaments*, 3rd, rev. ed. (Downers Grove, IL: IVP Academic, 2010), 175.

a pattern." "Example" (ESV) is a reasonable translation in 1 Corinthians 10:6, 11. Thus, even in the key verses, the *word* "type" or "antitype" does not have a technical meaning. It is the passages, not the word, that show us that a deep and meaningful connection in meaning exists. The passages say much more than the word. It is easy to ignore this fact, especially in the light of the later historical development of a technical meaning for the word *type*. The technical meaning *seems* at first glance to fit the verse, within the context of the New Testament. But it is still the case that the technical meaning is a later development. Of course it is partly *based on* the verses we have listed. But the idea of a meaning connection of a typological kind belongs to the passage as a whole. The original readers did not have the later technical meaning in mind when they read the word. For them, it was the *passage* that conveyed the full meaning.

In sum, we can learn from studying the case of Adam in Romans 5:14, the flood in 1 Peter 3:21, the incidents in the wilderness in 1 Corinthians 10, and the discussion of the priesthood, the tabernacle, and its ordinances in Hebrews 3–10. But the passages contain much more information than the Greek word τύπος ("copy/example") possesses by itself.

Words and Concepts

Studies of typology in the past have often relied on the Greek word τύπος ("type") as a starting point. And this is understandable, because our English words *type* and *typology* are etymologically related to the Greek word. But etymology is not a good guide to meaning. The Greek word, as we have seen, is broader in meaning. Subsequent to the writing of the New Testament, Bible students have developed a much more specialized meaning, which is conveyed in English with the word *type*.

In this connection, we need to pay attention to what is called the word/concept distinction.[4] A word is a lexical item within a particular

---

4   James Barr, *The Semantics of Biblical Language* (London: Oxford University Press, 1961); Moisés Silva, *Biblical Words and Their Meaning: An Introduction to Lexical Semantics* (Grand Rapids, MI: Zondervan, 1994); D. A. Carson, *Exegetical Fallacies*, 2nd ed. (Grand Rapids, MI: Baker, 1996), ch. 1.

language, such as Greek. A "concept" usually means someone's idea or mental picture of a larger field of investigation. The two—word and concept—are usually not identical. Words can be used to *express* concepts. But typically it takes whole sentences or paragraphs to explain a concept adequately. It takes *many* words.

Let us illustrate. Τύπος is a word in Koine Greek, the language of the New Testament. A word in one language cannot be expected to be a perfect match for any one word in another language. And indeed this is so in the cases of τύπος. and similar Greek words. The summary above shows that, depending on the context, several different English words, such as *mark, trace, copy, image*, might serve as the most apt translation, that is, the most apt representation in English of the meaning of the corresponding Greek word. One lesson is that even translating a single occurrence of a foreign word can be challenging. But an additional lesson is that we cannot expect to read out a particular person's view or theory—a concept—merely by looking at a single word. Rather, we read or listen to whatever the person says.

With respect to the issue of types, the lesson is that it is no good trying to develop a theory of types by looking at a word in the Greek lexicon. Rather, we have to read the New Testament as a whole. We have to look at all the cases where the New Testament uses material from earlier in the history of the working out of God's plan. We have to see what the New Testament teaches about the relation of the earlier situations and events to the future.[5] It would be a mistake merely to confine ourselves to verses that happen to use or not use a particular word.

What Is a Type?

So what is a type? We have seen that we cannot properly build a concept of "type" just by looking at a Greek word. So how do we do it? How

---

5   Fortunately, excellent work is already available. Especially noteworthy are G. K. Beale and D. A. Carson, eds., *Commentary on the New Testament Use of the Old Testament* (Grand Rapids, MI: Baker; Nottingham, England: Apollos, 2007); G. K. Beale, *Handbook on the New Testament Use of the Old Testament: Exegesis and Interpretation* (Grand Rapids, MI: Baker, 2012).

do we make a positive step? It is up to us. We just have to single out for attention regular patterns of relations that we see in the teaching of the Bible. We might say, "See, here is a pattern. Let us study it more thoroughly. Let us call this pattern 'X' [in our case, 'type']. Then we can have a convenient label under which to classify what we are doing." But then maybe there is more than one fruitful way to do it.

The situation may, in fact, be more difficult. What if reality itself does not offer us clear, sharp boundaries? For example, is there, in fact, a clear, sharp boundary between what is and what is not a type? The question itself is ambiguous because, as we said, it depends on what we choose to mean by the word *type*. If we are going to use a word or a phrase with a special, narrow, stipulated meaning, we can define the word either more narrowly or more broadly. Still, we might hope that reality will guide us. After all, God has created the world. He has made it in an orderly way. He has made it with meanings. There is order among the kinds of creatures he has made. There is order also among the correspondences and analogies between different events and people and institutions.

To illustrate, let us consider the case of horses. Suppose that we were Adam. Suppose that we have never seen a horse, and we do not have any word for "horse." Then we see one. Let us say that we see several. After we have seen several, we can intuitively see that this animal is a distinctive kind of animal, distinct from cows, pigs, dogs, and so on. So we can confidently give it a distinct label: *horse*. It does not seem to be a problem.

So could it be the same way with "types"? Before we ever study the question, we know that God has created reality with order. Maybe that order includes a distinctive kind of thing that we could label "a type." Just as the reality is that horses are a distinctive kind of animal, so also might there be a distinctly organized reality about types? The reality might be that there is a certain fixed group of things and events that have a clear set of delineating characteristics, separating them from everything else and making it suitable for us to craft a particular label for the group—the label *type*.

But then maybe not. Maybe there is no clear, obvious boundary out there in the world of reality. Maybe some things, like the Old Testament priests, are clearly types, but other things are not so clear. Maybe there is a gradual kind of transition between many kinds of relations between Old Testament institutions and New Testament fulfillments. Maybe it is complicated. As we have observed, God made the world with order. But sometimes he may have decided on a very complex order, an almost unfathomable order. Our ability to expand the categories "analogy," "symbol," "type," and "prophecy" into perspectives on the whole of the Bible (chapters 15 and 29) suggests that there may be no clear, sharp, natural boundaries to the idea of a "type."

The History of Interpretation of the Bible

It is not so simple for another reason. There is already a *history* in the church, from the second century AD onward, of interpretation of the Bible. (And there is a history of interpretation of the Old Testament, beginning even before the New Testament was written.) The history of interpretation in the church does happen to contain uses of the words *type* and *typology* as technical terms. Should we, then, just use the words the way that they have come to be used in the history of church interpretation of the Bible?

It would be nice if we could. But the history is not entirely uniform. In fact, in the first few centuries of the church, there was considerable fluidity. The later history includes some attempts to distinguish "typological interpretation," which its advocates see as good, from "allegorical interpretation," which they see as bad. But different people have made the distinction in different ways. And we also find cases where one person labels a particular interpretation "allegorical" and another person labels it "typological." We find one interpreter who claims there are very few if any real types in the Bible. Another finds them all over the place. Different people mean slightly different things when they talk about types or typology. We cannot merely affirm the past, because the past is not uniform.

If we do look at the past, we are likely to find various kinds of things in biblical interpretation. We will find the good; we will find the bad.

We will find mixtures of good and bad. And by what criteria do *we*, with our finiteness, decide between good and bad?

The ultimate judge between good and bad ideas about Scripture must be Scripture itself. As the Westminster Confession of Faith puts it,

> The infallible rule of interpretation of Scripture is the Scripture itself: and therefore, when there is a question about the true and full sense of any Scripture (which is not manifold, but one), it must be searched and known by other places that speak more clearly. The supreme judge by which all controversies of religion are to be determined, and all decrees of councils, opinions of ancient writers, doctrines of men, and private spirits, are to be examined, and in whose sentence we are to rest, can be no other but the Holy Spirit speaking in the Scripture.[6]

But that means there is no easy solution. We must humble ourselves before God; we must ask for his help through the Holy Spirit. We must listen respectfully to the past, but not without critical discernment.

Our Way Forward

There is much to learn from the past. As we said, we find bad examples of interpretation; we find good examples; we find mixed examples. And this is true in the area of typology, as it would be in any other subdivision of the task of interpretation. It would be profitable to take a tour through the past. But it would also be very complicated. In order not to have this present book excessively long, it seems best to refer readers to other sources for extended discussion of this past.[7] We shall focus on studying the Bible itself.

---

6   Westminster Confession of Faith (1647), 1.9–10.

7   Fairbairn, *Typology of Scripture*, 1.1.1.1–41; Richard M. Davidson, *Typology in Scripture: A Study of Hermeneutical Τύπος Structures* (Berrien Springs, MI: Andres University Press, 1981), 17–93; K. J. Woollcombe, "The Biblical Origins and Patristic Development of Typology," in G. W. H. Lampe and K. J. Woollcombe, *Essays on Typology*, Studies in Biblical Theology 22 (Naperville, IL: Alec R. Allenson, 1957), 39–75; Jean Danielou, *From Shadows to Reality: Studies in the Biblical Typology of the Fathers* (London: Burns & Oates, 1960); Leonhard Goppelt, *Typos: The Typological Interpretation of the Old Testament in the New*, trans. Donald H. Madvig (Grand Rapids, MI: Eerdmans, 1982), 23–58.

Appendix C

Distinctiveness in the Study of Typology

THE STUDY OF TYPES has a long and informative history. This book builds on the past. But it may be of interest to indicate briefly how it differs from past studies.

Main Differences

The main differences are four: (1) the acceptance of the lack of a clear, sharp boundary between types and other structures of meaning; (2) the recognition of affinities between one-level analogies and types; (3) the explicit affirmation of meaning in relations between texts ("import"); and (4) a perspectival approach to meaning.

None of these four points is completely new. None of them represents a sharp break with past methods of study. I suspect that quite a few people in the past have tacitly recognized difficulties and complexities in one or more of these areas. Nevertheless, it can be a help when we formulate the four points explicitly and try to reckon with them explicitly.

The last of the four points underlies the other three. If indeed meaning is perspectival at a deep level, then the idea of a type or an analogy or a symbol may become the starting point for building a perspective on *all* meaning (as in chapter 15). Consequently, the boundaries between types and symbols and analogies will not be sharp. This lack of sharp boundaries is what is in view in point (1). As we indicated in chapter 15, however, we must be careful not to overestimate the implications. The lack of a *sharp* boundary is not the same as having no boundary at all.

There will also be natural affinities between one-level analogies and types, which are instances of two-level analogies (point [2]). Affinities exist between the two, because the distinction between one-level meaning and two-level meaning is not sharp.

Finally, with regard to point (3), meaning can be treated, as in chapter 12, from three perspectives: a static perspective, a dynamic perspective, and a relational perspective. These three perspectives do not lead to three distinct meanings, but to overlapping views on the same holistic communication. Consequently, the relations between texts, and their contributions to meaning, cannot be neatly isolated from the conception of what a single passage means *in isolation*. No passage is in fact isolated. So treating a passage as if it were isolated is inevitably artificial. Such a focus on a single passage is useful for noticing details and internal relations within the passage. But it always takes place within an environment—other texts, a situation of personal communication, and the thoughts of those who are communicating. Leaving the relations out of focus does not make them go away.

Basis in the Trinity

We cannot fully justify this perspectival approach to meaning within this book. But we may briefly note that it is based ultimately on the Trinity.[1] We have assumed within our framework for typology that types derive from God's meaning. And we have also assumed that God rules all of history and gives each event its meaning. These meanings are not isolated, as if they were like grains of sand. They belong to one unified comprehensive plan of God. God has one mind and one plan, because he is one God. Consequently, we cannot isolate bits of knowledge, though as human beings we can *focus* on one bit and

---

1   Vern S. Poythress, *Knowing and the Trinity: How Perspectives in Human Knowledge Imitate the Trinity* (Phillipsburg, NJ: P&R, 2018).

leave the rest temporarily in the background. The one bit functions as a perspective on the whole, because the bits cannot be isolated. So it is with the meaning of types.

Separate Rules for Types?

One of the results is that this book does not assume that "types" are a distinctive kind of thing, in such a way that there is a clear and sharp boundary. There are many cases that are clear instances of types. But then there are also cases that are less clear. There is no natural way to mark out what is a type, in distinction from what is not a type, in such a way that there is a sharp and clear and distinct boundary. There is no natural "border," as it were, between types and non-types. The world is not organized that way.

We may illustrate using an analogy. There is no natural border between Canada and the United States. The Great Lakes *do* offer a kind of natural boundary. But the western part of the Canadian-American border at the 49th parallel is just an arbitrary line. It does not correspond to natural features of the landscape. Similarly, the northern end of the boundary between Canada and Alaska is an arbitrary line (the 141st meridian).

The example of the Canadian-American border is not a perfect example, because the border is defined legally. An individual cannot change the border merely by saying that he is going to adopt a new perspective. But there is no corresponding legal definition of a type. There is no organization that lays down the law. And if there were, it would not be very helpful because, like the 49th parallel, it would ignore the continuity of the landscape.

Now that does not mean there is no distinction between a type and a non-type. It means only that (1) the distinction is a rough-and-ready one; (2) people are free to define the distinction in more than one competing way, if it seems useful for their purposes; (3) no possible definition with a sharp boundary is going to do justice to all the aspects of continuity between material on the two sides of the boundary; and (4) one may stand in the center of the "territory" of what is a type, and use it as a continuous perspective on the whole field of meaning.

It also means that it is futile to search for a special set of rules that will apply naturally to types and only to types.

It means that many disputes as to whether a particular person, event, or institution is a "type" can never be settled for all future time. It all depends on how expansively one treats the term *type*.

Mixed History of the Study of Types

The history of the study of types is mixed. It is mixed partly because the relational meaning belonging to types is a matter of subtlety. So mistakes are possible. In dealing with meaning, our imaginations may be overactive or underactive.

Our imaginations may be overactive. We read in meanings that are really ours and not the Bible's. If the meanings come from some other place in the Bible, the meanings may still be orthodox. (Remember our earlier illustration, where someone thought that the three gifts of the wise men [Matt. 2:11] correspond to the three persons of the Trinity. The Trinity is an orthodox doctrine, but it is not the meaning of the three gifts.) But the danger exists that they may be heterodox, contrary to the Bible, without our realizing it. For example, Philo's interpretation of Genesis 6:9 and other parts of Genesis seems to imply that salvation comes by mental purification. This is contrary to the Bible's message that salvation is through grace, on the basis of the work of Christ (Eph. 2:5–10). It may seem to us psychologically that we are setting forth the meanings we have drawn from the text of the Bible. But we are fooling ourselves.

Or our imaginations may be underactive. We may be "dull," "slow of heart," in the words of Luke 24:25. We may notice nothing but the obvious. For example, we may read about the Old Testament priests and have no notion that God has given them as a type for the priesthood of Christ.

In addition to these challenges, there is the challenge when people try to come up with a theory of types, together with an interpretive framework for dealing with them. In a sense, this book is such an endeavor. But people may bring trouble or confusion on themselves if they assume, without further reflection, that "types" are a distinctive "thing," separate from all other kinds of meaning.

Appendix D

Clowney's Triangle of Typology

[This appendix reproduces an article originally published in *Unio cum Christo*.[1] It is used with permission. In its topics, it overlaps with chapter 6. We provide it as a further explanation, parallel to chapter 6.]

EDMUND P. CLOWNEY created a triangle diagram to explain the function of types in the Old Testament. The triangle has since become known as "Clowney's triangle." It has proved fruitful, and a number of people have incorporated it into their principles for interpretation and their interpretations of individual types.[2] Let us reflect on its significance.

What Is Clowney's Triangle?

The triangle appears in print in Clowney's book *Preaching and Biblical Theology*.[3] For purposes of reference, it is reproduced in Figure D.1.

1   Vern S. Poythress, "Clowney's Triangle of Typology," *Unio cum Christo* (October 2021): 231–238, https://frame-poythress.org/wp-content/uploads/2021/12/2021Clowneys Triangle.pdf, accessed March 10, 2023.

2   See, for example, the course NT 123 at Westminster Theological Seminary, campus. wts.edu/~vpoythress/nt123/nt123.html, 1C6aModr.odp, slide 87, accessed August 25, 2020; Vern S. Poythress, *Reading the Word of God in the Presence of God: A Handbook for Biblical Interpretation* (Wheaton, IL: Crossway, 2016), 247–50; Vern S. Poythress, *The Miracles of Jesus: How the Savior's Mighty Acts Serve as Signs of Redemption* (Wheaton, IL: Crossway, 2016), 65–67 and elsewhere; Vern S. Poythress, "Christocentric Preaching," *Southern Baptist Journal of Theology* 22/3 (2018): 47–66 (48), https://frame-poythress.org /christocentric-preaching/, accessed August 25, 2020.

3   Edmund P. Clowney, *Preaching and Biblical Theology* (Grand Rapids, MI: Eerdmans, 1961), 110.

Figure D.1: Clowney's Triangle of Typology

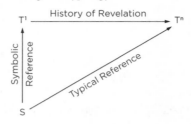

In the text that accompanies the diagram, Clowney explains what the diagram represents.[4] It summarizes the nature of sound reasoning about types. Since Clowney's own explanation is reasonably clear, we will move on to illustrate how it applies to a particular case, namely the tabernacle of Moses (Ex. 25–27; 36–38).

An Example: The Tabernacle

The tabernacle is a physical structure, a tent. In addition, it has symbolic meaning. So it is a symbol, which is designated S in Clowney's triangle (fig. D.1).

As a first step, Clowney advises us to consider what is the meaning of the symbol within its original historical context. For the tabernacle, we ask about its symbolic meaning at the time when God instructs Moses to set it up. It signifies that God has undertaken to dwell with his people: "And let them make me a sanctuary, that I may dwell in their midst" (Ex. 25:8). This meaning is designated "T^1" in fig. D.1. Step 1 is the movement from the symbol S to its meaning $T1$. It is represented in fig. 1 by the vertical arrow.

In step 2 we ask how this truth about God dwelling with his people comes to climactic manifestation (T^n), as the history of revelation continues to unfold. It comes to a climax in Christ, "For in him the whole fullness of deity *dwells* bodily" (Col. 2:9; see John 2:21; 1:14). Therefore, the tabernacle is a type of Christ. Christ is the "antitype" of this type. In general, S designates the type. T^n designates the antitype, to which

---

4   Clowney, *Preaching and Biblical Theology*, 110–12.

the type points. The relation between the two is "Typical Reference." The completed diagram appears in fig. D.2.

Figure D.2: The Tabernacle as a Type of Christ

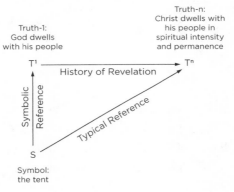

Clarifying the Triangle

We may try to make a few clarifications in the triangle by relabeling. Instead of *S* we may write out "Symbol." Instead of *T¹* we may write out "Truth-1" or "Truth in Anticipation." Instead of *Tⁿ* we may write out "Truth-n" or "Truth in Fulfillment."[5] Instead of "History of Revelation" we may write "Fulfillment," to indicate more directly that the history is leading to a fulfillment. Instead of "Typical Reference" we may write "Typological Reference," because the word *Typical* can be misunderstood to have its more common meaning, "exhibiting the essential characteristics of a group," rather than the more specialized meaning "symbolic" (and forward-pointing).[6] (See fig. D.3.)

At some point, someone decided to add a fourth arrow to Clowney's triangle, in order to include application. So Clowney's triangle became a rectangle. (See fig. D.4.)

5   Clowney says, "[T]he fullness of that truth revealed in Christ" (*Preaching and Biblical Theology*, 110–12).

6   *Merriam-Webster Dictionary*, online, merriam-webster.com/dictionary/typical/, accessed August 25, 2020.

Figure D.3: Clowney's Triangle with Relabeling for Clarification

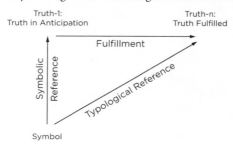

The downward arrow moving from "Truth Fulfilled" to application to us is not actually the reverse of the upward-pointing arrow on the left side ("Symbolic Reference"). It would be more appropriate if the movement to application were represented by an arrow pointing out of the page toward the reader, to whom the truth is intended to apply. But we cannot represent this third dimension easily, so I think we should be content with the two-dimensional representation.

Figure D.4: Clowney's Triangle with Application

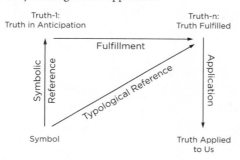

The Value of Clowney's Triangle

What is the value of Clowney's triangle? It gives us guidance about how to do typological reasoning responsibly. We have to avoid inventing types arbitrarily. We also have to avoid overlooking genuine typological correspondences because we cannot conclusively "prove" them by some artificially high standard of proof.[7]

7   Clowney, *Preaching and Biblical Theology*, 111–12.

To show the challenge, we might consider two opposite extremes. On the one side is the stereotype of the untrained reader who invents types by following his fancy. On the other side is the stereotype of the doubting scholar, who may find only a very few, because he must have "proof."

Let us consider these two dangers, and how Clowney's triangle addresses them.

The Danger of Arbitrary Typology

First, consider the danger of fanciful typology. An interpreter can find a type inappropriately if he introduces loose or fanciful connections, and then claims that such-and-such a text gives us a type of Christ or the church or some spiritual truth.

I encountered one gentleman who told me that the three gifts of the wise men in Matthew 2:11 stood for the Father, the Son, and the Holy Spirit. We can feel the arbitrariness of this claim. There are indeed three gifts. And there are three persons in the Trinity. But the connection is merely in the number three, not in the context of Matthew. Such an interpretation pays no attention to how the Gospel of Matthew is telling us about the wise men. Unfortunately, the interpreter who finds an artificial typology is apt to overlook genuine symbolic relations that the text presents. In Matthew we find repeated emphasis on fulfillment. The theme of "the king of the Jews" (2:2) builds on the Old Testament promise of the Messiah. The star of Bethlehem is connected to Numbers 24:17, and also more broadly to the promise of light that comes with the Messiah (Isa. 9:2; 60:1). The gifts from the wise men correspond to the gifts of "gold and frankincense" that the nations will bring according to Isaiah 60:6.

Here is where Clowney's step 1 is important. Clowney's step 1 tells us to anchor our reasoning in what God revealed when he originally communicated a particular symbol. The tabernacle had a meaning for Israelites. God explained it to them through Moses. We look back at this meaning from a later point in history. We can read in the New Testament about the coming of Christ. But the fulfillment in Christ is an enhancement of

the meaning already given earlier. It does not cancel the earlier meaning or overlay it with something completely unrelated. Step 1 tells us to
honor the truth that has been revealed at an earlier point. The climactic
manifestation of truth in Christ will indeed be climactic. In certain aspects it will surpass what could have been seen earlier in history. But it
will surpass the earlier points by fulfilling them, not by negating them.

In sum, one temptation for the untrained but enthusiastic Bible
reader is to generate arbitrary meanings and to claim that they are types.
Whatever the text stimulates in his mind, however fanciful, becomes
for him a typological meaning. Step 1 serves to rein in his fancies. It
disciplines his mind and heart by telling him to pay attention to what
God says in the context of earlier texts and earlier history.

The Danger of Minimizing Typology

Let us now consider the opposite danger, the danger of minimizing or
neglecting typological meanings.

This minimization is a danger especially for scholars with a certain
mindset. It can be tempting to overreact to fanciful readings by refus-
ing to see any but the most obvious symbolic meanings. Some scholars
tell us that we can find types in the Old Testament only when the New
Testament *explicitly* tells us that there is a type. Or a scholar may claim
that symbolic meanings are only relevant for the immediate historical
circumstances. He treats each moment in history as if it were so distinct
that the message of God is only for that moment, not for us (contrary
to Rom. 15:4 and 1 Cor. 10:6, 11).[8] He breaks the unity of redemptive
history and the unity of the plan of God into fragments, each fragment
being its own distinct moment in time.

Clowney's step 2 is important at this point. It tells us to travel forward in the history of revelation. We need to see that the truth that
God reveals at one point in history is not isolated, but belongs to his
comprehensive plan.

8   Clowney also notes the importance of divine authorship: "Such a method [of understanding "organic connection"] does not commend itself to those who deny or de-emphasize
the primary authorship of Scriptures" (*Preaching and Biblical Theology*, 111).

All things in the Old Testament are moving to fulfillment. All the times of history are connected intrinsically, according to the comprehensive plan of God. The meanings are connected through the passage of time to later and fuller meanings. That is one of the reminders that we get from Clowney's step 2. Every symbolic meaning that we find in the Old Testament does not stand in isolation. No meaning is just abandoned and dropped along the way, to be permanently forgotten. All is moving toward the climax in Christ, which comes not only with his first coming but his second coming (2 Cor. 1:20). The interpreter who avoids this richness of meaning, out of fear of making a mistake, is not doing justice to the unity and profundity and beauty of the plan of God, summed up in Christ (Eph. 1:10).[9]

It helps to observe that some connections of meaning are more obvious than others. Some connections are stronger and more salient than others. We do not need artificially to find a direct allusion from one passage to another, when in fact the texts provide only a broader thematic unity. But having said that, Clowney's step 2 encourages us to practice a kind of humble boldness in looking for unity in meaning between earlier and later times, between Old Testament and New Testament.

Moreover, a sensitive examination of the Old Testament shows that symbolic meanings are everywhere. All things and all events are what they are according to the plan of God. And the plan of God is deep.

Some symbolic meanings are obvious. The meaning of the tabernacle of Moses, as a symbol of the presence of God and his dwelling with his people, is obvious, because God tells Moses explicitly what the meaning is (Ex. 25:8). But meanings are not always that explicit. Consider something a little less explicit. The meaning of the sin offering includes substitutionary death. The death of the animal is symbolic of the need for substitutionary death to atone for sin. But the full implications are not completely spelled out in Leviticus 4.

---

9 "But a better grasp of biblical theology will open for us great riches of revelation" (*Preaching and Biblical Theology*, 112).

We can see the symbolic dimension more clearly if we link Leviticus 4 to the reality of what the people were experiencing. Guilt is real. We have to understand that the people in those times, like us, experienced guilt. God teaches that he is holy. The people need forgiveness. And here, in the sin offering, God gives them a symbolic representation of how to get forgiveness. But people know, deep down, that an animal's death is not an adequate equivalent for the guilt of sin and the death it deserves. So they also may sense that the animal sacrifice points beyond itself to something definitive, something that would surpass an animal.

It would be superficial to pass by the account and dismiss it by saying that it is all merely outward ceremonies, or, as some interpreters claim, that it belongs to a "primitive mentality." Such interpreters show their ignorance of the human heart. They skate on the surface of the text. They do not realize that God, speaking in the text, can challenge the heart at a deep level.

And at that level, everything in the Old Testament concerns in one way or another the relation of God to man. We see guilt and pardon, death and life, alienation from God or fellowship with him, curse or blessing. The issues always have symbolic depth, concerning ultimate relationship with God and eternal destiny, ultimate curse or ultimate blessing.

The result is that typology is pervasive in the Old Testament.

The Larger Significance of Clowney's Triangle

Clowney himself was deferential about the significance of his triangle.[10] The triangle is not a mechanism that automatically generates answers. It cannot substitute, by itself, for discernment and genuine understanding of the meaning of the word of God. Rather, it is a pointer and reminder about the structure of the history of redemption. When it is appreciated in this way, and used as a clue to the broader issues of biblical interpretation, it is a most fruitful contribution to biblical understanding, and in particular the understanding of symbolic meanings.

---

10 "This diagram is of only limited usefulness" (*Preaching and Biblical Theology*, 110).

Appendix E

Christocentric Preaching

[This appendix reproduces an article originally published in *The Southern Baptist Journal of Theology*.[1] It is used with permission.]

Abstract

The principle of *sola Scriptura*, when applied to church officers and to preaching, implies that preachers are given authority by Christ to proclaim and teach the content of Scripture, but not to add to or subtract from that content. This limitation constrains the content of preaching and teaching, but leaves much freedom with respect to form and selection of texts and topics at any particular time and place. As part of the total process of teaching, we can affirm the value of grammatical and historical study, study of human spiritual and moral examples, study of the process of redemption leading to Christ, study of types and analogies with Christ, study of the nature of God, and more.

When we apply these principles to Genesis 15:1–6, it follows that we can have many kinds of study of the passage. We take into account

---

1   Vern S. Poythress, "Christocentric Preaching," *Southern Baptist Journal of Theology* 22/3 (2018): 47–66, https://frame-poythress.org/wp-content/uploads/2019/03/2018SBJT-22.3 -Poythress-Christocentric-Preaching.pdf, accessed March 10, 2023. An earlier version was presented at the annual meeting of the Evangelical Theological Society, November 15–17, 2017. The paper was part of a larger session, "Expository Preaching and Hermeneutics: Preaching Christ, the Text, or Something Else?"

its literary place in Genesis 15 and in the whole of Genesis; we take into account the historical setting of patriarchal times. We take into account themes that link the work of God in Genesis 15:1–6 to the climactic work of Christ—themes like promise and fulfillment, blessing, offspring, inheritance, fear, and protection. All these are linked together by their coherent, mutually reinforcing presence in Genesis 15:1–6. The centrality of Christ in the life of the NT church implies his centrality in the preaching and teaching of the church. But there may be a spectrum of ways through which this centrality is wisely expressed and maintained.

———

I would like to address the topic of Christocentric preaching.

Let me begin with a short homily on Genesis 15:1–6. In this homily I will be illustrating the use of Clowney's triangle of typology, which represents a two-step process: finding the meaning of a symbol (S) in its own time (truth T^1), and then discerning how the truth is fulfilled in Christ (truth T^n).[2] Application is best worked out as a third step, after discerning the role of Christ. (See fig. E.1.)

Figure E.1: Clowney's Triangle, Summarizing Steps for Typological Reasoning[3]

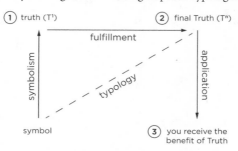

---

2   Edmund P. Clowney, *Preaching and Biblical Theology* (Grand Rapids, MI: Eerdmans, 1961), 98–112, especially 110, where the triangle is found in its original form.

3   From *Preaching and Biblical Theology*, 110, with some relabeling.

Proclaiming the Word

[1] After these things the word of the LORD came to Abram in a vision: "Fear not, Abram, I am your shield; your reward shall be very great." [2] But Abram said, "O Lord GOD, what will you give me, for I continue childless, and the heir of my house is Eliezer of Damascus?" [3] And Abram said, "Behold, you have given me no offspring, and a member of my household will be my heir." [4] And behold, the word of the LORD came to him: "This man shall not be your heir; your very own son shall be your heir." [5] And he brought him outside and said, "Look toward heaven, and number the stars, if you are able to number them." Then he said to him, "So shall your offspring be." [6] And he believed the LORD, and he counted it to him as righteousness. (Gen. 15:1–6)

In this life, what grips you? What grabs your attention and energy? Abraham was concerned to have a son who would be his heir. That concern does not necessarily strike us as gripping. So what grips you? What grips me? The desire for happiness? Family? Achievement at work? Increase in knowledge? Most of us know that the right answer should be something like "God himself" or "the glory of God." But that might not be the same as what *actually* grips our attention and desire. Whatever good things we may experience in this world are gifts from God. They are tokens and expressions of his blessing. At their best, they express personal communion with God, and we experience the presence of God through them. But in sin we are tempted to seize the gifts apart from the Giver.

Abraham belongs to a culture different from our own, but at a fundamental level his desires are the same. A son who is an heir is a blessing from God. It betokens *the* fundamental blessing, communion with God: "I will be your God" (see Gen. 17:7–8). A line of descent offers a shadowy symbol of ongoing life. The ongoing life represents Abraham's life blood, extending from generation to generation. It is a shadow of eternal life, in communion with the living God, the God who is the fountain of life. Moreover, in Abraham's case his offspring is special. God's promises in Genesis 12:2 and 13:15–16 already suggest that Abraham's offspring is also the offspring of the woman. Through this line climactic salvation will come.

How will you have communion with God, the God of all life? How will Abraham? How could God bring it about for you and me? How—when we, like Abraham, are doomed to die because of our sin? It is by God speaking and promising: God says, "Your very own son shall be your heir" (15:4). God who knows the inmost heart knows the question behind Abram's question. He understands the feeling of impossibility. It is as if he says, "Come outside, Abraham. I want to show you something."

"Come outside, Christian, I want to show you something." "Look toward heaven." In the silence of the night, in the countryside, what do you see? Stars. Many of them. It is magnificent. They testify from age to age about the power and beauty and magnificence of the one who made them (Ps. 19:1–2). Theirs numbers testify to the abundance of God's power, his power to multiply and make fruitful. The stars of heaven link us symbolically to the reality of heaven and the one who dwells there. Each star links us to the beauty and brightness and purity and abundant power of God. The stars thereby represent communion with God. God says to Abraham, I grant you blessing, beyond the bounds of earth. Blessing that signifies the reality of communion with God. The blessing of a son. But not one son only. A multitude. A multitude testifying to the fruitfulness of God, analogous to the multiplication of stars. The blessing of communion with God is such that it multiples and deepens beyond calculation. The name "Isaac" means "he laughs" (Gen. 21:3, 6). Envision laughter, the laughter of joy from God, multiplying beyond Isaac up to the stars of heaven, to uncountable joy, joy "inexpressible and filled with glory" (1 Pet. 1:8). "So—" says God, "so shall your offspring be" (Gen. 15:5). God promises fullness of joy, overflowing life, life forevermore (Ps. 16:11).

The promise is as if God took a star, a star symbolizing heavenly presence, and brought it down for us. He brought it down by putting words of promise in our ear, so that we could absorb it, as if to eat it with our own mouth. The promise expresses the light of God. He brought down light in the form of a son.

And so he did, in the climax of history. God, the eternal light (1 John 1:5), sent God of God, light of light, down to the earth, and he became man, "which we looked upon and touched with our hands" (1 John 1:1). The Son and heir is our Lord Jesus Christ. "We have seen his glory, glory as of the only Son from the Father" (John 1:14). The morning star (Rev. 22:16) has come to us, the Son and "the heir of all things" (Heb. 1:2), "the radiance of the glory of God."

Here is fullness of life, fullness of joy—in him. Believe what God has said, as Abraham did. Reject the folly of the world. Believe, in order that you may participate in eternal life, the life in communion with God through this Son. In him you inherit communion with God, and with that communion all that is God's. Abandon the grip of this world, to lay hold of God and his life in his Son. By being joined to the Son, you are counted as one of the stars yourself. In Christ, you are an heir of Abraham: "And if you are Christ's, then you are Abraham's offspring, heirs according to promise" (Gal. 3:29).

Exploration of Significance

I could use my whole space to give an expository sermon on Genesis 15:1–6. But that would leave many questions. So I have decided to discuss the principles guiding interpretation and preaching, with Genesis 15:1–6 as an example. Given the limitations of a single article, I must be sketchy; I cannot provide full justifications.

Qualifications and Clarifications

At the outset, let me include two qualifications.

First, I believe in Christocentric preaching in a certain sense. But I do not consider myself a typical representative of that approach,[4] for

---

4 For more representative approaches, see, for example, Clowney, *Preaching and Biblical Theology*; Dennis E. Johnson, *Him We Proclaim: Preaching Christ from All the Scriptures* (Phillipsburg, NJ: P&R, 2007); Edmund P. Clowney, *The Unfolding Mystery: Discovering*

reasons that will appear. I may disappoint those who expect a robust defense of a classical understanding of Christocentric preaching.

Second, I do not endorse Christomonism, under which I include two defective approaches: (1) the strategy of preaching *only* on Christ incarnate, and (2) the strategy of preaching Christ apart from the context of the Father and the Spirit. A restriction to the incarnate Christ is in tension with the NT teaching about his preexistence. What about the issue of the Trinity? The work of Christ takes place as the execution of the plan of the Father, by his anointing, in the power and presence of the Holy Spirit (Acts 10:38). Accordingly, Christ-centered interpretation and Trinity-centered interpretation should be seen as two sides of the same coin. How so?

We know Christ in the context of knowing the Father and the Spirit, through the power and illumination of the Spirit of Christ, who proceeds from the Father (John 15:26). Proper understanding of Christ naturally includes the Trinity. So my approach might be called Trinity-centered preaching. Rightly understood, Christocentric preaching is also necessarily Trinity-centered preaching.

Conversely, Trinity-centered preaching is Christ-centered. Trinity-centered preaching ought to acknowledge the centrality and preeminence

Christ in the Old Testament; With Study and Application Questions (Phillipsburg, NJ: P&R, 2013); Edmund P. Clowney, *Preaching Christ in All of Scripture* (Wheaton, IL: Crossway, 2003); Charles D. Drew, *The Ancient Love Song: Finding Christ in the Old Testament* (Phillipsburg, NJ: P&R, 2000); Sydney Greidanus, *Preaching Christ from the Old Testament: A Contemporary Hermeneutical Method* (Grand Rapids, MI: Eerdmans, 1999). In addition, there are broader discussions of the history of redemption and the centrality of the role of Christ in that history: Geerhardus Vos, *Biblical Theology: Old and New Testaments* (repr., Edinburgh/Carlisle, PA: Banner of Truth Trust, 1975); O. Palmer Robertson, *The Christ of the Covenants* (Grand Rapids, MI: Baker, 1980); O. Palmer Robertson, *The Christ of the Prophets* (Phillipsburg, NJ: P&R, 2004); O. Palmer Robertson, *The Christ of Wisdom: A Redemptive-Historical Exploration of the Wisdom Books of the Old Testament* (Phillipsburg, NJ: P&R, 2017); Graeme Goldsworthy, *Gospel-Centered Hermeneutics: Foundations and Principles of Evangelical Biblical Interpretation* (Downers Grove, IL: IVP Academic, 2006); Graeme Goldsworthy, *Christ-Centered Biblical Theology: Hermeneutical Foundations and Principles* (Downers Grove, IL: IVP Academic, 2012). For my own approach, see Vern S. Poythress, *The Shadow of Christ in the Law of Moses* (repr., Phillipsburg, NJ: P&R, 1995); Vern S. Poythress, *Reading the Word of God in the Presence of God: A Handbook for Biblical Interpretation* (Wheaton, IL: Crossway, 2016); Vern S. Poythress, *God-Centered Biblical Interpretation* (Phillipsburg, NJ: P&R, 1999).

of Christ and his work in the redemptive reconciliation to God, who is Father, Son, and Spirit. Knowledge of the Father and the Spirit is mediated by the words and work of the Son.[5]

This mutuality involving Christ as center and the Trinity as center is confirmed by the examples of apostolic preaching in Acts. Preeminently, the apostles expound Christ and his work. But their exposition includes attention to God in his trinitarian work, as illustrated by the reference to the Father and the Spirit in Acts 2:33:

> Being therefore exalted at the right hand of *God*, and having received from the *Father* the promise of the *Holy Spirit*, *he* [Jesus] has poured out this that you yourselves are seeing and hearing.

The same holds for the instruction found in the NT letters (e.g., 1 Cor. 2:2; Eph. 1; 2 Tim. 3:15; 1 Pet. 1; 1 John 1).

Freedom in Preaching, within Limits

To provide a framework for assessing preaching, let me now briefly take up the topic of freedom and constraint in preaching. The only constraints should be scriptural.

I hold to a principle of *sola Scriptura* for ethics. No extra ethical principles have to be added to the canon of Scripture in order for Christian living to be complete. One can see this principle of sufficiency of Scripture in Psalm 119:1:

> Blessed are those whose way is blameless,
>   who walk in the law of the LORD!

---

5 Thus a focus on Christ offers a *perspective* on the Trinity, and conversely a focus on the Trinity offers a *perspective* on Christ. This use of perspectives follows the pattern discussed in John Frame, "A Primer on Perspectivalism (Revised 2008)," https://frame-poythress .org/a-primer-on-perspectivalism-revised-2008/, accessed August 31, 2017; and more elaborately in Vern S. Poythress, *Symphonic Theology: The Validity of Multiple Perspectives in Theology* (repr., Phillipsburg, NJ: P&R, 2001) and John M. Frame, *Theology in Three Dimensions: A Guide to Triperspectivalism and Its Significance* (Phillipsburg, NJ: P&R, 2017).

Does someone want to be blameless? The only thing that he needs to do is to "walk in the law of the LORD." Nothing else needs to be added.

The principle also applies to officers of the church, as can be seen from 2 Timothy 3:16–17. The famous passage about the breathing out of Scripture by God ends with the goal: "that the man of God may be *competent*, equipped for *every* good work" (v. 17). The phrase "man of God" focuses on those responsible for ministry of the word. Scripture is sufficient to make them "competent."

Attempts to add to scriptural commands most often end up in the long run unintentionally undermining Scripture, as Jesus observes in his critique of tradition in Mark 7:6–9:

> And he said to them, "Well did Isaiah prophesy of you hypocrites, as it is written,
>
> > 'This people honors me with their lips,
> >   but their heart is far from me;
> > in vain do they worship me,
> >   teaching as doctrines the commandments of men.'
>
> You leave the commandment of God and hold to the tradition of men." And he said to them, "You have a fine way of rejecting the commandment of God in order to establish your tradition!"

The basic principle governing church officers, including preachers, is that they have no genuine *legislative* authority, but only *executive* authority. They cannot rightly legislate; that is, they cannot invent extra ethical principles and bind the people of God to them; neither can they annul the rules of Scripture or implications deducible from Scripture. Rather, they are given the responsibility of carrying out what God has already said (executive authority).

Now this principle of sufficiency has implications for expository preaching. The preacher or teacher must teach the teaching of Scripture. He is not authorized to add or subtract. When he speaks the word of

God, which it is his duty to do, his words have authority derivative from God. But only then. In sum, this means that he is authorized to teach "the whole counsel of God" in a sense similar to Acts 20:27. That is the main constraint on preaching.

There is also freedom in preaching, as an implication of the Reformation doctrine of the freedom of the Christian man. How so? The principle of *sola Scriptura* also governs *how* the preacher does his preaching. Scripture does not command us to use just one style. So in fact there is vast freedom for the teacher to use his God-given wisdom as to just how he expresses and conveys teaching. He may use verbal illustrations; he may use blackboard or slides. At a particular time or place, he may expound the teaching of the whole Bible by topic; he may expound the meaning and implications while focusing on a single passage like Genesis 15:1–6. He may focus on explaining the relations of one or two passages in Genesis to the whole of Genesis. He may explain how, in the context of the whole canon, an OT passage has links forward to the work of Christ on earth. All of these approaches and more may operate within the general task of teaching the whole counsel of God.

Of course in the long run, in the case of a person who preaches or teaches regularly, he should consider also whether his teaching is balanced and avoids always returning to a few pet topics or pet verses.

The Place of Expository Preaching

Now, within this framework, what about expository preaching? What is it? To some extent, people may operate with different definitions and different conceptions. At the very broadest, it might mean only that the content of teaching is orthodox and is built on canonical content. This constraint is the one already mentioned, concerning "the whole counsel of God." But often expository preaching is considered more narrowly. It often means focusing on expounding one verse or one passage from the Bible. This latter sense is one way, but only one, of carrying out the task of teaching.

If we were to say that it is the only way or the best way, that would be a matter of human tradition. I believe it is a tradition with wisdom and it can serve to instruct aspiring preachers. The principal people who advocate expository preaching do not themselves claim that single-text preaching is absolutely the only way to preach—only that it is generally preferable. In particular, they offer it as wise counsel for young men who are still gaining their feet with the practice of preaching. With that understanding I agree. But we should nevertheless remember the principle of *sola Scriptura*. It implies that the tradition as such has no exclusive claim on us, as the only proper way to teach the word of God. No passage in Scripture restricts preachers to this method. And a restriction of this sort is contradicted by the sermons in Acts and by the NT letters, none of which is exclusively focused on expounding one OT verse or passage.

A focus on biblical exposition is useful. But it produces a danger that we would bring in expectations from tradition about how it ought to be done. The principle of *sola Scriptura* for ethics and for the "how," the method of teaching the word of God, makes me conclude that there is not only one way or one method or one technique for having "the word of Christ dwell in you" (Col. 3:16), but many. Many ways of teaching may be faithful to the teaching found in Scripture itself. All of these good ways necessarily contrast with heretical and false teaching, as well as with teaching done by people whose lives do not commend their words.[6]

Centrality of Christ for Spiritual Life

Though there is vast freedom, the Bible shows us the importance of Christ for the long-range spiritual health of the church. There are several motivations for keeping Christ central in the whole life of the church, preaching included.

First, as we have seen, preaching in Acts and the letters in the NT provide examples of the centrality of Christ.

Second, Christ is central in the gospel, which is the central proclamation of the NT. The gospel is both the gospel that Christ proclaimed

---

6   Note the link between life and teaching in 1 Tim. 4:6–16 and other passages.

(Mark 1:15) and the gospel about Christ that the apostles and other early preachers proclaimed (Rom. 1:1–3; 1 Cor. 15:1–8; Col. 1:28). The gospel needs to be central in the church, which is the body of Christ, whose members are those who follow Christ.

Third, the NT indicates that union and communion with Christ is central in salvation and in Christian growth (e.g., 2 Cor. 3:18; Eph. 1; Col. 2:3). Neglecting the centrality of Christ is not responsible and leads to spiritual unhealthiness when the sheep of Christ's flock are not wisely fed. The centrality of Christ should therefore be continually considered, and should be a regular focus for people who feed the sheep.

Fourth, the NT indicates at various points that the OT is centrally about Christ. Most prominent is Luke 24:25–27, 44–49, but we may add John 5:39, 45–46; 2 Corinthians 1:20; Hebrews; and 1 Peter 1:10–12. These passages certainly need to be taken into account in our interpretation of the OT. But we do not have space enough to consider them at length.

The upshot is that Christ should be central in preaching as well. But how? That question returns us to an affirmation of freedom within the boundaries of the whole counsel of God. The interpreter who respects the word of God must respect the many thematic and rhetorical unities that belong to each individual passage. He must also respect the unity that belongs to the whole biblical canon, unity in doctrine, unity in accomplishment of redemption in Christ, and unity in the history of redemption, as progressing through time.[7] Those unities give unity to preaching. But still there is diversity. Diversity of passages, and diversity of various aspects of each passage.

Affirmation of Variety

The unities are perhaps more attended to. So let me take the time to affirm a variety in the ways that we study Scripture. Variety need not be understood as opposed to the centrality of Christ. I can affirm in

---

7 Note, in particular, the focus on the history of redemption and the history of revelation in Vos, *Biblical Theology: Old and New Testaments*.

principle the positive value of a focus on grammatical and historical study of the communication of God through human authors to an ancient audience. That kind of study contributes as one aspect of the whole, that is, the total process of teaching Scripture.

I can affirm the value of a focus on redemptive-historical movement, leading forward to the once-for-all appearing of Christ on earth at the proper historical moment ("the fullness of time," Gal. 4:4). This focus, properly executed, would be a valid form of Christotelic exposition. The focus on grammar and language, the focus on history and the immediate historical and social environment, and the focus on redemptive movement forward to Christ represent moments within a rich and complex meditation on the word of God that is addressing us (Rom. 15:4).

But I treat these various foci as moments within a larger whole. These moments can be isolated from that whole only at the cost of distortion and illusion. In fact, we always have a larger background, hermeneutically speaking, constituted by our previous understandings and assumptions and practices in living, a background that we do not explicitly address, but which helps to guide our research on a single passage. Truth in Christ is not composed merely of isolated bits, like marbles in a bag.

Illustration of Variety with Genesis 15:1–6

We may illustrate with Genesis 15:1–6. It is valid and useful to do a careful study of the words, phrases, and larger linguistic textures of the passage. As one example, after examining the flow of the six verses, we may judge that verse 5 forms a kind of literary peak, with verses 4–6 forming a somewhat broader mountain top. So we try to appreciate how the earlier verses lead up to this peak, and how the peak functions as the main point for the entire episode.

In addition, it is valid and useful to study the historical environment, which includes previous promises to Abram and the social contexts of the time. Included in social context would be the cultural atmosphere of placing value on having sons and having an inheritance to pass on. We may also study how Genesis 15:1–6 fits into a larger context:

the further developments and the ceremony in 15:7–21; the section on the generations of Terah beginning in Genesis 11:27; the larger story of early history and the patriarchs found in Genesis as a whole; the context of the Pentateuch; and the context of the history of Israel continuing in Joshua, Judges, and beyond. Because God has a plan from the beginning, we may also consider how all this history leads to Christ. The history includes the promise of offspring, offspring traced through the line of Seth, the line of Noah, the line of Abraham, and the line of David. Genesis 15:5 offers us one point on this developing line.

I also affirm the positive value of meaningful connections between passages, connections in many dimensions, through many themes. So, for example, human beings long ago, in Abram's time, were human like us. They serve therefore as moral and spiritual examples, good and bad and mixed. The climactic example is found in the humanity of Christ. We may ask of a passage, "What are human beings doing, and how are they analogous to Christ and to us?" In Genesis 15:1–6, what do we learn about Abram? We see his faith and also his insecurities and possible doubts, which he brings before the Lord. He is like us. And Christ is the climactic human being who trusts God with all his heart.

All of the events in the OT are redemptive-historical preparations, along a timeline leading according to the unfolding plan of God to the coming of Christ. A sermon may choose to focus on this aspect of preparation. Genesis 15:1–6 represents one episode along this long timeline. How does it fit into the whole? As father of the faithful, Abram exercises faith, and is the fountainhead for a line of offspring of faith (as in Heb. 11 and Rom. 4).

Since God is always the same God, I affirm a systematic-theological, God-centered approach that focuses on the question, "What is God doing, and what do we learn about him?" The climactic revelation of the character of God is in Christ: John 14:9; Hebrews 1:1–3. In Genesis 15:1–6, God appears as merciful, compassionate, promise-keeping, redemptively active, and miracle-working. He is the same God still today.

I affirm a typological approach that looks for symbols that have meaning in their own historical location and also point forward to a final, climactic realization in Christ. Edmund Clowney has shown how to avoid arbitrariness in treating typology by focusing first on the meaning of symbols in their own time. As a second step, we see how the truth symbolized at an earlier time is further unveiled in Christ.[8] (See fig. E.1 above.)

Typology in Genesis 15:1–6

How might this approach work with Genesis 15:1–6? The subsequent narrative in Genesis 15:7–21 has more obvious symbolical material than verses 1–6, and nothing about symbolism should be forced. One of the liabilities in the medieval fourfold method was to appear to suggest that we treat every passage of Scripture the same way. To practice such a uniform approach would be to ignore the unique character of genuine symbols and differences in genre.

I may nevertheless suggest that there are elements in Genesis 15:1–6 that have some degree of symbolical overtones. Verse 1 presents us with a vision, which connotes intimacy with God and thus symbolic depth. Verse 2 speaks about offspring and inheritance. In Genesis, physical offspring and inheritance are tokens of blessing in the context of a holistic personal relation to God. They thus betoken also spiritual fruit and spiritual inheritance. "Your reward" in verse 1 links with the theme of inheritance. "Your shield" in verse 1 functions to guarantee God's care, and thereby suggests the larger pattern, where God promises to "be God" to Abraham (Gen. 17:7, 8). Fruitfulness is suggested in verse 5, as confirmed by 17:6. Covenantal promises are suggested in verse 5, as confirmed by 17:4.

Or consider the theme of life. The tree of life in 2:9 (3:22) symbolizes real life in fellowship with God, and thus eternal life (3:22). This eternal life is still a prospect even after the fall, as is made visible by the promise concerning the offspring of the woman (3:15). The tokens of life and blessing that are found in 15:1–6 evoke this larger theme of blessing, which has climactic form in the blessing of eternal life. In

8 Clowney, *Preaching and Biblical Theology*, 98–112.

verse 5, the stars betoken the power of God. The fact that the stars are used as a central illustration to confirm God's promise may invite us to slow down and experience more deeply what it means to actually look at stars and be in awe, as would have been Abram's experience.

A sermon focused on verse 5 could dwell on how Christ brings to fulfillment the covenantal promises in the verse. Christ inaugurates the new covenant (1 Cor. 11:25); produces fruitfulness (Isa. 53:10–12); receives an inheritance that is also ours when we are in him (Ps. 2:8; Rom. 8:17).

I affirm a fulfillment approach that stresses the superiority and climactic character of the revelation in Christ and the work of God in the earthly life, death, resurrection, ascension, and rule of Christ. So, for example, Christ is heir to the whole world, not simply the land of Canaan. Christ has dominion over all, not only over animals and land. Christ is fruitful in bringing many sons to glory (and the spiritual fruit is surpassingly glorious, 2 Cor. 3).

Christ as fulfillment encompasses the earlier emphases in covenantal promises. Christ in perfect humanity fulfills earlier human examples. Christ in his work in the fullness of time fulfills the acts of preparation. Christ is God, and as God he climactically manifests the character of God. The cross and resurrection show the mercy and justice and wisdom of the Father. Christ as antitype fulfills the symbols.

We can also consider focusing on themes. The major themes in Genesis include blessing, offspring (and fruitfulness), and land. They are articulated in terms of promise, waiting/development/trial/threat, and fulfillment. These all have typological functions, in that physical blessings, offspring, and land betoken the centrality of spiritual communion with God. Also, the redemptive plot that consists in the movement from distress to deliverance is typological in its relation to the antitype of redemption accomplished by Christ.[9]

Here in Genesis 15:1–6 are found many of these themes. In particular, the obstacle is that Abram has no proper heir. It is a trial,

---

9   Vern S. Poythress, *In the Beginning Was the Word: Language—A God-Centered Approach* (Wheaton, IL: Crossway, 2009), chs. 25–26; Vern S. Poythress, *The Miracles of Jesus: How the Savior's Mighty Acts Serve as Signs of Redemption* (Wheaton, IL: Crossway, 2016), part 2.

corresponding to the trials of Christ and of Christians. The answer is given in terms of the character of God and his promises. Near fulfillment is found in Genesis 21, when Isaac is born, after overcoming the threat in Genesis 20. This deliverance is typologically related to the climactic deliverance in the death and resurrection of Christ.

Illustrating Christocentricity for a Single Verse

Having considered themes in Genesis and in the passage 15:1–6, let us now illustrate aspects of Christocentricity at the level of a single verse. Christocentricity belongs to OT verses by virtue of relations with other verses and passages.

Let us consider a less prominent verse with Genesis 15:1–6, namely verse 3: "And Abram said, 'Behold, you have given me no offspring . . .'" One way of considering the larger significance comes from reflecting on why a situation with no offspring comes to exist at all. This verse 3 has a thematic contrast with the fruitfulness promised in Genesis 1:28, which includes offspring by implication: "Be fruitful and multiply and fill the earth . . ." What makes the difference between the blessing described in Genesis 1:28 and the situation of frustration in Genesis 15:3? The obvious watershed is the fall of Adam. Given the fall, the favor of God that Abram experiences in 15:1–6, even in the midst of his temporary frustration, is a picture of grace. And Abram's response to God relies on this grace. Grace solves the demerit from the fall. As a result of the fall, Adam and his descendants lack proper standing before God. God acts to overcome Abram's lack.

Now grace is possible only through Christ. In Genesis 15:1–6, the vision, the word of God, and the blessing are all mediated to Abram in a manner that must be consistent with God's justice. Grace is free from the standpoint of Abram's side, but from the standpoint of God it must be consistent with justice. And this requires dealing with demerit by means of substitution.

(This overall context, by the way, excludes the interpretation of verse 6 as meaning that God accounted Abram's faith as righteousness in an analytic sense, that is, because his faith was itself a righteous act. That interpretation ignores the necessary presence of grace.)

Phrases and Clauses

Now let us illustrate some ways in which Christocentricity belongs to texts by virtue of relations, at the level of phrases and clauses. In Genesis 15:4, consider the phrase "the word of the LORD." God spoke to Abram. This phrase in context resonates with all the earlier speeches of God to man in Genesis. Ever since the fall, God's speech needs to be mediated to avoid death of the recipient. The mediator is the Son, the Word. Because of the necessity of mediation, we can confidently infer the presence of Christ and his work when God speaks to Abram. Christ's role in Genesis 15:4 anticipates his incarnation and verbal ministry on earth.

Genesis 15:4 also resonates with the speech of God in Genesis 1, which powerfully brings about what it specifies: "And God said, 'Let there be light,' and there was light" (Gen. 1:3). In like manner, in 15:4–5 the word of God guarantees an heir beforehand and specifies authoritatively the nature of the heir. Both of these kinds of speech, in creation and in covenantal promise, are reflections within time that reflect the archetype, the eternal Word who is spoken by God, specifying the nature of God.

Embedding the Word of God

Consider also that the word of God can be embedded in the word of God. Genesis as whole book is the word of God, and in it is embedded the quotation at Genesis 15:4 from what God said at a particular point in the life of Abraham. Moreover, 15:4 could have included another level of embedding in turn, by quoting from what God said to Abram at Genesis 12:2 or 12:7 concerning Abram's offspring. Genesis 15:4 does not elaborate using the exact words of the earlier speeches in Genesis 12, but there is nevertheless an allusion to them. It is a kind of indirect embedding of an earlier divine speech. We may include also God's mention of offspring in 13:15–16.

How does it happen that the word of God can embed the word of God? I have argued elsewhere that embedding of this kind involves a kind of miniature transcendence.[10] Human understanding, as a finite, created imitation of divine understanding, is capable of standing back from immediate involvement in a situation and grasping the whole. In this case, the whole is the earlier oral communication to Abram, which is actually several wholes that are brought together in an act of miniature transcendence.

Now miniature transcendence is possible to mankind because man is made in the image of God. The original, the archetypal image is not man but the divine Son, as seen in Colossians 1:15 and Hebrews 1:3.

Man's thoughts exercising miniature transcendence echo the thoughts of God. And on the divine level the Son is the original image echoing the Father. The word of God can echo the Word, thereby reflecting the relation of the Father to the Son in the original divine instance of reflection.

Do you think that these reasonings are a stretch? The divine speech and activity is the archetype on which specific manifestations depend. In creation and providence, God does not depend on eternal abstractions outside himself, but on himself as the absolute origin. Thus there is a genuine relation between the original instance of communication in the relation of the Father to the Son, and ectypal instances in the world.

The Theme of Coming

Now let us look again at the expression "came to him" in Genesis 15:4. This expression describes a communication that, figuratively speaking, *moves* from God to man. Note also the particular style of the expression, "the word of the LORD *came* . . . ," instead of the simple expression, "God said," or "God spoke." The metaphorical idea of movement hints at a differentiation between God who is the origin and the word that comes out from him, traveling out as a word distinct from the speaker. This differentiation adumbrates the fuller NT revelation of the distinction between God the Father and the Word, the Son.

In Genesis 15:4, a revelation originates in God, which man cannot control or compel, and which is a free act of God. In the situation after

---

10 Poythress, *In the Beginning Was the Word*, chs. 11 and 12.

the fall, man cannot merit it and indeed has demerit, making communication from God problematic. The coming of the word is a coming
of God that is by grace. As such, it anticipates and foreshadows the
climactic coming in Christ. As Hebrews 1 says,

> Long ago, at many times and in many ways, God spoke to our fathers
> by the prophets [and, we may add, through Abram, functioning as
> a prophet in receiving the word, Gen. 20:7; Ps. 105:15], but in these
> last days he has spoken to us by his Son . . . (Heb. 1:1–2)

God sent forth his word to Abram. "But when the fullness of time had
come, God sent forth his Son, . . ." (Gal. 4:4).

Christocentricity in a Word

Let us now consider the level of individual words. The words, of course,
function in interaction with literary context. So a focus on one word,
like the earlier choices of focus, never leaves behind context. It would
be comparatively easy to take a word like *heir* (Gen. 15:2, 3, 4). The
general idea of an heir and an inheritance makes sense only against a
background defined by ownership and gift. The original of both is to
be found in God. God created the world and owns it. Adam receives
the world as a gift and is like an heir. He forfeited his position in the
fall. Abram's heirship is a type of the climactic offspring who inherits,
namely Christ as the last Adam.

Instead of continuing to reflect on the word *heir*, let us consider a
more challenging case: the word *after*, used at the beginning of Genesis
15:1 (Hebrew אַחַר). The word *after* functions together with the phrase
these things to show a chronological link with the preceding chapter. As
usual, the word functions in a context that colors its force and function.

What are we to say? Genesis 15 comprises one of a considerable
number of episodes unfolding the promises of God to Abraham. First,
a promise comes (Gen. 12:1–3). Then there is a time of unfolding and
development. And in Genesis we also have the early events in the initial stages of fulfillment. History thus unfolds God's plan of salvation.

Meditation on the serious implications of the fall shows that the continuation, that is, the history of redemption, is a kind of miracle and surprise of grace. And this grace, we know, can only be through Christ.

The progressive unfolding in the articulation of promises is shown in the ways that Genesis 15:1–6 adds to earlier articulations to Abram. "Fear not" (v. 1) is new. So is "I am your shield" and "Your reward shall be very great" (v. 1). Yet these promises are not absolutely new. The promises of blessings and care from God in Genesis 12:1–3, 7 and 13:14–17 already should provide Abram comfort in the security of God's promises, and therefore are cause for not fearing. However, making *explicit* the exhortation not to fear is significant encouragement. So also, the promise in 12:3 concerning God's curse on enemies hints that God is Abram's shield. But the explicit statement in 15:1 is more definite. "Organic growth" in revelation is rightly an idea applied to this sequence, and indeed well beyond Genesis into the entire OT period. This growth unfolds on the basis of the grace founded in the work of Christ, a work that is reckoned with beforehand as God blesses fallen people in Genesis.

We can see the role of Christ especially in Revelation 5. I am thinking of the worthiness of the Lamb—the Lamb that has been slain in sacrifice—to take the scroll. Interpreters differ concerning the contents of the scroll. On the basis of parallels with heavenly books in Daniel, I take it that the scroll is the book laying out God's plan for history, a history of redemption. The plan can unfold, as represented symbolically by the breaking of the seals, only because of the Lamb. We might observe that in Revelation 6 the results of opening the seals are more specialized, not necessarily the entirety of history. That is true. But the principle articulated in the symbolism is general: it concerns the worthiness of the Lamb as the driving center of redemption. This image is applicable beyond the specific details given as results of opening the seals. The principle is applicable, therefore, to the word *after* in Genesis 15:1.

In fact, at a principial level, the unfolding of history is trinitarian. It is according to the plan of the Father, executed by the Son, and consummated by the Holy Spirit. Doctrinal principle suggests that this execution of history extends not only to core events of redemption, where it is obvious and most vividly articulated, but concerning the movement from creation to consummation that characterizes the prefall situation as well as postfall.

The actions of God in history reflect the eternal trinitarian relations of action. The Father begets the Son eternally. This eternal begetting has a reflection in the causal unfolding of time on the level of the creature. Thus, the before-and-after structure articulated in the word *after* in Genesis 15:1 reflects the priority and posteriority of begetting and begotten in the Trinity.

All this, I aver, represents implications of the teaching of the Bible as a whole. General principles concerning the Trinity have salient connections with the particular instances that manifest those principles. The particulars include every one of the once-for-all, never-to-be-repeated particularities of words, phrases, clauses, and paragraphs such as found in Genesis 15:1–6.

The principles, expressing unity in the Bible, and the not-repeated particulars, expressing the diversity in the Bible and in history, are, as Cornelius Van Til argued, equally ultimate.[11] As such, they reflect the equal ultimacy of unity and diversity in God, the one God in three persons. And that expression is necessarily Christocentric, because it is revelational, mediated by the Son.

Conclusion

The relations between words and context and the relations between passages, when extended to the whole canon and the larger vistas of history, provide resources in which we find many meaning connections that involve the work of Christ. In addition to these sources of meaning, we can affirm the principial importance of Christ in teaching in the church, because of the centrality of Christ in NT preaching and teaching, in the process of sanctification, and in NT affirmations concerning the significance of the OT.

---

11 Cornelius Van Til, *The Defense of the Faith*, 4th ed. (Phillipsburg, NJ: P&R, 2008), 45–51.

Bibliography

Baker, David L. *Two Testaments, One Bible: A Study of Some Modern Solutions to the Theological Problem of the Relationship between the Old and New Testaments.* 3rd., rev. ed. Downers Grove, IL: IVP Academic, 2010.

Barr, James. *The Semantics of Biblical Language.* London: Oxford University Press, 1961.

Beale, G. K. *Handbook on the New Testament Use of the Old Testament: Exegesis and Interpretation.* Grand Rapids, MI: Baker, 2012.

Beale, G. K., and D. A. Carson, eds. *Commentary on the New Testament Use of the Old Testament.* Grand Rapids, MI: Baker; Nottingham, England: Apollos, 2007.

Beekman, John. "Toward an Understanding of Narrative Structure." Dallas: Summer Institute of Linguistics, 1978.

Boucher, Madeleine. *The Mysterious Parable: A Literary Study.* Washington: Catholic Biblical Association of America, 1977.

Burch, Robert. "Charles Sanders Peirce." In *The Stanford Encyclopedia of Philosophy*, edited by Edward N. Zalta (Spring 2021 ed.), https://plato.stanford.edu/archives/spr2021/entries/peirce/.

Carson, D. A. *Exegetical Fallacies.* 2nd ed. Grand Rapids, MI: Baker, 1996.

Chase, Mitchell L. *40 Questions about Typology and Allegory.* Grand Rapids, MI: Kregel, 2020.

Clowney, Edmund P. *Preaching and Biblical Theology.* Grand Rapids, MI: Eerdmans, 1961.

Danielou, Jean. *From Shadows to Reality: Studies in the Biblical Typology of the Fathers*. London: Burns & Oates, 1960.

Danker, Frederick William, ed. *A Greek-English Lexicon of the New Testament and Other Early Christian Literature*. 3rd ed. Chicago: University of Chicago Press, 2000.

Davidson, Richard M. *Typology in Scripture: A Study of Hermeneutical Τύπος Structures*. Berrien Springs, MI: Andrews University Press, 1981.

Duguid, Iain M. *Is Jesus in the Old Testament?* Phillipsburg, NJ: P&R, 2013.

Fairbairn, Patrick. *The Typology of Scripture: Viewed in Connection with the Whole Series of . . . The Divine Dispensations*. New York and London: Funk & Wagnalls, 1911. Available in several reprints and online, https://www.monergism.com/typology-scripture-ebook.

Frame, John M. *The Doctrine of the Christian Life*. Phillipsburg, NJ: P&R, 2008.

Frame, John M. *The Doctrine of the Knowledge of God*. Phillipsburg, NJ: Presbyterian & Reformed, 1987.

Frame, John M. *Perspectives on the Word of God: An Introduction to Christian Ethics*. Reprint, Eugene, OR: Wipf & Stock, 1999.

Frame, John M. "A Primer on Perspectivalism," 2008, http://frame-poythress.org/a-primer-on-perspectivalism-revised-2008/, accessed March 10, 2023.

Goppelt, Leonhard. *Typos: The Typological Interpretation of the Old Testament in the New*. Translated by Donald H. Madvig. Grand Rapids, MI: Eerdmans, 1982.

Hamilton, James M. Jr. *Typology—Understanding the Bible's Promise-Shaped Patterns: How Old Testament Expectations Are Fulfilled in Christ*. Grand Rapids, MI: Zondervan, 2022.

Johnson, Dennis E. *Him We Proclaim: Preaching Christ from All the Scriptures*. Phillipsburg, NJ: P&R, 2007.

Johnson, Dennis E. *Walking with Jesus through His Word: Discovering Christ in All the Scriptures*. Phillipsburg, NJ: P&R, 2015.

Kaiser, Walter C. Jr., and Moisés Silva. *Introduction to Biblical Hermeneutics: The Search for Meaning*. Revised and expanded ed. Grand Rapids, MI: Zondervan, 2007.

Leithart, Peter J. *Deep Exegesis: The Mystery of Reading Scripture*. Waco, TX: Baylor University Press, 2009.

McEwen, William. *The Glory and Fullness of Jesus Christ: In the Most Remarkable Types, Figures, and Allegories of the Old Testament*. Grand Rapids, MI: Reformation Heritage, 2022. Updated from earlier editions, beginning in 1787.

Meek, James A. "Toward a Biblical Typology." ThM thesis, Westminster Theological Seminary, 1981.

Philo of Alexandria. "The Unchangeableness of God." In *Philo*, vol. 3. Loeb Library. London: William Heinemann; Cambridge, MA: Harvard University Press, 1968.

Pike, Kenneth L. *Linguistic Concepts: An Introduction to Tagmemics*. Lincoln: University of Nebraska Press, 1982.

Poythress, Vern S. "Christocentric Preaching." *Southern Baptist Journal of Theology* 22/3 (2018): 47–66, https://frame-poythress.org/wp-content/uploads/2019/03/2018SBJT-22.3-Poythress-Christocentric-Preaching.pdf, accessed March 10, 2023.

Poythress, Vern S. "Clowney's Triangle of Typology." *Unio cum Christo* (October 2021): 231–38, https://frame-poythress.org/wp-content/uploads/2021/12/2021ClowneysTriangle.pdf, accessed March 10, 2023.

Poythress, Vern S. "Counterfeiting in the Book of Revelation as a Perspective on Non-Christian Culture." *Journal of the Evangelical Theological Society* 40/3 (1997): 411–18.

Poythress, Vern S. "Dispensing with Merely Human Meaning: Gains and Losses from Focusing on the Human Author, Illustrated by Zephaniah 1:2–3." *Journal of the Evangelical Theological Society* 57/3 (2014): 481–99, https://frame-poythress.org/dispensing-with-merely-human-meaning-gains-and-losses-from-focusing-on-the-human-author-illustrated-by-zephaniah-12-3/.

Poythress, Vern S. "Divine Meaning of Scripture." *Westminster Theological Journal* 48 (1986): 241–79, https://frame-poythress.org/divine-meaning-of-scripture/.

Poythress, Vern S. *God-Centered Biblical Interpretation*. Phillipsburg, NJ: P&R, 1999.

Poythress, Vern S. *In the Beginning Was the Word: Language—A God-Centered Approach*. Wheaton, IL: Crossway, 2009.

Poythress, Vern S. *Interpreting Eden: A Guide to Faithfully Reading and Understanding Genesis 1–3*. Wheaton, IL: Crossway, 2019.

Poythress, Vern S. "Introducing the Law of Christ (*Lex Christi*): A Fruitful Framework for Theology and Life." Version 1.0, https://frame-poythress .org/introducing-the-law-of-christ-lex-christi-a-fruitful-framework-for -theology-and-life/, accessed September 2, 2021.

Poythress, Vern S. *Knowing and the Trinity: How Perspectives in Human Knowledge Imitate the Trinity*. Phillipsburg, NJ: P&R, 2018.

Poythress, Vern S. *The Miracles of Jesus: How the Savior's Mighty Acts Serve as Signs of Redemption*. Wheaton, IL: Crossway, 2016.

Poythress, Vern S. *The Mystery of the Trinity: A Trinitarian Approach to the Attributes of God*. Phillipsburg, NJ: P&R, 2020.

Poythress, Vern S. "The Presence of God Qualifying Our Notions of Grammatical-Historical Interpretation: Genesis 3:15 as a Test Case." *Journal of the Evangelical Theological Society* 50/1 (2007): 87–103, https:// frame-poythress.org/the-presence-of-god-qualifying-our-notions-of -grammatical-historical-interpretation-genesis-315-as-a-test-case/.

Poythress, Vern S. *Reading the Word of God in the Presence of God: A Handbook for Biblical Interpretation*. Wheaton, IL: Crossway, 2016.

Poythress, Vern S. *The Returning King: A Guide to the Book of Revelation*. Phillipsburg, NJ: P&R, 2000.

Poythress, Vern S. *The Shadow of Christ in the Law of Moses*. Reprint, Phillipsburg, NJ: P&R, 1995.

Poythress, Vern S. *Theophany: A Biblical Theology of God's Appearing*. Wheaton, IL: Crossway, 2018.

Robertson, O. Palmer. Classroom lectures. Westminster Theological Seminary, 1972–74.

Silva, Moisés. *Biblical Words and Their Meaning: An Introduction to Lexical Semantics*. Grand Rapids, MI: Zondervan, 1994.

Tabb, Brian J., and Andrew M. King, eds. *Five Views of Christ in the Old Testament: Genre, Authorial Intent, and the Nature of Scripture*. Grand Rapids, MI: Zondervan, 2022.

von Rad, Gerhard. "Typological Interpretation of the Old Testament." *Interpretation* 15 (1961): 174–92. Translated from German, 1952.

Westminster Confession of Faith. 1647.

Woollcombe, K. J. "The Biblical Origins and Patristic Development of Typology." In G. W. H. Lampe and K. J. Woollcombe, *Essays on Typology*, Studies in Biblical Theology 22. 39–75. Naperville, IL: Alec R. Allenson, 1957.

Yates, T. P. "Adapting Westminster Standards' Moral Law Motif to Integrate Systematic Theology, Apologetics and Pastoral Practice." Thesis, North-West University, 2021. http://www.bethoumyvision.net/.

General Index

Scripture Index

Also Available from
Vern S. Poythress

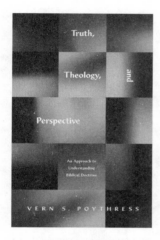

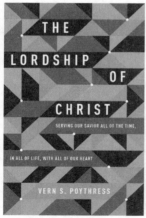

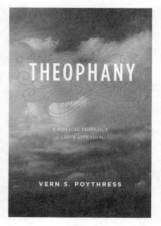

For more information, visit **crossway.org**.